THE REAL MIDDLE-EARTH

Magic and Mystery in the Dark Ages

THE REAL
MIDDLE-EARTH

Magic and Mystery in the Dark Ages

BRIAN BATES

SIDGWICK & JACKSON

First published 2002 by Sidgwick & Jackson
an imprint of Pan Macmillan Ltd
Pan Macmillan, 20 New Wharf Road, London N1 9RR
Basingstoke and Oxford
Associated companies throughout the world
www.panmacmillan.com

ISBN 0 283 07353 5

1 3 5 7 9 8 6 4 2

A CIP catalogue record for this book is available from
the British Library.

Typeset by SetSystems Ltd, Saffron Walden, Essex
Printed and bound in Great Britain by
Mackays of Chatham plc, Chatham, Kent

Contents

Acknowledgements

The Real Middle-earth is a subject that rambles like the roots of a great oak – well beyond the boundaries of conventional disciplines. Over the decades spent researching this fascinating topic I have benefited from the generous help of people who have each, in their ways, explored the territory. It started with that great British writer on Zen and Tao, Alan Watts, who, from his retreat on Mount Tamalpais, encouraged me to rediscover the magic and mystery of ancient England. And then I was fortunate to have the advice, wisdom and Glaswegian humour of the eminent psychiatrist R. D. Laing. Both these men are long gone to the Otherworld, but I still honour their wit, their shapeshifting, and our many discussions into the wee hours.

Much more recently, friends and colleagues who advised me are legion; they know who they are, and I thank them all. I have space to mention a few, starting with anthropologist Dr Susan Greenwood, who teaches Shamanic Consciousness with me at the University of Sussex. I am grateful for her informed views on imaginal states of mind, and for her letting me read the draft of her forthcoming book *Nature, Religion, and Magical Consciousness*. Historian John Russell engaged with me in many lively and humorous discussions on the nature of historical evidence, the powers of wizards, and perspectives on Tolkien's Middle-earth. Romani spiritual teacher (chovihano) Jasper Lee, and Lizzie Gotts, introduced me to the 'little folk' of the Jal tradition, and I am also grateful for Jasper's healing presence after the car accident. Oneida tribal elder Professor Apela Colorado shared with me her profound understanding of the spiritual worlds of indigenous peoples and provided inspiring and practical support for my work in rediscovering knowledge from ancient Europe; stained-glass artist and sacred landscapes researcher Kathy Shaw kindly took me to visit the ancient yew of Ankerwyke and outlined her fascinating insights into the imagination-charged environment of ancient times; architect Susanne Nessensohn shared with me her visions of the Celtic Otherworld, and also her sensitive insights into King Redwald; and anthropologist Dr Merete Jakobsen provided invariably stimulating discussions of her research into shamans, the implications or magic – and the enchantment of stories.

For sustaining me throughout the writing I am grateful to Rachel Turner for her superb coaching; my literary agent Ed Victor, and my editors at Macmillan, Gordon Wise and Ingrid Connell, for knowledge-able advice and encouragement throughout. Also thanks to Jacqui Butler for her resourceful picture research. Last but not least, my family; Beth, Pearl and Robin unfailingly provided me with great ideas and loving support.

Illustration Acknowledgements

1 & 2 – © National Trust Photographic Library / Joe Cornish
3, 8, 9, 10, 14, 20, 22 – © Ancient Art and Architecture Collection
4 – © Roman Baths, Bath and North East Somerset Council
5 – © Brian Bates
6 – © St Edmundsbury Borough Council / West Stow Anglo-Saxon
    Village Trust
7, 17, 18 – © Werner Forman Archive
11 – © Michael Holford
12 – © AKG London
13, 16 – © J. S. Selfe
15 – © National Trust Photographic Library / Ray Hallett
19 – British Library, MS Harley 603, fol. 22r
21, 26 – © Antikvarisk-topografiska arkivet, the National Heritage
    Board, Stockholm
23 – © Sheffield Galleries & Museums Trust
24, 25 – National Museum of Denmark

THE ANGLO-SAXON KINGDOMS c. 700 AD

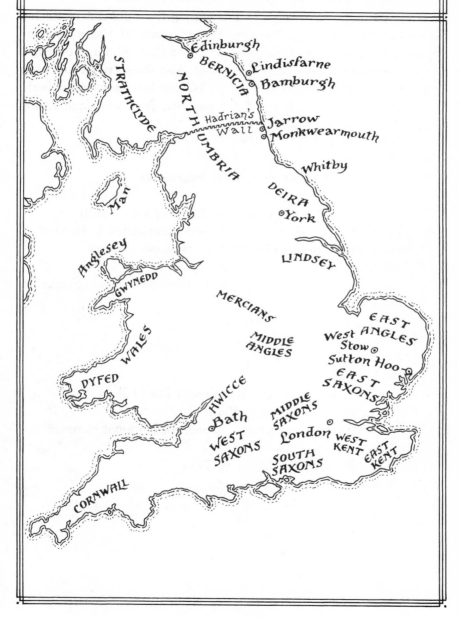

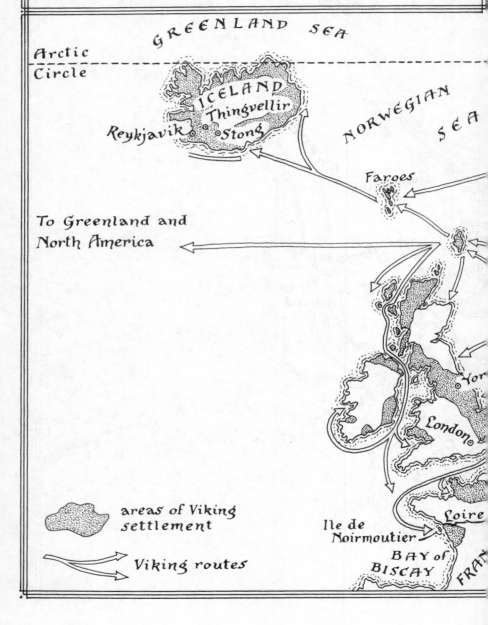

NORTH~WESTERN EUROPE c.800~1000 AD

GREENLAND SEA

Arctic Circle

NORWEGIAN SEA

ICELAND
Thingvellir
Reykjavik
Stong

Faroes

To Greenland and North America

York
London

areas of Viking settlement

Viking routes

Ile de Noirmoutier

Loire

BAY of BISCAY

FRAN

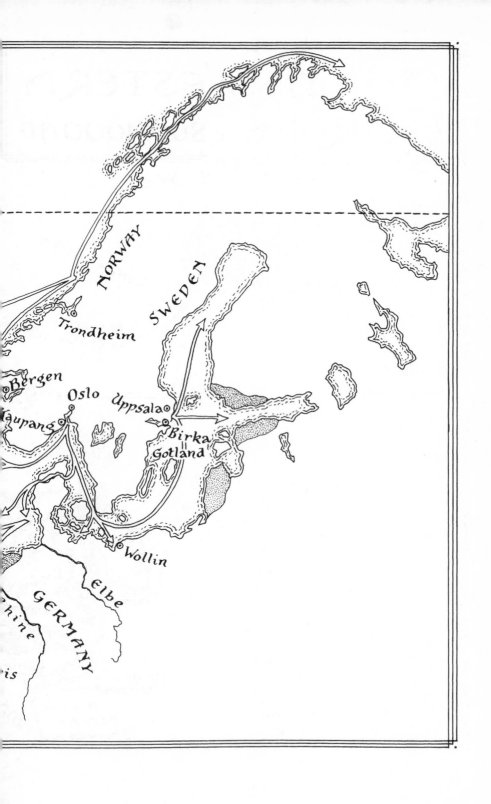

NORWAY

SWEDEN

Trondheim

Bergen

Oslo

Uppsala

Kaupang

Birka

Gotland

Wollin

Elbe

GERMANY

Rhine

Paris

REDISCOVERING
THE REAL MIDDLE-EARTH

1. The Real Middle-earth

The gods and goddesses lived in the bright spaces of the Upperworld, along with the light elves. Far beneath, in the cavernous shadows of the Lowerworld, lurked the spirits of the dead; they were accompanied by dark elves and the dragon called Nidhog. And in between, reached by a bridge formed of a rainbow called Bifrost (Trembling Pathway), lay the enchanted landscape of Middle-earth. It was a magical realm inhabited by men and women, and surrounded by an infinite ocean. In the ocean swam a serpent so huge he encircled all of Middle-earth and bit on his own tail. In the mountains bordering the ocean lived the giants. This landscape of three realms, one above the other, is how the peoples of historical north-west Europe saw their world during the first millennium, that early period sometimes called the Dark Ages (so-called by scholars to mark the relative lack of written records during the first thousand years of English history, and the absence for several centuries of Christianity). The great cultures of those times, the Celts, Anglo-Saxons and Norse, infused their lives with a remarkable imagination and sense of spirituality. The natural landscape of Europe took on a whole new meaning – a deeper, enchanted dimension, making it a realm of magic and mystery. These were the people of the Real Middle-earth.

Today, the term Middle-earth conjures a fictional realm of spirits and sorcery made famous by J.R.R. Tolkien's epic fantasy *The Lord of the Rings*. His invented tales of the wizard Gandalf, Bilbo Baggins, the hero Aragorn, the fire-demon Balrog, rings of power, Queen Galadriel, quests through ancient and evocative landscapes – the whole fantastical world of magic and adventure – have made his among the most popular novels over the last fifty years.

But now there is another remarkable story to be told: Middle-earth really existed. Historical research has revealed that, stretching from Old England to Scandinavia and across to western Europe,

there arose about two thousand years ago a largely forgotten civilization which foreshadowed Tolkien's imagined world. Tolkien readily
admitted in his letters that the concept of Middle-earth was not his
own invention, but an old Anglo-Saxon term for the magical world
inhabited by people in the first millennium (AD 0–1000). And it is
this culture, made up of many colourful early European tribes now
identified under the umbrella titles of Celts, Anglo-Saxons and
Norse, on which he based *The Lord of the Rings*.

Until recently, historians tended to regard these peoples as
primitive, violent and obscure barbarians, living in the shadows of
the more widely documented Romans who formed an empire over all
of Europe in those early times. But research in a wide range of disciplines is revolutionizing our view of the past. We now realize that
at their best these ancient civilizations were characterized by some
remarkable perspectives on the nature of reality.

The people of the Real Middle-earth had a vision of life animated
by beings beyond the material world – elves, dwarves, giants and
fire-breathing dragons. They believed that real wizards cast spells,
and flew on eight-legged horses. A life-force enchanted everything.
Berserker warriors were believed to change into bears, and heroes
journeyed on perilous quests for truth in the land of the giants. The
cosmos was held together by an interlaced web of golden threads
visible only to the wizards. And at the centre of it all lay Middle-
earth, inhabited by people and suffused with a magical power.

While their many tribal cultures were rich and varied (and in
this book I point out some of the differences between them), in com-
parison with the twenty-first century their commonalities were
strong. Even in the mundane realities of everyday life, these peoples
of ancient Europe shared the experience of living in a natural, un-
engineered world markedly different from today. In particular, their
imaginative and inspired view of life makes these people sufficiently
homogeneous for us to approach their remarkable cultures as a single
destination for a journey back in time.

Totalling perhaps two or three million people at the beginning
of the first millennium, they lived in a landscape of trees, streams,
hills and a carpentered world of wooden buildings. They followed a
self-sufficient style of life based on farming, hunting and weaving.

Technologically their culture was quite simple, and in ancient Europe throughout the first millennium, living conditions could be physically harsh. They were of necessity a quintessentially pragmatic people. These were no airy-fairy daydreamers. But what makes them so special is that they imbued their lives with an all-embracing imagination. Today, in a more secular and rational age defined by science and engineering, we tend to approach our lives from a more objective perspective. And yet the huge interest today in such fictional versions of their culture as Tolkien's *The Lord of the Rings* confirms our hunger to reconnect with the imagination of our ancestors.

And ancestors they were. Travelling back in time a hundred generations or so takes us to the beginnings of this remarkable civilization. The people who populated it now have, through the mathematics of biological progeny, hundreds of millions of descendants. And interbreeding with later tribal incomers means that everyone of north-west European heritage living today, anywhere in the world, has one of these people in their early family tree. The magical world of Middle-earth is our personal heritage.

Keys to the Forgotten World

In this book I have brought together historical, literary, psychological and archaeological research on this forgotten world to reveal once again the civilization I call the Real Middle-earth. The primary sources on which this scholarship is based are necessarily varied and patchy for several reasons. One is that the Anglo-Saxons and Norse, in particular, wrote down little of their beliefs and traditions. Theirs were oral cultures. They told stories, some of which, fortunately were written down at the end of the millennium, including the great Anglo-Saxon poem *Beowulf*. They memorized healing remedies, a small corpus of which were recorded by Christian monks and are available to us now, a thousand years later, in Anglo-Saxon documents such as the magical healing manuscript called *Lacnunga*, kept in the British Library. They used runes as symbolic writing for the magical purposes of divination and spell-casting, and only in a limited fashion for naming or explaining things. Archaeologists have excavated many objects such as swords which are marked with runes, apparently for identifying not only the owner of the weapon, but also the spirit beings which give it a special power.

By about AD 600 we have documents which were drawn up as legal property boundaries, or to make functional arrangements for laws and social order. Some of these contracts give us glimpses into the ways in which they visioned their lives – such as the inclusion of a monster called Grendel as a landmark among the more prosaic features of named trees and streams. So we are able to gain at least some insights into the real Middle-earth from these early writings.

However, the Romans, who had many encounters with the early Germanic and Celtic peoples in Europe when expanding their empire, did write reports in Latin on the customs and beliefs of these still tribal peoples. Some of them have survived, and serve as an early kind of anthropology. The reports of the Roman official Cornelius Tacitus, in particular, writing in the first century AD, afford clear and vivid accounts of their lives. Like all writers, Tacitus had his own particular perspective which somewhat coloured his reporting. He thought Rome was becoming indulgent and decadent, and he sought to portray the tribal people he observed or read about in a positive light, as an instructive example of what he believed the citizens of his home city state were losing – an early example of the 'noble savage' phenomenon. Nevertheless he is a prime source of historical material, describing for example the significance of Nerthus the goddess of Earth, who was drawn in a sacred cart through early Germanic territories bringing peace wherever she stopped. Other Roman writers also left valuable accounts, including descriptions of the Celtic warrior queen Boudicca, who led an uprising in Britain against the brutality of the Roman overlords in AD 61.

In the second half of the millennium, the Christian missionaries who travelled among the tribal peoples also left some accounts of the people they were attempting to convert. They also battled to replace the pre-Christian spiritual practices by sermonizing, and promulgating both Church and secular laws outlawing some of the practices. Some of these writings have survived, and tell us what the people of the real Middle-earth were doing rather in the form of a 'negative' through which we can read a positive 'print' of early magical and spiritual traditions. For example, Wulfstan, an early Archbishop of

York, left instructions to all priests to 'promote Christianity eagerly, and thoroughly obliterate any [trace of] heathenism' by forbidding 'the veneration of springs and magic involving dead bodies and omens and charms and the veneration of human beings and the evil that people perpetrate through various others [kinds of] trees and at stones and in all sorts of errors in which people persist the more they should not.' In breathlessly attempting to banish these activities, he has provided us with documentation about them which now, a thousand years later, helps us to understand some of the magical practices of Middle-earth.

Naturally, many of the written records in monasteries were often biased against the indigenous pre-Christian views. When Christianity was imposed by missionary activity sponsored from Rome, it usually evangelized and sought to destroy the spiritual beliefs which preceded it. And in the eleventh century social, political and religious upheavals in Europe changed the nature of official belief and repressed many of the ancient traditions. However, our knowledge of the real Middle-earth is greatly enhanced by the fact that Iceland did not officially convert to Christianity until the year AD 1000. The relatively late date of this conversion, and the fact that it happened as a result of a deliberate and democratic decision, meant that the old beliefs and practices were largely tolerated long after that date, and more fully documented.

Working from documents now lost to us, as well as traditional folk stories, one writer in particular called Snorri Sturluson recorded accounts of the pre-Christian beliefs of Iceland. Similarly, in the storytelling tradition that thrived and began to be written down in the thirteenth and fourteenth centuries, tales known as sagas recreated life in the pre-Christian period, sometimes containing vivid accounts of early practices. We have to allow for some literary elaboration in these stories, and slippage in accuracy with the intervening passage of time, but life did not change so rapidly in those days, and many of the old ways may still have been current even generations after the offical conversion. These sagas provide us with such valuable details as the appearance and trance techniques of Thorbiorg the seeress, who travelled the countryside to foretell events on behalf of individuals and whole communities.

In recent years the work of archaeologists has become an

increasingly finely developed science. The techniques of recording, dating and analysing materials recovered from the ground, are sometimes of breathtaking sensitivity. But particularly, the written reports of excavations are these days often placed in a context of other historical information – the digs are not merely reported, but analyzed as to their import in understanding spiritual beliefs, as well as the everyday world of the people of Middle-earth.

A Journey Through Middle-earth

In this book I have sought to select material which throws light on the magical world of the first millennium – the beliefs and practices of those people which express their religion, healing and especially the enchanted view they took of their lives and their environment. We look first at the tribal peoples who made up the populace of this magical time, the ways in which they coalesced to form the potent combinations of cultures, and how they conjured a quality of imagination which transcended the challenging environment in which they lived.

Then we review the way in which they lived their daily lives, constructed their houses, designed their clothes, grew and cooked their food. These are the sorts of prosaic details which help us to get closer to and empathize with them as people. If we can identify with them, it helps us to enter more fully into the more fantastic aspects of their beliefs, such as dragons, giants and elves.

After that we explore the hidden history of Middle-earth, a world of magic, mystery and destiny. A starting point is the forest, for trees were hugely significant features of their understanding of life. Timber was a staple material, of course, for building, fuel, tool-making and so on. But the people's connections with trees went much deeper, and even provided a template on which they imaged their entire spiritual cosmos.

The magic and mystery can also be discovered in surprising places. When the Romans arrived, they subjugated the indigenous Celtic peoples; and when the Saxons came afterwards, the Romans had not long withdrawn from the island. Over a period of a relatively few years, as Roman functionaries and retired soldiers followed the armies which had protected them, they left behind magnificent villas, even entire walled towns. Hundreds of fine Roman-built villas lay empty and ripe for occupation. Astonishingly, the Saxons avoided these buildings as if they were harbingers of doom. Investigating this phenomenon reveals more about the special relationship the Saxons had with their environment, and their strongly-developed views about destiny.

The landscape of Middle-earth England was both geographical and mystical. The hidden history reveals, for example, their belief in the existence of dragons. A creature of fantasy to us, the dragon is shown to embody philosophical views for them about the dark side of wealth, and the inevitable life-cycle of civilizations. Dealing death to dragons turns out to be a deep and subtle element of their understanding of life. We encounter some of the bloodiest battles with these beasts, and enter their lairs and treasure hoards.

The people of Middle-earth, whether Celts, Anglo-Saxons or Norse, all had a view of nature which we would call enchanted. They ascribed to the natural world a palpable energy called life-force. Also they felt that the environment was imbued with spirit in a way that could be manifested. Their world was inhabited by elves, and other supernatural presences associated with water, wells, plants and the heavenly galaxies. This used to be boxed and wrapped by modern anthropologists as primitive 'vitalism', which patronized the indigenous cultures' ascription of a kind of sentient consciousness to inanimate aspects of nature. However, we can now see that in Middle-earth, the enchanted landscape incorporated attitudes to health and healing which are only just re-emerging in the medical practices of today. We sample some of the rituals, spells and insights of enchantment.

In the second half of the thousand years of Middle-earth culture, their views of life were influenced by what was then an imported, evangelical religion – Christianity. The struggle between these two traditions and their practitioners – Middle-earth wizards and Christian priests – is usually portrayed as a religious rivalry. But it was just as much a power struggle for control of the magic – even the spells – for as we shall see, the Christians believed in magic too, so long as it was mediated by God.

In first-millennium Europe, people encountered a much greater number of wild animals than we see today in our urban and suburban environments. The relationship of people with these animals is instructive, for it touches upon their understanding of the human soul. We document the ways in which certain people were believed to change into animals, and to take on their powers – and the consequences they suffered.

They also believed that individual lives were inextricably linked with all other people, beings and events. This is reflected in the beautiful and complex designs of Celtic, Saxon and Norse jewellery, which often had a characteristic interlaced pattern.

The connectedness of all events meant also that their experience of past, present and future was different from ours. They believed that future events could be predicted by people with the gift of foresight. We shall consider the techniques and trances of these seers – often women who were honoured highly in early Europe.

Then we consider the remarkable presence of dwarves and giants in Middle-earth life, and the roles they were believed to play in the unfolding of events. The dwarves specialized in a magical way of thinking, and the construction of subtle spells. The giants, terrifying but surprisingly wise, reveal a challenge to the way in which people thought of their lives even in the times of Middle-earth.

Wizards' initiation into occult knowledge often included surrendering to Otherworld journeys – being 'taken' to the realms of spirit – by demons. We track a spell recorded in a tenth-century wizard's notebook, which tells of such a journey. Here, an apprentice wizard is gripped by a spider monster and carried off to other realms.

Finally, we embark on a last voyage – the funeral of a great East Anglian king in which he is buried along with his entire ship. Such burials, including those in which the ship is launched onto the waters with the coffin aboard and fired with burning arrows, took the honoured dead on a passage to the Otherworld. The destination is the garsecg, the mystical sea surrounding our Middle-earth, and which ensures an eventual return to this life. It is a fitting end, for it is also a vision of return.

After the close of the Middle-earth period of history, we eventually moved first to a heavily Christianized, and then later to a more secular, scientific age, where the meaning of life was to be incorporated within rational enquiry. But now, in the twenty-first century, we are finding that while science can explain the biological dynamics of life to a remarkable degree, there are limits to its power to explain the 'why' of life. We need to reconnect with the language of our imagination to address these deeper issues. Our ancestors in first millennium Europe gained insights into some of these questions in their enchanted view of life. Our hunger for the recovery of this lost knowledge, and the stories in which it is encoded and preserved, have led us to witness the return of the real Middle-earth.

2. The People of Middle-earth

The people of the real Middle-earth lived in small communities – extended families belonging to tribes and clans – over north-west Europe and Scandinavia. Their culture lasted for a span of about a thousand years (AD 0–1000), until social, political and religious forces began to change its character. At the beginning of the first millennium, their population may have totalled only two or three million. Their tribes were led by chieftains (in Anglo-Saxon the term translates as 'head-kinsman') who were later called kings or queens. They were more than elected leaders – they were often regarded as sacred. In early European and Norse tribal culture people identified with their ancestors, and leaders in particular would name a long personal heritage, going back many generations. Ultimately, the chieftains claimed their earliest ancestor as the god Woden (called Odin in the Norse culture). This sacred heritage filled them with 'mana' or life-force. They carried the fortunes of their tribe in their personal presence.

The early communities were bonded together by shared rituals and customs particular to each, such as calendar festivals, hunting practices, techniques of magic and by totems or icons which symbolized the spirit of the tribe. Dialects, details of costume and shared stories about heroic figures, were as important to their identity as they still are today in badging and branding subcultures in our less homogeneous contemporary social worlds.

The terms we use today to denote these people of first millennium Europe, such as Celts, Anglo-Saxons and Norse, are really 'umbrella' titles which subsume a myriad of tribal groups. For example, among the 'Anglo-Saxon' or Germanic stream of peoples, inhabiting the lowland areas of the north-west coast of Germany and southern Denmark, were the Frisians, with the Saxons competing with them from the north, and squeezed by the Sugamri and Batavi in the marshes to the south. The Cherusci were settled in heavily forested land on the Weser River, near the Chatti. In the eastern reaches of Germany lay the Burgundiones, with a chief named by the Romans as Gunther uth Clotar. They were under pressure from the Lugians to their east, themselves pressed by the Vandals for agricultural land, and also by the Langobardi to the north. Northern Germany was the home of the Cimbri. They were a successful and powerful tribe until they were decimated by the Roman legions whom they challenged in protecting the southern borders of their tribal territory.

The Goths were an eastern German confederation of tribes which ranged as far as southern Scandinavia. In central Germany the Hermundris' lands were a mixture of forest and open flat land. Their neighbours were the Langobardi. In southern Germany were the Marcomanni and Quadi, and in the south-west, the Suebi. Many tribes stretched across the lands now in Holland and Belgium, including the Batavi, the Frisians and the Bructeri, who, around the third and fourth centuries, became part of the tribal merging that became known as the Franks, who gave their name, grammar and laws to modern France. Among the many other tribes were the Saxons and their cousins the Jutes and Angles who, along with the Frisians, populated England after the fall of Rome.

These Middle-earth cultures thrived, grew and battled all around north-west Europe and Scandinavia. In England, particularly, they came together like ingredients in an alchemical cauldron. The smallness of Britain as an island meant that when new ethnic groups settled, they mixed with, or dominated, earlier settlers. This mixture of traditions conjured a rich blend of magic, and eventually inspired Tolkien to write *The Lord of the Rings* as an attempt to invent a legendary story which captured this essence of ancient England. In historical and cultural terms, the coming together of these peoples in England is a microcosm of what happened at various levels of intensity elsewhere. In this book I refer to sources dealing with peoples on the European mainland and in Scandinavia, but use England as a touchstone for examining the ways in which the magic was expressed.

There were four main cultural influences during this thousand years. First were the early Celts, who were living as a settled society in Britain, when the Romans invaded the island in AD 43, and stayed for four centuries. The Romans contributed a lot to the culture of England, but in terms of the magic of Middle-earth, they were more like a contrasting intermission, as we shall see. When they left around AD 410, the Saxons invaded and settled, pushing many of the Celts into Wales and Cornwall. They were followed by the Norse, or Vikings, in the eighth century, which saw them colonize the eastern part of the country. These three peoples – the Celts, the Anglo-Saxons, and the Norse, make up the people of the Real Middle-earth.

I begin the book, then, with a brief overview of the conventional history of these tribal incomers to England – the kings, warriors, battles, religious rivalries, social structures and economies – the 'noisy history' with which we are already somewhat familiar. It comprises our more usual sense of the history of ancient times. This will help to establish the context in which the culture of Middle-earth emerged.

England proved to be a volatile meeting ground for the tribal peoples of ancient Europe. Academics used to distinguish between them on linguistic grounds as falling under the 'umbrella' terms of the Germanic Peoples (including Scandinavia), and the Celtic peoples. However, in a shifting kaleidoscope of migrating tribal groups, it seems likely that the importance of this variation in their language may have been overstated. Distinctions between the two groups are small compared with their commonality of experience consequent upon living as tribal peoples. Many scholars now regard all of these tribal peoples as sharing some beliefs and practices.

Certainly warfare took place between tribes of the two peoples, but the process of migration, invasion and settlement of the later Germanic groups on an island formerly occupied by mainly Celtic peoples is now understood as a much more complex array of relationships, from cooperation all the way to open antagonism.

The history of this period, while increasingly documented by archaeologists and historians, has been generally ignored in favour of the earlier cultures of Greece and Rome, although schoolchildren in north-west Europe are now beginning to be introduced to the history of their ancestors. Denigrated as the 'Dark Ages', it was considered, until recently, a regrettably primitive period which dominated Europe between the fall of the enlightened age of Roman occupation, at about AD 400 years, until the full advent of Christianity across Europe, and into Scandinavia, around AD 1000.

But research in a wide range of disciplines is revolutionizing our view of these people, and enables me in this book to develop a very different perspective. While I do not claim that the indigenous peoples of ancient Europe represent some sort of utopian society, they are far from being peoples of the '*dark* ages' in a negative sense. Indeed, seen from the viewpoint of what they offer us today, the best of their ancient culture represents a millennium of knowledge and insight in areas of life in which we might even be relative paupers today.

Celts

While humans of some kind have lived in England since at least 500,000 BC – the date of rhinocerous bones with flint marks of human butchering, found in the south of England in the 1990s – we know too little about them to assess the subtleties and heritage of their culture. But we do know that from at least 600 BC, immigrants from the European continent continued to cross the choppy waters of the narrow English Channel in small boats. The flotillas of extended families beaching their boats on England's (then called Albion) shores were from many small tribes, and their numbers built up gradually over several hundred years. They were known collectively by the Greeks as Keltoi, or Celts, and they spoke languages that have survived into modern times as Welsh, Cornish, Breton, Manx, Scots Gaelic and Irish. They were the first people to contribute to the magical culture I have identified as the Real Middle-earth.

To meet a Celtic person today who lived two thousand years ago, at the beginning of the Middle-earth period, would be like meeting ourselves in a long-forgotten dream. They would be instantly familiar to us. Looking into their eyes, we would see not an alien being from another world, but an intelligent person. Their culture was highly developed. Their 'scientific' knowledge was of course much less than ours today, but they knew a lot about things that we have forgotten over the centuries. And skull measurements show that the brain capacity of people living in the first millennium was exactly the same as our own.

The writers of ancient Rome described the Celts as tall, well built people, strong and healthy. They had fair or reddish hair. Their skin would be ruddier or more tanned than most modern north-west Europeans, through living an outdoors life. They enjoyed a wide range of fresh foods, although they could suffer in times of famine, for crops sometimes failed. They also had fewer cures for infectious illnesses than we do now. But those who survived to maturity seemed to live a healthy life, albeit shorter than now – a person in their fifties was considered venerable.

The Celtic women were impressive too – they were 'nearly as tall as the men'. Cassius Dio, a Roman writer of the fourth century AD, reported the appearance of Boudicca, a Celtic warrior queen of the Iceni tribe, a wealthy and powerful society who lived in what is now Norfolk and northern Suffolk. 'In stature she was very tall', says Cassius, writing from her reputation and from documents that we no longer have: 'A great mass of the tawniest hair fell to her hips; around her neck was a large golden necklace; and she wore a tunic of divers colours over which a thick mantle was fastened with a brooch. This was her invariable attire.' It is unlikely that a Celtic queen would leave her hair 'wild' while at court, for they were known to be well-groomed people. But this vivid account is of a warrior woman preparing for combat. Celtic women were renowned for their strength and bravery, fighting in battle alongside the men.

The Roman's descriptions of the Celts was of a dynamic and fiery culture. Physical fitness, sports, and war skills were popular, especially among the elite warrior class. So were lavish feasts. Strabo, who died in about AD 21, was one of the world's first travel writers. He described the Celts in his *Geographica* as heavy drinkers, with wine for those who could afford it and beer of wheat for the commoners, spiced with cumin. At feasts they passed around vast and ornate cups and imbibed from them. According to Strabo, 'they do it rather frequently'. Perhaps if we met them, the aroma of feasting, wine and beer could be smelled on their breath.

An encounter with an early Celt would probably be a colourful experience, too, so much so that the Roman writer Strabo thought

their love of personal ornamentation to be rather naive and boast-
ful. They decorated themselves with heavy twisted gold necklaces,
ending in clasps with animal motifs. Gold bracelets gleamed on the
arms of high-born men and women. Brooches were enamelled and
cloaks were fastened with imposing buckles. Examples of their beautiful gold torques dating from the first century BC have been found
in Norfolk, Suffolk and Staffordshire. The torque at Snettisham,
Norfolk was part of one of the largest hoard of Celtic gold and siver
treasure discovered in Britain. More than 11 kilograms of gold and
16 kilograms of silver jewellery were unearthed. The hoard lay in the
East Anglian territory of Queen Boudicca. Perhaps she even wore
some of it.

Fabric clothing was dyed and stained from natural vegetable
colourings, in a variety of hues and stripes from bright reds, to greens
and yellows – in contrast to the former, dreary stereotype of the
'Dark Ages' during which people were imagined to be poverty-
stricken savages, trudging about in grime. This view is now outmoded.

The Celts lived in roundhouses made of turf or wattle and daub,
with thatched roofs. Usually they were constructed in small hamlets
of between about fifty and a hundred people. These must have been
essentially extended family settlements. Each community grew barley
and wheat, and raised pigs, sheep and cattle. They were ruled by
chieftains or elite families. For protection they often formed alliances
with other small groups, and sealed the arrangement by gift-giving
and entertaining each other to sumptuous feasts.

So why did the early settlers come to Britain? There are theories
of land shortages and over-population on the continent, but the
'bottom line' answer is they migrated to Britain for wealth. 'Albion'
was an island rich in natural resources, a temperate climate for
farming and plenty of land – although the island is small, it was not
yet crowded. We can gain a sense of how the island would have
continued to attract incomers from Bede's account written some
several hundred years later.

Bede

Bede was born around 673, and died in 735. He is a very important figure in the scholarship of Middle-earth, for his texts are reckoned to be well researched by the standards of his time. And, while seeking to put Christianity in a positive light, his work is considered to be more objective in intention than many early monastic volumes which were, for example, hagiographies praising uncritically the virtues of certain Church figures. He was also the most voluminous writer of his time, as far as we can tell, and was highly influential in his day.

Bede was born in the region of the modern Newcastle-upon-Tyne, and lived there all his life except for occasional, short periods spent away at the monastery of Jarrow where he was a monk. He lived the life of an academic priest, attached to the monastery, and wrote his texts in Latin, as was standard practice for monastic scholars. Those of his sources we can document showed that he had read widely, probably in the library at Jarrow which contained numerous books brought back from the continent. Bede read widely from Christian Latin literature, and also knew some pre-Christian Greek writings. As Bede lay dying, he wrote a short poem. The existence of this poem was noted by a man called Wilberct, who happened to be in the room with him, transcribing Bede's oral translation into Anglo-Saxon of St John's Gospel. The poem is written, unusually, in Anglo-Saxon rather than Latin, and in words which reflect a Northumbrian dialect, which is probably how he spoke. The actual sound of his speech cannot be recreated, but the words used, spellings and so on, show he is writing in the vernacular of his region.

The Bede's *Ecclesiastical History of Britain*, his language, even allowing for poetic licence, gives a sense of what the incomers found here. He says that Britain 'extends 800 miles in length towards the north, and is 200 miles in breadth ... where it opens upon the boundless ocean.' He goes on to detail some of the natural qualities of this small island: 'Britain excels for grain and trees, and is well adapted for feeding cattle and beasts of burden. It also produces vines in some places, and has plenty of land and water-fowls of several sorts; it is remarkable also for rivers, abounding in fish, and plentiful springs.' He describes great quantities of river fish like salmon and eels, even whales hunted off the coasts, and many sorts of shellfish, such as mussels, in which are often found excellent pearls of all colours, red, purple, violet and green, but mostly white.

Bede also describes a great abundance of cockles, 'of which the scarlet dye is made; a most beautiful colour, which never fades with the heat of the sun or the washing of the rain; but the older it is, the more beautiful it comes'. Bede mentions that Britain has both salt and hot springs, and from them flow 'rivers which furnish hot baths, proper for all ages and sexes and arranged accordingly'. There were treasures, too: '. . . Britain also has many veins of metals, as copper, iron, lead and silver; it has much and excellent jet'.

So a wealth of natural resources supported a successful economy, which through trade made the elite class gold-rich. It also made the people of the island not only subject to waves of fresh immigrants throughout the thousand years – but also the victim of vicious raids, piracy, inter-tribal warfare, competing warlords and extortion by the Romans and Vikings (both of whom referred to enormous enforced payments as 'tribute').

These perennial curses of plunder, pillage and bloody conflict have been well documented in other, more conventional history books. These are the material facts. However, there is another dimension. A subtle culture lay hidden beneath the noise and harshness of battle. This is the magic of Middle-earth – more intimate and democratic than religion, more substantial than superstition, more manifested than fantasy. The people who lived out their lives during this long period of history, in this place, imbued their lives with an imagination so rich that it entertains us still.

Romans

After the Celts came the Romans, who stamped their military overlordship on ever-increasing amounts of territory, and milked those tribes for wealth to support the glory of Rome. Julius Caesar invaded Britain twice, first in 55 BC then again in early 54 BC. The indigenous Celtic tribes were regarded by the Romans as 'barbarians' – a term derived from the Greek and mimicking the 'bar bar' sounds of 'savage' language. The Celts had either to submit to the Romans as overlords, or risk being wiped out by a huge military invasion. On his second attack, six powerful tribes in the east of England submitted to them. Among them were Boudicca's Iceni. Their story was eventually to become a tragic example of what happened to the Celtic tribespeople of Britain under Roman rule, as we shall see. But then Caesar had to leave to deal with troubles on the continent among the great territories he was controlling. He never came back. For a century life went on without the Romans.

In AD 43 a new emperor called Claudius had been hustled into power during a crisis caused by the murder of the notoriously corrupt Caligula. Looking for adventures which would promote his prestige, he studied Caesar's journals about Britannia, and decided that the island was rich enough to warrant launching a new invasion. He sent an enormous detachment of 40,000 troops to take and colonize the island. Faced by this military might, many of the Celtic tribes swallowed their pride and succumbed to being 'client kingdoms', among them the Iceni. Their tribal ruler Prasutagus, and all the other client-rulers, received military 'protection' – an early and large-scale example of a protection racket. They were also required to take enormous 'loans' from the Romans, thus leaving them in debt to the sovereign government. They had to take the loans, for much of their wealth was being plundered by the Roman government. These payments, or 'tributes', were sent back to Rome.

Prasutagus married Boudicca in about AD 48 or 49. As Queen of the Iceni, she bore two daughters (names unknown), who are believed to have been in their early teens when their father died in AD 60 or 61. Boudicca then became Regent of the Iceni, and the guardian of her daughters' inheritance. When Prasutagus died he left in his will half of his wealth, in lands, personal possessions and monies, to the Emperor Nero. This was required of him, as a client-ruler 'indebted to Rome'. He left his remaining wealth to his wife, for their daughters, assuring a dowry to their future husbands, and income to pay their Roman tributes.

The Roman governors, assuming themselves to be unassailable, felt this was not enough. So they publicly stripped and flogged Queen Boudicca, and raped her two daughters, before confiscating much of their wealth. This action was far more than a mere public humiliation. Early tribal cultures regarded their chieftains as descended from gods. The Iceni held Boudicca to be sacred. The Roman's had knowingly destroyed the soul of her culture, and the Iceni now had nothing left to lose. Boudicca raised an army of farmworkers, women, even children numbering up to 100,000. In righteous revenge, they burned the Roman city of London (Londinium), leaving a thick layer of red ash which exists still below the streets of the city. They sacked two other Roman towns, but were finally defeated in a battle with elite Roman troops. Mass slaughter followed, and the remaining Iceni were forced into slavery. It was genocide on a massive scale. Calgacus, leader of the Caledonians in the far north of Britain, led another rebellion against the Romans some twenty years after Boudicca's, and said of them, 'They create a desolation and call it peace.'

On the island of Mona (Anglesey) in AD 60, the Romans sought to break the status and influence of the Druids over the indigenous Celts. Here, in an ancient Druidic sanctuary, some of the leaders of rebellions against Roman rule had sought protection. The Roman leader Suetonius decided to hunt down not only the rebels, but destroy the Druids at the same time. The scene at Mona is vividly described by Tacitus. Facing down the well-drilled Roman troops was a native force including 'black-robed women with dishevelled hair like Furies, brandishing torches'. Close by stood the Druids, 'raising their hands to heaven and screaming dreadful curses'. Transfixed by this spectacle, the Roman legions had to be urged forward by Suetonius to put these strange people to the sword. After the successful assault, Suetonius had the sacred groves of Mona cut down so that, as Tacitus put it, Mona's 'barbarous superstitions' could no longer be practised.

The Romans seemed less concerned about introducing their gods and beliefs on the Celts than simply gaining political and military dominance. Britannia became the wild outer fringe of the extensive Roman Empire. The Romans built roads, villas and even garrison-towns. The ruling aristocracy, numbering thousands, but dominating an island of perhaps a million people, was modelled on Roman lines, although many of the Celtic peoples continued to live in the ways of old, in small groups with local chieftains.

Of course, the Romans brought benefits. They recorded much about the people they encountered – England enters the history books with the writings of the Romans. And certainly the Romans were well connected throughout Europe, providing trade and other links with an empire that extended to the Holy Land, North Africa and central Europe as far north as the Rhine and the Danube.

But then eventually the empire started to fall apart, with Rome stretched in AD 406 by attacks on its northern border, which was effectively the river Rhine in Germany. In 407/8 the Rhine froze over, and the Vandals, Alans and Suebi unleased a massive invasion cross the ice and swarmed into Gaul (France) to attack the Roman encampments. Two years later, Roman rule was collapsing back to defend Rome itself. In 410 the Emperor Honorius issued an edict to the cities in Britain instructing them to take responsibility for their own defences. Troops of centurions were pulled out of Britain to help to deal with this threat.

Historical re-enactment groups who have recreated replica Roman armour of this period and worn it, have remarked on how noisy it is. Metal knocks against metal. The martial clanking of an approaching Roman garrison must have frightened many an enemy. But it must have sounded like music of the gods as they finally left the country, never to return.

Saxons

England had been subject to the military dictatorship of Rome for four centuries, so when the Romans summarily withdrew, they left a power vacuum. Chiefs of ancient tribal fiefdoms all over England embarked on a frantic round, forming alliances as they competed for territory over shifting borders and boundaries. Such intense inward-looking activity and lack of central organization meant that the country as a whole was ill-prepared for dealing with any outside threats. Some of the evidence for this state of affairs is clear in *The Anglo-Saxon Chronicle*. This was a compilation of the annual diaries of events of the previous year kept in monasteries in various parts of England. The original compilation was probably put together in the early 890s at the court of King Alfred. Several versions of it have survived until modern times. And in their pages, the chroniclers have recorded a post-Roman story of continuous rolling battles and alliances, fuelled by treachery and triumph.

The first chieftain to gain wide prominence is named in *The Anglo-Saxon Chronicle* as Vortigern. We have little information about him, and we do not know what evidence was available to the writers of the *Chronicle*, or indeed to what extent they may have been relying on folklore and legend. It is possible that Vortigern is a title for 'overlord'. He is reckoned to be a warlord ruler of the south-eastern kingdom of Kent, and the first Celtic leader to emerge as leader of post-Roman Britain.

There is uncertainty about exactly when he achieved this position. Some sources say that he came to the overlordship of Britain in AD 425, although dating gets pretty awry here. The *Chronicle* reckons a later date of 449. But what is not at issue is what he did about the marauding Picts – the tribal people raiding and robbing down the northern coasts of England. 'Picts' was the name applied to them from the third century AD by the Romans, possibly translating from the Latin as the 'painted ones', referring either to the use of warpaint, or possibly a native custom of tattooing.

In exchange for their keeping the Picts at bay, and guarding the south coast to prevent the Romans from re-invading, Vortigern offered land on the Isle of Thanet, off the coast of Kent, to a substantial contingent of Saxon mercenaries. According to the *Chronicle*, warriors from Jutland, under their leaders Hengist and Horsa, landed at Vortigern's invitation at Pegwell Bay, just south of modern Ramsgate. Hengist's name means 'horse', and his companion Horsa means stallion. These may be given names, or status titles within their tribe. Possibly these tribespeople had horses as a totem animal, perhaps sailing with horse-headed ships. By tradition, they came with a banner of a white horse, preserved to this day as the emblem of Kent.

According to the *Volsunga Saga*, a thirteenth-century Icelandic story of Sigmund the Volsung, an early and legendary family, Horsa was a high-born leader of Saxons. And Bede, in his eighth-century history of England, records that Horsa was a king descended directly from the pagan god Woden, as Saxons invariably claimed of their chieftains, suggesting that the incomers were indeed high-born tribal leaders. Bede says they were Jutes, although some historians think it more likely that they were Franks, and sailed therefore not from Denmark but from the mouth of the Rhine.

All of these tribal groups were closely related, probably having, in the opinion of linguistic experts, only slightly divergent dialects. Their versions of ancient Germanic language formed the basis for modern German, Dutch and English wording, the southern English accents (Jutes and Saxons), and the midland and northern accents (Angles). From the latter comes 'Angle-ish', or English.

The first sight of the Saxon peoples who contributed so much to Middle-earth magic was far from enchanting. They must have looked terrifying. Plunging from their low, lean boats onto the beaches of England, beards and moustaches stiff with saltwater spray, these were elite warriors armed to the teeth. Bristling with swords, spears, shields, axes, bows, metal helmets, knives and chains, they beached in their dozens, scores, even hundreds in search of a new homeland for their clans.

Certainly these warriors came dressed to kill – literally. They were a sort of Saxon samurai. Even their hairstyles reflected their elite status, and tribal affiliations. Roman writer Sidonius, writing at the time of these first invasions, describes fifth-century Frankish warriors – whose exclusive right to speak their mind freely in Dark Age Gaul gave us our 'speaking frankly' phrase. They pulled their hair from the back of the head and fixed it on top, leaving their necks bare and bright. He describes their 'red pates', and they may have vividly painted their faces and necks. Coolly staring from these colourful heads were eyes 'faint and pale, with a glimmer of greyish blue', according to Sidonius. They were clean shaven, except that 'instead of beards they have thin moustaches which they run through with a comb'. They must have resembled Captain Hook from Peter Pan, but without the whimsy.

A Roman official called Cornelius Tacitus reported that the young warriors of the Chatti tribe, in western Germany, allowed their flowing hair and beards to grow unchecked until they had killed an enemy. The wild, unkempt locks of these men hungry for the status of a haircut would not have been an encouraging sight. And Sidonius reveals that in Bordeaux the north German Saxon fighters shaved their hairlines and '. . . with the growth thus clipped to the skin, his head is reduced and his face enlarged'. The big-faced Saxons charging up the beaches must have been an alarming sight. Some-times they embellished their appearance with luxuriant moustaches which, judging by the combs, tweezers, shears and clippers found in archaeological digs, would have made them impeccably groomed assassins.

The most dramatic hairstyles among this array was that of the Suebians, a tribe from the south-west of Germany. They can be seen in Roman sculptures of Germanic tribesmen with their hair tied up in a knot at the side of their head. This was a sign of status as a freeman, according to Tacitus, and several hundred years later, Sidonius confirms that this hairstyle was still in vogue and copied by other tribes. Young warriors were obviously the role models of popular culture in those days, a more brutal version of our sportsmen and rock stars.

Even the Romans had employed Saxons on a small scale to repel invaders along the east coast. But the Romans had the military muscle to contain the mercenaries. With England in a now much weakened state, the Saxon warriors coming in saw opportunities for the taking. They kept arriving in scores and hundreds. Entries in *The Anglo-Saxon Chronicle*, say 'Aelle and his three sons, Cymen, Wlencing and Cissa, came into Britain with three ships.' Another, for 514, records that 'In this year the West Saxons came into Britain with three ships.'

The new Anglo-Saxon invaders were not centrally organized, and their spread across the landscape was slow and uneven. Historians have long debated just how this transition could have happened. It used to be thought that the Saxons wiped out the Celts, or forced them to the west, Wales and Cornwall. Certainly, this was the case for some of them. A letter sent by the Celts to the Romans said of the Saxons, despairingly, 'The barbarians drive us into the sea, and the sea drives us back to the barbarians. Between these, two deadly alternatives confront us, drowning or slaughter.' Then the evidence accumulated to show that it was a more complex and varied pattern. In some areas there was cooperation, in others the Saxons were the rulers and the Celts a kind of underclass. At West Heslerton, in Yorkshire, an Anglican settlement excavated in the 1980s, revealed 201 burials. The skeletons were of two distinct physical types. Most of them were short and of stockier build, while a minority – about one-fifth of the total – were taller and probably of a higher status, because they were buried with their weapons. Archaeologists think it likely that the shorter people were indigenous Celts, while the taller were Angles, who had invaded and become the dominant upper class. Nevertheless, there is little Celtic influence in place-names and root words in England, which one would expect if cooperation had been the norm. And certainly there were pitched battles between some Celtic tribes and the Saxon incomers, some perhaps featuring that part-legendary Celtic hero, Arthur. So while there probably were examples of cooperation, in sum, the Saxons did take over, and the Celts were subjugated again, as they had been when the Romans came to the island.

By the end of the sixth century, the liaisons and confederations of tribal groups coalesced into larger kingdoms. By the end of the sixth century, some of their names can still be traced in today's counties and old shires. Kent was named from the Cantiabi, the Celtic tribe who occupied the territory before the Saxons took it over. Sussex and Essex were the lands of the the South Saxons and East Saxons respectively. The region on the east coast of England known as East Anglia today was the homeland of the East Angles. The other two Angle kingdoms were those of Northumbria (land north of the Humber) and Mercia (middle Angles – now the Midlands). Wessex, home to the West Saxons, eventually extended over most of England south of the Thames, when Alfred the Great became the first regional leader to successfully unify much of the country – a military necessity in the face of Norse invasions in the ninth century.

By this time, competition and intermarriage had led to amalgamation of kingdoms, so that at the beginning of the ninth century only four Anglo-Saxon kingdoms remained: East Anglia, Mercia, Northumbria and Wessex. Also by now, Christianity had been officially adopted by all the Anglo-Saxon royal houses, although the populace did not necessarily follow them until some time later. Baptism was an attractive move for kings like Alfred, for it connected them with the powerful political alliances connected with the Church on the continent. The kings added to their Woden ancestry a Christian blessing on their ruling as His representatives on Earth.

Christianity spread downwards from the kings and their court to the people, although the process took some time.

The Anglo-Saxons themselves remained well aware of their origins, even centuries after they first settled in England. In 738 the English missionary, St Boniface, reports the continental Saxons saying of the English, 'We are of one blood and one bone.'

Vikings

The final phase of the noisy history was as bloody as the earlier ones. *The Anglo-Saxon Chronicle* and other sources report bluntly what happened in AD 789: three fast ships appeared suddenly on the south coast of Devon. This was in the territory of Beorhtric, then king of the West Saxons (who later died in 802, the victim of an allegedly 'accidental' poisoning by his wife). His local administrator, one of the officials then called 'reeves', was named Beaduheard. He was notified about the ships. Immediately he leapt on his horse, and rode over to the ships from Dorchester with a few men. He assumed that the foreigners were merchants who needed supervising, rather than the armed marauders they turned out to be. Reeves were usually men of high status, in charge of great royal estates and receiving large gifts of land from the king for their services. They were used to being obeyed. The sources tell us that when Beaduheard reached the ships and encountered the Norsemen, he 'admonished them in an author-itative manner', and gave orders that they should be driven to the royal town. And at that point he and his companions were summarily executed by the Norsemen.

This event set the tone for many years to come. More 'fast ships' began to arrive, and brought raids intermittently from around 780 until the Normans took over the island in 1066. They were oared by people who came to be called, in *The Chronicle*, 'northmen', 'Danes', or 'Vikings'. Some scholars reckon the name Vikings to have origi-nated as a description of people who came from the shores of the Oslo Fjord, know as the Viken. Among the English, it was soon taken into the general vocabulary as a term for the feared pirates with whom they became painfully familiar. Their language became today's Danish, Swedish, Norwegian, Icelandic and Faroese.

Raiders along the east coast of England helped themselves to the easy pickings of Christian wealth in unguarded monasteries. Silver and gold chalices, book-mounts, personal ornaments and coinage were melted down by the still-heathen Norsemen. The monastery of Whitby in Yorkshire was raided in 867, and a stone mould for casting ingots found at Whitby Abbey may have been used by Vikings for melting down and sharing out the looted treasures.

Contemporary Christian commentators such as Wulfstan regarded the Vikings as the agents or instruments of divine punishment for the sins of the English people.

Gradually, from the end of the eighth century until the middle of the eleventh, England was transformed by a large influx of Norse invaders. The raids increased in frequency, the Norsemen started staying in England over winter, and then settling, particularly in eastern England. In 866 they captured York, and by the early 870s the Vikings controlled the greater part of eastern England from York to London. In 865 the first payment of a Danegeld is recorded – tribute payments. For the promise of peace the people of Kent paid the Vikings money and were rewarded with treachery, says *The Anglo-Saxon Chronicle* accusingly, and that 'under cover of the promise of money, the (Viking) army went secretly inland by night and ravaged all the eastern part of Kent'.

The political battle for territory split the country until finally, King Alfred came to the throne of Wessex in 871 until his death in 899. In the year of his accession, nine major battles took place against the Vikings. At the beginning of 878 Alfred narrowly escaped capture in a surprise attack on his residence at Chippenham. He fled to the Somerset marshes and hid until he could reorganize his forces. He rallied the West Saxons and won a decisive victory at Edington in Wiltshire. In 886 Alfred 'occupied' London, and in the words of *The Anglo-Saxon Chronicle*, 'all the English people that were not under subjection to the Danes submitted to him'. Alfred ended his reign as 'king of the Anglo-Saxons' the dominant ruler in England.

His successors established a united English kingdom by the middle of the tenth century. The last Viking king of York was Eirik Bloodaxe, who was expelled by the Anglo-Saxons in 954 during the reign of Alfred's grandson, Eadred. The struggle for power continued, and Edgar (Eadred's son) had a second coronation at Bath in 973 to confirm his status as the most powerful of the rulers of the British Isles.

The Death and Rebirth of Middle-earth

The Norse invaders were originally from the same ethnic stock as the Anglo-Saxons, and much of their culture was the same. But they had not been subject to the same influences of Christianity, and now they brought a resurgence of the magical beliefs of Middle-earth.

With this late refuelling, the culture of the Real Middle-earth had lasted for about a thousand years, from the times of the early Celts. When King Edward the Confessor died in 1066 without a male heir, Harold, a powerful and very wealthy member of the Wessex aristocracy, claimed that Edward had promised him the succession to the throne – and had himself crowned king in Westminster Abbey on 6 January, the day after Edward had died. However, it transpires that he had already promised the succession to the throne to William of Normandy, who came to England to fight Harold for the kingship. Harold lost the throne to William on 14 October 1066 at the Battle of Hastings. His earlier oath of allegiance to William had proved his undoing. After his death, it was said that Harold had been 'too free with his oaths'.

While history is a seamless, interwoven flowing river of human experience, there are points in the stream to which we can point and say the current changed. This was one of those times. With Harold's death and the takeover of the royal house by the Normans, a new aristocracy arrived. And by this time, political and religious upheavals in Europe had brought in a more strictly Christian religious epoch, in which the old ways became marginalized or even outlawed. The Norman invasion of 1066 was the beginning of the end for Anglo-Saxon England as the invaders brought in a new layer of elite rulers. The magical culture of Middle-earth gave way to what we think of as the beginning of the Middle Ages, and a new era.

Through the centuries, an incipient denigration of pre-Christian Anglo-Saxon culture followed and has persisted. The magic was dismissed by historians as 'superstition', 'primitive', 'dark ages' – an embarrassing interlude of history between the Romans and the

Normans. Only now have these attitudes to the Anglo-Saxons begun to be reversed as archaeology and history reassess the past. And today, there is a renewed hunger for magic and mystery in a modern world in which technology has failed to deliver peace, and science has proven to be an inappropriate language for finding answers to the deeper questions about our existence. The realm of human imagination is once again considered as important as our rational mind. We need both. Middle-earth has returned.

3. How They Lived

A fire spits, seethes and crackles in the central stone hearth. Smoke seeps from it, filling the plank-walled room with a sweet, resinous aroma. It jumps in the draught from the open door, then drifts higher, into the oak roof-beams of the timber hall, and escapes like a ghost through the roof thatch. I am in the main hall at West Stow, an Anglo-Saxon village. Or rather, a village recreated from, and built on the site of a community that thrived here for two hundred years in early Anglo-Saxon England.

West Stow was built originally around AD 420, in north Suffolk, shortly after the Roman overlords abandoned England. It was typical of hundreds of small settlements of the time. They were established near to rivers, with an area cleared for farming. The larger communities, with a hall and houses, was a 'vill' or village – smaller ones, perhaps just two or three houses around a farm, were hamlets.

West Stow is a microcosm of how people lived in first millennium England. These communities were typical of a mid-point in the Middle-earth millennium. Earlier Celts lived in roundhouses, later Anglo-Saxons and Vikings built larger communities – though the vast bulk of the population of England continued to live rurally until the nineteenth century.

Stow means the 'special place' or the 'sacred place'. And while every pioneer settlement in a new country is special in a way, most Middle-earth place-names did not include words which can mean 'sacred' – although there are a few dozen towns and villages still surviving to this day, which were named after gods or goddesses. West Stow may have had some sacred presence of its own, perhaps even a resident shaman or wizard, attracting people from other settlements to its ceremonies. We know that it had been inhabited from the earliest times of Stone Age hunter-gatherers. Archaeological evidence shows that six or seven thousand years ago, people camped on the low hill, made flint tools, and hunted from there. And around 2000 BC a tribal chief was buried at the west end of the hill at Stow. He was entombed in a round-shaped burial mound surrounded by a broad ditch. His body was buried with a single stone bead. Later settlers cremated their dead, and buried some of them in the ditch, so continuing the connection with the afterlife suggested by the burial mound.

The hill was later occupied and farmed, probably by Celts, for some generations, starting around 200 BC. They cleared some of the woodland for their fields, built circular huts, rubbish pits, ditches to keep livestock in the fields and farmed small plots of crop-growing land. Archaeological evidence suggests that the community was abandoned by about AD 60. This was the territory of the Celtic Iceni tribe and, ominously, AD 60/61 was the time of Queen Boudicca's doomed uprising against the occupying Roman military forces. After she was defeated, many of her people were slaughtered or consigned to slavery. That may have been the dark fate of the people of West Stow.

With the Romans gone, the system of central government collapsed. The early Anglo-Saxon villages like Stow functioned as tribal organizations – extended families or groups of families, with chieftains. Remarkably, the nearby Roman town of Icklingham lay abandoned and deserted (we shall return to this phenomenon of the avoidance of Roman ruins by later settlers in Chapter 5). No further towns were built for another two hundred years – in Suffolk, for example, Ipswich was founded in the early 600s. Until then, tribal chieftains ruled as early kings over extensive rural areas. They drew their wealth partly from trade, and from war tribute from other kingdoms. But the backbone of their kingdoms relied on revenue from the hundreds of little villages like West Stow, for whom they provided military protection in return.

West Stow was abandoned in around AD 620, when its resident families apparently moved a mile upriver to build a new village near to the larger communities then being set up. We can imagine the buildings left to the forces of nature: the thatch blowing off the roofs, deserted buildings leaning and breaking and the decaying timbers crumbling back into the soft ground. The discarded detritus of generations disappeared beneath the spreading vegetation, to lie undiscovered for over a thousand years.

And then, in 1847 men working to raise gravel for use as ballast in barges on the River Lark discovered skeletons and numerous urns at West Stow. Gradually, over the next hundred years, the site revealed its secrets. Major excavations took place from 1965 to 1972 under the supervision of Stanley West, when Bury St Edmunds Council joined him in establishing a trust to rebuild the village. Archaeologists excavated the buildings, and then the houses, huts and halls were reconstructed on the same site, using the ancient building techniques, tools and materials that would have been available to the original inhabitants.

If we could travel back in time and approach the original village, we would walk up the rise to the hill on which the settlement sits. Our first sight of it would be the grey firesmoke drifting in the wind above the surrounding trees – fires were needed all year round for cooking and blacksmithing, and in the winter for heating. And on a cloudy, damp day, smoke would have seeped from the thatched roofs, making the village look as though it were steaming.

The path to the village would pass the fields cleared for farming on each side. By the fifth and sixth centuries AD the farmers of the real Middle-earth had an effective and well-ordered system of land management. Land was shared among the people who had cleared it for agriculture, and the fields were laid out in strips, each strip fenced and farmed by one extended family. They were expected to take full responsibility for it, and to respect their neighbour's patch.

In the late seventh century, King Ine declared that: 'If free peasants have a common meadow or other land divided into shares to fence, and some have fenced their portion and some have not, and if cattle eat up their common crops or grass, those who are responsible for the gap are to go and pay to the others, who have fenced their part, compensation for the damage that has been done there.' Each year, in rotation, one-third of the arable land was left to lie fallow, to replenish its productivity.

Tolkien reflected these practises in *The Hobbit*, when he described how his hobbits loved a well-organized life in their 'Shire', with their fields farmed with good husbandry.

Approaching the village, we would have had to blow a horn to warn of our arrival, and to make clear that we were not bandits sneaking up surreptitiously. There was no general law enforcement then, and communities had to look after their own safety, so we might be met by young men from the village with spears and knives in hand. But once we were accepted as peaceful visitors, it is likely that we would be welcomed and offered food, and even a sleeping place in a barn or workhut for the night. Tacitus, writing about the Germanic peoples who were the ancestors of the people of West Stow, remarked on the fact that 'they regard it as bad to turn anyone away'.

Today, the village has a timeless quality. The natural cladding of the replica houses, built each in their own space as originally, makes the buildings appear to grow out of the ground, with soft edges and attractively uneven angles, each house full of individual character. Archaeological excavations have revealed that the people of West Stow comprised three or four large, extended families, consisting of parents, children and the children's children, together with slaves. Each family group seems to have lived in its own groups of houses, surrounding larger individual halls which were for a family to sit and eat together, drink and entertain. In its prime, the village would have had two or three halls for its principal families, and archaeologists found remains of 69 smaller houses, workbuildings and stores on the site. The village population fluctuated over the decades between 60 and up to 200 people at any one time.

The remains of the houses consisted of a pit about thirteen feet long and up to five feet deep. Their smallest dwellings were built on an A-shaped design and planked over, for storage and to keep the floor dry. The structure comprised a framework of strong, thick beams of wood embedded in the ground at one end, and bolted together at the top with wooden pegs hammered through holes. Fastened onto this framework were walls made of long, pliable sticks of willow or hazel called wattles, woven together and then daubed with a mixture of clay and straw which dried like plaster. The insides were kept dry and warm by placing a layer of thatch or turf onto the roofs, and plank floors often had an excavated pit under the floor for a cool food store.

Tolkien recreated this atmosphere of intimacy with nature in *The*

Hobbit, by placing Bilbo Baggins and other hobbits of his fantasies in 'houses' cosily tunnelled into hillsides, or built low to the ground, and covered with turves of grass for insulation. However, Bilbo Baggins's comfortable rooms had windows and doors borrowed from the England of Tolkien's writing – the middle of the twentieth century. In the real Middle-earth, windows were formed of wattle shutters. Glass – made of beechwood ash fired in a charcoal furnace with washed sand – was not yet available in ancient England.

On a summer's day like this one, West Stow's smaller buildings would be humming with activity, for most of them were used as summer workshops. In the larger ones people slept, with clay hearths in the centre of the floor holding a woodfire.

Around and among the houses, the sights and sounds would be those of a pre-industrial farm community. The creak of wooden water mills accompanied the grinding of corn, the munching of tethered goats, and clucking chickens; perhaps the commands of an ox-herd taking the community's few oxen to plough the nearby fields. More distant sounds would include the forge hammers ringing on metal in the blacksmith's hut, placed for symbolic reasons, as we shall see later, on the edge of the settlement.

Archaeologists discovered that the hall located in the centre of West Stow was larger and more complex than the others. It may have been the hall of the chief of the settlement, or even a hall that all the families used. As visitors we might have been taken to this hall to meet the headman of the settlement. The door of the original building unlocked with the turn of a large key made of bone. The main hall was about thirty-two feet long and fourteen feet wide, with a central fireplace. The open-plan rooms were open to high rafters. When doors and shutters were closed, the only natural light filtered through chinks in the smoke holes and gaps around the door. The people working at the reconstructed village have noticed that the central fire makes smoke which rises into the loft areas, and thereby discourages flies and mice. Dried meat stored there in the smoky atmosphere stays edible for a very long time.

Cutting and preparing the timbers to build the hall would have taken a lot of work. The trees had to be chopped down, branches axed and sawn off, and then the trunks split with wedges. Oak was the main timber, being hard and long-wearing, but relatively easy to split. The structure of the building was held together by making holes in the timbers with iron pokers like drill-bits, two of which were found on the site by the archaeologists, and driving wooden pegs in through two pieces of wood. Ash would be used for the rafters, and hazel for the battens on which the straw or reed thatch was fixed.

The volunteers at West Stow declare that the original inhabitants of the village would have made a better job of the buildings than they have. In the reconstruction there are very narrow cracks between the planks of the walls, caused by using wood which was not properly aged. It shrinks as it dries, forming gaps between the planks. The original builders, with generations of wood-building experience, would have established a continual supply of ageing timber, felling and cutting it several years before using it for building. The experiment of reconstruction has engendered a great respect for the skills of our fifth-century ancestors.

Even so, the upright planks of this rebuilt hall look strong and solid. A building with walls like this has actually survived since Anglo-Saxon times – the tiny wooden church at St Andrews, Greensted, in Essex is the oldest such building in the world. Dendrological evidence shows that it was built in the eleventh century. The builders cut massive oak trunks, split them, and then laid them upright side-by-side. Thin strips of wood were then set into internal recesses to bind the uprights together and provide draught-proofing. The original oak sill-beam was replaced only in the nineteenth century, with a brick one.

Entering one of the recreated houses, my first impression was of cosiness. Houses like these are several steps up from a basic shelter, but a long way short of the cocooning provided by the more sophisticated Roman constructions. The wood of the frame, walls, benches and tables – all of it is suffused with the soft, warm aroma of woodsmoke, even when the fire is not burning.

The walls of the main hall would probably have been decorated with carving and tapestries. There might have been a ceremonial sword – often the symbol of the leader or chief (and buried with them). The hilt of such a sword often had fine design worked on it, the blade perhaps pattern-welded and inscribed with protective runes. To bury such a valuable object with its owner was a potent sign of respect.

Hunting bows and arrows which fell, or were even deposited, in marshy bogs have been preserved by the conditions until modern times. Recovered examples show exquisite craftsmanship. Replicas of these ancient weapons made at the West Stow Anglo-Saxon village are elegant, formed from fine-grain ash, a shallow groove smoothed into the back of the bow so that when flexed the grain of the wood narrows rather than opens up. This retains the flexibility and long life of the wood. The weapons have a fine balance, and can shoot arrows a considerable distance.

Mentions of halls in literature sometimes suggest that running down either side of the room, against the two longest walls, were raised benches topped with linen-covered mattresses stuffed with straw or horsehair. The planked floor was strewn with dried rushes and aromatic, creamy-flowered meadowsweet. Clothes and domestic implements hung from pegs driven into the beams of the wooden frame. Inside, the material comfort level was of course much less than today, and the fire in the middle of the floor must have made for a smoky atmosphere, but the rooms have a cosy and comforting feel.

Beds, tables, chests, boxes, stools and chairs are all referred to in later Anglo-Saxon literature and in archaeological reports. The hall may have contained at least one fine chair. An illustration on a pot from a cemetery excavated at Spong Hill, Norfolk shows a person seated on a chair with a low back. The chair appears to show panels on the sides and back, and would have to have been held together with mortise and tenon joints and pegged together. Slash marks on the arms and back of the chair suggest a cushion.

If we were sitting in the hall of the original village, the men around us would have been wearing oufits of woollen leggings, soft leather shoes, and tunic tops with belts; the women wore longer tunics. Our main source for the appearance of these peoples is Tacitus. Describing how they looked on the continent some generations before they settled in England, he said that '. . . all wear a cloak, fastened with a clasp, or in its absence, a thorn'. He reported that only the richest men wore underclothes, suggesting that the manufacture of such garments was costly. Those that Tacitus saw were tight-fitting, '. . . throwing each limb into relief'. They also had overcoats of wild animal skins. He noted also the use of sheepskin coverings, often with the fur worn inside, and the outside of the skins sewn into shape. He reports that the women had the same dress as the men, except that very often '. . . trailing linen garments, striped with purple, are in use for women: the upper part of this costume does not widen into sleeves: their arms and shoulders are therefore bare, as is the adjoining portion of the breast'. The women also wore jewellery, such as brooches, necklaces and rings.

Archaeologists at West Stow and similar settlements have analysed traces of fabric preserved on metalwork found in graves – buttons, belts, brooches and other things attached to clothing – and discovered that these garments were made of wool, linen and hemp. At West Stow the people have made replica clothes from the same materials, and found them to be light, warm and comfortable. Working clothes in Anglo-Saxon England could be simple, but also attractive. The vegetable dyes they used have proven in recent experiments to result in beautifully coloured clothing, producing a wide variety of bright shades and deep, soft hues.

Shoes, belts and bags were made from leather from cattle hide. Shoes would generally be round-toed, flat soled and reach to the ankle or just below. They were stitched or laced together with leather thongs, not nailed as in some Roman examples.

Things changed slowly in those days, but even so influences from outside, and creative new ways of doing things from inside, affected ways of living. At West Stow the clothes changed fashion over the two hundred years of residence – at least for the women. Imported jewellery and accessories from southern Scandinavia – found only in women's graves – include wrist clasps for fastening sleeves. Until the seventh century, women seemed to have worn large brooches on the shoulders, with a string of beads hung between them on the chest. But then a different style, featuring festoons of rings and dresses a little more like the Mediterranean 'tunic', came into fashion. The clothes for both men and women may have included some fine stitching, embroidery, colours and patterns.

Judging by the surfeit of bone combs found in graves, people kept their hair and beards well-groomed.

Hearing them talk would seem uncannily familiar. Much of the language of Middle-earth is directly antecedent to modern English. Linguists reckon that, for example, the people of the Anglii tribes spoke a language (Angli-ish, which became English) which had a rhythm and sound which would feel familiar to our ears today, even though we might not understand any individual words.

With the influx of settlers, their Germanic language of Anglo-Saxon rapidly became the most used in place of the Latin of the departed Roman elite, and even the Celtic languages spoken by people who had been taken over by the Romans. These languages were used fully in a culture in which people did not write, but passed down their history, laws, heroes and villains, religions and magic through oral tradition – teaching and learning, genealogies and allegiances, memorizing, spells and incantations, and poetry and stories.

Tacitus reported that Germanic tribes had a 'marked preference for spontaneous forms of community: communal feasting and hospitality'. He wrote that for the Germans, 'To close the door against any human being is a crime'. From ancient manuscript descriptions we can imagine how such an indoor feast would look. Inside the air hung heavy with the odour of mutton-fat candles, wood-smoke and roasting meat spitted over roaring log fires set in trenches down the centre of the hall, or cooked in kitchen huts just outside. Side benches were fronted with boarded trestles. Blazing torches in wall brackets would have arced great shadow shapes up into the high, smoke-blackened roof-beams. The chieftain of the settlement would be seated at a ceremonial chair at the head of the hall. If he was rich, he might wear gold arm-rings.

Once the food was grown, baking and cooking were carried on much as they were on the American frontier a century ago. The people of Middle-earth knew and used yeast. Fruits and vegetables were generally smaller and perhaps less sweet than those of today, and included cabbage, onions, leeks and turnips as the heavy staple items, plus lettuce, peas and parsley. Apples (which could be stored through the winter) and berries were the main fruits, either picked wild or grown domestically. Cherries, pears, plums and nuts were available.

Meat was a luxury, but for an important feast, a necessity. Large, black cooking pots suspended above the fire would be winched noisily to the ground, and racks of spitted fowl pulled from the flames and chopped onto trenchers, while bakers carried boards of steaming bread and cakes which were removed with tongs and placed carefully on the trenchers. Perhaps the aroma of roasted venison would gradually camouflage other smells. Pitchers of ale and mead would be pushed along the tables. Beer and alcoholic apple cider were the common drink, and mead, made from honey, was a more expensive drink for the aristocracy.

The knife handles, made of horn, were sometimes carved into the likeness of horses' heads, and metal spoons had wooden handles of unique designs for each, sitting smooth and lightly in the hand. The food was served on wooden platters, and in bowls, made on a pole lathe operated by working a foot pedal. They were carved and decorated in animal shapes, but exaggerated, so they seemed to have some supernatural quality.

So in practical terms, this is how the people of the real Middle-earth lived. Let us now explore their magic.

4. The Magic of the Forest

I am sitting beneath the wisest tree in England. It is an extraordinary and ancient yew, estimated to be about 2500 years old. It lies near the banks of the River Thames, opposite the area known as Runny-mede. Runnymede now refers to a specific island, but historical geographers reckon that in medieval times, it may have referred to a scattering of islands surrounded by what was then a wide estuary of the Thames. The river has since been re-routed, making these small islands into riverside land. Runnymede is famous as the site of the signing of the Magna Carta on 15 June 1215 – a document drawn up over nine days of negotiations between the barons – the high-ranking landowners of Norman England – and King John. The Magna Carta gave to the barons a share of the power which they believed was being wielded unethically by the king. It is sometimes proposed that the Magna Carta was signed at Runnymede because the site was near to London and yet open countryside. On those small islands, it would have been difficult to conceal an ambushing army, either on the king's or the baron's side. But there may also be a deeper reason, a significance which propels us back deeper into history, beyond the Magna Carta and into the age of Middle-earth.

In Anglo-Saxon times, Runnymede was known as Rune-mede . . . the area of the casting of the runes. Historians have suggested that, for kings and chieftains, this area may have been a sacred place, significant for divination and auguries. Wizards who specialized in such rituals foretold the wealth of the land in the coming season, the health of kings and princesses, chiefs and warriors, and the likely outcomes of battles. The history of the area as a royal divination site may have been why it was chosen as a location for signing such an important document as the Magna Carta.

Perhaps the most propitious site in Rune-mede, where the signing could have taken place and fortunes told centuries earlier, was at the ancient tree beneath which I am sitting. Now known as 'Ankerwyke', it would then have been well over 1,500 years old, and already massive. Also, as if in recognition of its special significance, a nunnery was built a mere thirty yards or so from the tree. Records show that it was constructed there in 1265, not long after the Magna Carta was signed, and possibly on the very spot where the historic agreement was made. The stone walls of the nunnery, the remains of which are still some twenty feet high in places, are built on an alignment which would have afforded a direct view of the ancient tree just outside a fine arched window and door, still present in the ruins. Looming over the kingly rune-castings, the tree must have been 'witness' to many secrets.

To visit the tree, I had journeyed a few miles west of the M25 motorway. Here the roar of the great London cityscape fades into the background, giving way to the birdsong of winding country lanes and the soft greenery of countryside. Near the village of Wraysbury, there are pockets of ancient forest stretching back to Anglo-Saxon times. From the village, I walked for an hour across ancient fields, along trackways, and over wooden bridges linking ancient islands once separated by the estuary of the River Thames. Over the centuries the river has been re-routed, the water table is lower and the area between the islands drier, but the outlines of the water meadows can still be discerned.

Entering the ancient woodlands, the sensation is one of stepping back in time. All woods evolve with the centuries, but this one has had less human interference than most. Some of the oaks in nearby Windsor Park are still surviving after a thousand years. They are probably only the second generation descendants of trees which stood on this site in the times of Middle-earth. And in those times, the landscape looked different.

From an aeroplane today, the lush green landscape of England looks like a patchwork of farm fields, with scattered settlements connected by ribbon roads, and punctuated by great towns and cities. But if we could have made the same airborne survey two thousand years ago, at the beginning of Middle-earth, the land would have appeared radically different. Then, great woodlands of oak, beech, hornbeam, thorn and ash trees covered up to a third of the island,

broken by tracts of open heath and moorland and hilltops ridged
with scrub cover.

Already, for many centuries, early people had been cutting down
the trees for their needs. This continued throughout the Middle-
earth millennium. But the landscape encompassed perhaps a million
people on an island that now supports over fifty times that number.
Areas cleared for farming that were later abandoned, would have
quickly grown back secondary forest of willow, then birch, followed
by alder and hazel, then to oak and finally beech and spruce.
However, by the Domesday Survey in 1086, forest cover was down
to about 15 per cent. Today, surveys show deciduous woodland cover
in Britain to be as low as 1.5 per cent, with total forest cover of all
species of trees reaching about 7 per cent of the island. Compared
with today, much of the landscape of the real Middle-earth lay under
an exquisite blanket of foliage, green in summer, multicoloured in
autumn, and like a gossamer web of lacy branchwork in the winter.

The shadows of this old world still stretch across modern England,
for some woodlands of today retain their ancient names. Sometimes
they were named for the tribal peoples who lived in them. In the
seventh century an area of one of the large forests was called
Inderauuda, meaning 'in the wood of the Deirans', and today Wych-
wood in north-west Oxfordshire is the modern name of Hwicce
Wood, the forest home of the ancient Hwicce clans.

Tolkien says that the Great Wood of *The Lord of the Rings*, which
he called Mirkwood, was not his invention – his researches had led
him to the original name for the great mountainous forest regions
that had formed a barrier to the south of Germany. Mirkwood was a
very ancient name, weighted with legendary associations. So the
hobbits trekked through forests that once really existed.

Some of the forests of the Real Middle-earth were extensive. For
example, those woods called Dean, Morfe and Kinver, west of modern
Stourbridge, each once covered hundreds of square miles. One of the
most extensive wooded areas was the great Anglo-Saxon Andredes-
weald, described in the year 892 as 'thirty miles wide and stretching
one hundred and twenty miles from east to west'. Modern geographers reckon that this forest covered over 2,500 square miles, and
the fragments that have survived comprise the present wooded area

called the Weald, in the south-east of England between the Downs
of Kent and Sussex. On the small island of Britain, forests of this
magnitude would have dominated the landscape.

Trees also dominated the imagination of these peoples. Because
people lived in them, depended on them for shelter, fuel, weapons,
building and carpentry, hunting areas, and much more, they were
intimately attached to the forest. Furthermore, in the times of
Middle-earth the forest was treated like a place of magic and power.
The forest was treated like a place of magic and power. It was
like a great spirit which had to be befriended. For the Celts, the
word 'nemeton' denoted a sacred grove of trees. The old Irish word,
'fidnemed' referred specifically to a forest shrine. Tacitus wrote that
'The grove is the centre of their whole religion. It is regarded as the
cradle of the race and the dwelling-place of the supreme god to
whom all thing are subject and obedient.'

It is hardly surprising, for trees and forests seem to be a natural
template for the human imagination. Many ancient folk tales are set
in the woods. Perhaps it is the way our neurons are connected, like
great entanglements of treetops in a forest of ganglia, that draws us
to the image of branches passing messages.

Walking into the Wood

These thoughts primed my perceptions as I walked into the ancient
wood near the Thames, to visit the ancient yew. The air was pungent
with tree bark and the aroma of the dry ground cover crackling
beneath my feet. A few fronds of bracken quivered in the shadows,
and the grassy undergrowth was punctuated with delicate white
flowering plants. Mosses crept up the lower trunks of trees. Crossing
my path were narrow but clear animal trackways. Some of them
seemed still well used, worn away by the feet of badgers, weasels,
stoats, foxes and hares. The air must have been thick with the smells
of territorial markers beyond my human nasal sensitivity.

Eventually the track opened out into a leafy glade, dappled a pale
golden colour by the late morning summer sunlight. In the times of
Middle-earth this would have been a place where hunters lay in wait
for deer, hares and, for the brave, boar. The open ground afforded a

clear flight for their arrows, fired from their hiding places in the undergrowth. Ash bows made to replicate those found in bogs of Anglo-Saxon times can shoot goose-feathered arrows hard for 150 yards. But even if an animal could be hit from that distance, it might cause only a glancing wound. Good hunters tried, like the drawings in medieval manuscripts, to shoot their prey from as close as possible. Experts reckon that twenty yards was an ideal distance for impact of the arrow blow, and to give the sharp iron tip a chance to penetrate.

In ancient times, journeys into woods like this were dangerous. Bandits haunted pathways through the large stretches of unowned land. There were also risks from wild animals – especially the great, looming brown bears which were hunted for their pelts, usually with pits of sharpened sticks. They are shy animals, and were probably rarely glimpsed. But if surprised and disturbed by a traveller early in the spring, when they may have just emerged half-starved from winter hibernation, a dangerously hungry bear could move fast and kill with a swipe of its claws.

Boar also ran wild in the woods – and are re-emerging today in some areas of Britain. They would attack humans only if disturbed and startled, but their aggressive charge hurtled a heavy muscular body low down through the undergrowth like an explosion of aggression. Wolves acquired an awesome reputation over the centuries of Middle-earth, and often became an enemy of humans because they hunted the same prey. They rarely attacked people unless they were injured or desperately hungry – but there was always the possibility.

A rabbit hopped across my path further along. It was probably the most dangerous animal I would encounter today.

As I left the main footpaths and ventured under the tree cover, I saw a patch of soft, mossy ground pressed flat, possibly by a deer taking a rest. And a short distance away a deer-nibbled sapling gleamed, freshly stripped of bark a few feet from the ground. The Anglo-Saxons would have tried to protect young saplings from being browsed by deer by digging ditches and piling the earth as ramparts around the boundaries of woodland areas.

A giant willow stood massive and alone at the far end of a clearing, its leaf-laden branches climbing above roots thickly carpeted with columbine and purple garlic. All around me elder and sweetbriar shrubs flaunted petals in colours softened by the filtered sunlight. I breathed their sweet fragrance warmed and wafted by the summer breeze. Chaffinches flitted nervously from bush to bush, chattering to each other in harsh warning notes as I passed. When today we glimpse the breathtaking beauty of a woodland setting, it is hardly surprising to us that the people of the historical Middle-earth imbued nature with a spiritual presence. But, of course, for them it was far more than a matter of aesthetic beauty. Landscapes are taken in by the eye but actually perceived with the brain. That is where interpretation and meaning make sense of the signals from our sensory receptors. And they saw more than we would, gazing at the same scene. They thought of nature not only as an objective world, external to themselves, but as also reaching internally, with magical powers and imbued with the full richness of their imagination. Features of nature had many layers of meaning, levels of significance, allusions and messages. The forest was alive with the chatter of another world. Particular trees, for example, held magical potency.

I came across a huge, fallen giant beech tree, victim of high winds in the south of England in the 1980s. Massive tree rootballs lay exposed, towering fifteen or twenty feet high, ripped from the ground by the weight of the tree crashing down. The roots were truly magnificent. I rested awhile, leaning against the fallen trunk. I could identify the tree as a beech by its shape, its bark and leaves.

In Anglo-Saxon times, this would be just the beginning. Then, strips of beechwood, or even bark, were taken on which runes were carved, and for the making of runesticks for divination. Perhaps this is why beech ('boc' in Old English) shares its name with the ancient form of the word 'book'.

In those times too, houses were sometimes built next to, or even around trees. The tree embodied the destiny of the family living beneath it. The Norse had a concept called 'barnstokkr' (barn = 'baby'; stokkr 'tree trunk') which symbolized the eternal unfolding of generations of a family, and linked them with both ancestors and generations to come. The tree sanctified the well-being of these generations.

The Anglo-Saxon word 'treow' meant both 'tree', and 'trust' or 'truth'. The tree seemed to represent the very essence of spiritual reality in cosmology, and material trees manifested this deepest level of integrity. For this reason, trees were even thought to provide witness for the most serious of contracts between people. Sacred vows, such as marriages or pledges, were carried out in the presence of these spirits of nature – rather like a pre-Christian ceremony equivalent to swearing on a Bible. Not surprisingly, the Church authorities objected: one of their proscriptions admonished 'No one shall go to trees, or wells, or stones . . . or anywhere else except to God's church, and there make vows or release himself from them.'

As the wood deepened, ahead of me the grassy trackway twisted to the left beneath the huge, spreading canopy of an old ash tree. The base of the trunk was smothered with drooping blue flowers of columbine. As I came closer, I could see the bark had turned dark grey, and was crazed with a network of shallow ridges, like the map of another world. The ash tree produces elegant shoots, tall, straight, strong and clear of branches – ideal for the shafts of spears. The Anglo-Saxon word for this tree, 'aesc', meant not only 'ash' but also 'spear'.

But the ash also had an Otherworld dimension. As I stood at the base of the trunk and looked up, from this vantage point, the highest branches seemed to disappear into the sky. And when powerful winter storms raged through the woods toppling trees, the ash tended to stand its ground. In Anglo-Saxon times, this deep-rooted stability encouraged people to imagine that its roots sank into the ground as far as its trunk and branches stretched into the sky. The tree seemed to form a bridge between the spirits of the Lowerworld, and the Upperworld realm of the gods. The Norse identified the ash (or some say the yew . . . we shall come to that later) as the World Tree, the image that connected all worlds of spirit.

A 'maiden' ash like this one – self-sown, rather than planted, and never pruned – was especially powerful. It had magical powers. I picked up a long twig which had dropped down from the branches. It was narrow, strong, whip-like. It whistled when I snapped it through the air. In ancient times, riders would cut sticks of ash to use as crops, whipping or 'twitching' their horses. But the whip's usefulness far surpassed its practical qualities – the ash's magical powers warded off harmful magic directed towards the horse and rider. The twig or stick must have contained, for the Anglo-Saxons, the potency of the whole tree, stretching between the Worlds. It was like a lightning conductor for unseen forces. Malevolent spirits of the Otherworld may have tried to grip and grasp a rider, pulling him from his horse, or directing the animal to step into a hole, hobbling it. But grasping spirit-fingers were warded off by the slashing stick of ash in the rider's hand.

In Middle-earth, a central power of spell-casting was to draw energy into the confined and controllable space of a circle. Often the circle was carefully etched into the ground with a wizard's staff formed from a maiden ash tree, thereby containing and binding unseen forces.

In everyday life, people believed that such a circle drawn with ash could contain snakes, and prevent them from escaping. I picked up an ash wand which was among several that had blown down from the tree, and lay in the undergrowth. It was about four feet long – a little short for a staff – but very straight and smooth. I held it lightly, and concentrated. Then I drew a clear cirle around myself, dragging the end of the wand through the grass of the forest floor. Standing in the circle, I chanted some of the words of the charm in the Lacnunga spellbook: 'I circle myself with this rod and trust, against the sore stitch, against the sore bite, against the grim dread, against the great horror that is hateful to all, and all evil that enters this land.' I went to set the stick aside . . . but then kept the wand with me just in case of snakes. Or Otherworld intrusions.

A stand of six beautiful birches, growing tall and straight, arose right ahead of me. When I reached them, their bark was white and wonderfully stimulating to the touch; rough and textured. The surface was dry, but rain the previous day had still not dried from within the cracks and crevices of the trunk. Its beauty was appreciated in early England. The rune B was called 'beorc', a variant of the word 'birch'. It was a tree which in Anglo-Saxon times was associated with the feminine, and had the connotation of female purity. Perhaps its clean white trunk gave this impression. Where possible, stables built for horses were sited next to a birch, for its purity was protection against a feared feminine energy: witches. A birch hung with strips of red and white cloth outside a stable was believed to protect the horses from hag-riding. This might occur in the dead of night, when witches ghosted into the stable, stole the horses and rode them hard out into the darkness. The horses were later returned by the witches, but the animals were trembling with exhaustion, foaming with sweat, their nostrils flaring and eyes rolling.

Beneath the birches spread a low stand of creamy flowered elder shrubbery, giving off a heavy, fruity fragrance. Their leaves grow on stout twigs which are filled with a thick, white pith. I snapped one off. The pith is easily hollowed out by a finer stick or long blade to make a hollow tube, from which can be constructed pea-shooters or whistles. Elder gets its name from an Anglo-Saxon word meaning 'hollow tree', so perhaps they knew how to make pea-shooters and whistles!

The branches of the elder curved over and formed a tunnel, or hole. I crawled through it. Certain trees were regarded as having direct healing powers. Sometimes the way a tree had grown, or been hit by lightning, or rotted out in the centre, provided a space in the trunk through which people could pass. The tree formed its own circular passage, concentrating its spiritual and beneficent energies within the space. Such holes in trees through which people or animals could pass transferred to them some of the wisdom and energy of these sacred, huge growing things. So farmers of ancient times drove their animals through it to bring them good health.

This practice enraged Christian authorities, for it engaged directly with spiritual powers, rather than by grace of priests interdicting with God. In about AD 640, St Eligius was provoked to declare 'Let no-one . . . make flocks pass through a hollow tree or an aperture in the earth; for by so doing he seems to consecrate them to the devil.' He also insisted that, 'No Christian place fires at the temples or at the stones, or at fountains and springs, or at trees, or at places where three ways meet.' Placing fires meant lighting wildfires, or flames kindled from scratch, and holding celebrations by their light. Clearly various features of nature also held this magic – not only the wooden 'temples', but also stone circles, fountains and springs, and where 'three ways meet' – crossroads. Certainly they were consecrated to local spirits, emanations of the sacred essence of the natural features of the landscape.

I climbed over fallen giant trees, some from the hurricane winds of fifteen years previously, left here to rot. One was an oak, hundreds of years old. Its uprooted base jutted jaggedly into the air, probably a victim of the same storms. The underside of the logs where the bark remained moist, had sprung large mushrooms, some white and two red. Here the leaf litter was soft and damp, and twigs bent under my feet. The oak was considered to be sacred to Thor, or Thunor, the thunder god in ancient European and Norse mythology. Celts favoured the oaks for Druidic rites, and these trees were iconic as spirit beings.

The light softened and and the wood became misty as if behind a lens, as the sun warmed the leaf cover high above. A light breeze trembled and the leaves and shafts of light darted about here and there, seeming to illuminate a path across the woodland floor. I was nearing the wise yew tree.

The World Tree

As I approached the site of the ancient tree, I passed by a sweeping plantation of shrubbery. It was bladebrush, which has leaves with razor-sharp edges. The shrubs were originally planted centuries ago by women who lived in the nearby nunnery. They used switches of the shrub for whipping their naked flesh to scourge themselves of sin.

The tree suddenly came into view. It was massive in drawings of the nineteenth century, but is shorter now, for over the years it has lost top branches and trunk to lightning and other environmental hazards. But the tree has an immense presence. It is fronted by a small sign from English Heritage, marking it out as a tree of historical significance.

Yews are male or female, and this is the former. It has a very thick trunk, over thirty feet in circumference. The trunk is fantastically knotted, swirling and twisting all the way up, like the gnarled skin and beard of an ancient giant, which, to the people of the Real Middle-earth, is exactly what it was. But most remarkably, the trunk has, with age, lost much of its bark. It has peeled away to reveal the heartwood. This has the appearance of molten lava, honey coloured, flowing down the trunk of the tree. Its eddies and curlicues make fascinating shapes which appear to take on the form of horses, bulls, elves and other spirit creatures.

Tolkien reflected this image of the wise tree in his character Treebeard, a giant who appears in *The Lord of the Rings* with a straggly, long face, and a bushy beard bristling like a mass of twigs with mossy endings. His body is two or three times the size of a man. He is supported by strong, thick legs, and his broad shoulders connect directly to the head without any neck. Rough, thick, greeny-grey skin, like the bark of an elm tree, cover his trunk, but his arms have a smooth brown skin. Each of his feet rambles into seven toes, and when he walks, each stride covers about seven yards.

Tolkien personally felt that trees had a special presence: he said that the magical, fantasy realm of Lothlorien was beautiful because there the trees were loved; elsewhere they were represented as awakening to consciousness of themselves. In *The Lord of the Rings*, Frodo and his companions dozed under an enormous, ancient willow tree. As they drifted into sleep, they glimpsed the hoary branches stretching across the sky, and heard them creaking in the wind. Words drifted into their minds, words they could hardly hear, words that cast a spell over them and took them to a dream world.

The yew tree was like this – old beyond guessing. Great trailing wisps of twig hung from the heavy branches, drifting and swaying in the light breeze. It is a place for perennial spirits which live forever, peering from the branches at the ever-unfolding passage of time, the shifting landscape and many generations of human life.

For the people of Middle-earth, age conferred knowledge. It was a time where information was preserved only in the experienced heads of people as they matured, so that the wisdom of age was truly venerated – not as a romantic homage to a person who had survived a long time and now needed buttressing in fragile old age, but rather out of pragmatic respect for all that such a person had seen, heard, experienced and knew. So what could be more knowledegable than trees, the oldest living things in the landscape?

The world's oldest known wooden artefact, dating from the Hoxnian interglacial layer, 250,000 BC, is a yew spear, found at Clacton in Essex. Another yew spear, probably flint-tipped, has been found in Lower Saxony, where it had been deposited in the ground at about 200,000 BC. The spear was still lodged between the ribs of a straight-tusked elephant.

Possibly the two oldest examples of yew bows are from the Somerset Levels dated about 2700 BC. And the neolithic corpse of the 'Iceman' discovered in 1991 on the Italian–Austrian border had with him a yew longbow measuring 6 feet, even though the man himself was only 5 feet 2 inches tall. This bow may be even older than the Somerset ones, possibly from about 3500 BC.

So yew trees have played a part in human history since the earliest times. However, surviving yew trees are notoriously difficult to date. Although it is widely accepted that they grow to a great age, the oldest ones lose their centre. Because it rots out, fallen trees become hollow and cannot have their rings counted in cross-section because the tree is hollow. So what experts have done is to calculate the average circumference increase in younger yews, and extrapolate to larger ones. This is an inexact science, of course, for tree growth may slow with increasing longevity. But even allowing for this, the trees are hundreds and in some cases, thousands of years old. The oldest yews are reckoned to be as old as Stonehenge. Most of the stone circles in Britain, about 900 of them including Stonehenge, were built between 2600 and 1500 BC, as were the stone rows at Carnac in Brittany. There are at least half a dozen trees existing now that were in their prime at that time, and probably a dozen or so more that have been recorded but have now gone. By these sort of calculations, the yew tree beneath which I was sitting is at least 2,500 years old.

The special significance of yews is also apparent from the way they were sometimes planted on top of burial mounds. Taplow Court in Buckinghamshire created a sensation when it was investigated by Victorian archaeologists in 1883. A large burial mound, 15 feet high, stood 30 yards west of the site of a ruined church. This was a pagan mound within a Christian churchyard. When the barrow was opened it was found to be the grave of a Saxon warrior, buried with his gold buckles, jewelled studs, drinking horn and arms. These objects date his burial to about AD 600. On top of the barrow was an ancient yew, with a circumference of at least 21 feet. For a yew of that size the most likely origin is that it was planted by the Saxons when they interred their dead chief.

Yew trees in churchyards often predate the church, and it is likely that the trees were sacred for our indigenous ancestors long before the advent of Christianity to these islands. The policy of the early church was to Christianize pagan practices rather than always attempting to combat and destroy them. The missionaries of the 'new' Christian religion from the East built some of their churches on existing sacred sites, following advice from Pope Gregory in Rome. A letter he sent to St Augustine in Britain dated 12 July AD 594 bids him

> . . . not to destroy pagan temples, but rather to replace the idols with the relics of saints; to sprinkle the old precincts with holy water and rededicate them, because people come more readily to the places where they have been accustomed to pray. At festivals the people shall be allowed to build their booths of green leaves and to slay their bulls.

He reasoned that it was easier to draw people into a new way of worship if it held a visible and symbolic link with their spiritual life in the past.

I sat down on one of the roots of the yew, resting my back against the trunk. Above me, the branches stretched an unbelievable distance in every direction. Each branch was the size and weight of many entire smaller trees. Gazing up at the branches ranging into the sky, it was easy to see why the tree was such a potent image for the people of our ancient past.

Trees were not just external objects, but also formed a pathway for people to move into the spirit world. Far back, Norse legends tell us, the god Odin, archetypal wizard, climbed into a tree, from there journeyed through the realms of spirit, and came back with a map of the cosmos.

In the creation mythology of the historical Middle-earth, reported in its later Norse form by Snorri Sturluson, the original state of the cosmos was defined by two mighty polarities of force opposing one another. One was composed of fire, the other of ice. Between the two was a region of empty space, which exploded. The ice hissed, and fire spat, and between them they created a seething, swirling mist of potent liquid which filled three wells of wisdom, one of which was called the Well of Wyrd.

The cosmology of Middle-earth also featured, above the well, a central, unifying image: that of an enormous tree which was so high that it reached to the heavens, and with roots so deep that no one knew for sure where they ended. This World Tree formed an unimaginably vast organic map for the realms of the spirit, encompassing the upper worlds of the gods, middle worlds of people, and under world of wisdom within the corresponding parts of the tree: upper branches, lower branches and roots. Sometimes in the literature that surrounds the Norse myths the tree is described as an ash, or even 'an evergreen ash'. Scholars of this literature have declared that the evergreen yew was also held sacred, and a name for the yew in Old Norse is 'barraskr', which means 'needle-ash'.

We know that the early Germanic tribes, at the beginning of the Middle-earth millennium, had a 'World Tree', reflecting their notion that the heavens whirl about a central beam or pivot which pierces both earth and sky. This 'pillar of heaven' was known to the continental Saxons as 'Irminsul' and was represented by a huge wooden pillar erected as the focal point of their religion. The pillar was destroyed by the Christian Charlemagne. In Norse myth the pillar was known as Yggdrasil, 'Odin's steed', since on it the god Odin journeyed to the heavens. The English likewise venerated both standing stones (as at Stonehenge) and prominent trees. An eleventh century English penitential refers directly to the practice:

> Some men are so blinded that they bring their offerings to an earth-fast stone and also to trees and wellsprings, just as witches tell, and they will not understand how stupidly they act, or how the lifeless stone or the dumb tree can help them or deliver health when they themselves never stir from that place.

The ancient cultures of Middle-earth seemed to be based on a shamanically-inspired vision of life, as we shall see later. This means that their notion of the structure of the cosmos, and the spiritual realms, was discovered for them by wizards – people who could enter trance states which they believed could enable them to transcend the earthly realm, 'fly' into the Otherworlds of spirit, and return with descriptions of the geographies of those sacred places. In the legends of the Norse, the first such journey was taken by Odin, a figure later revered as a god, and who served as an archetypal template for the initiation of shamans in Middle-earth. His quests for wisdom in the Otherworld are hinted at in Beowulf and later Norse sagas, as we shall see in chapter 14.

The Cosmology

One of the experiences Odin underwent in his quest for knowledge is contained in the lines of an ancient Norse poem called *Havamal*, written in a form so condensed it is practically a hidden code. Stemming from an oral tradition of sacred poetry from very ancient times, the Havamal was written down by Snorri Sturluson in the thirteenth century as a part of his compilation of materials about Norse indigeneous beliefs, folkways and shamanic traditions from many sources.

The *Havamal* narrates Odin's own description of his initiation, his exploration of his inner worlds, and the map of the cosmos that he revealed during his spirit journeys. The concentrated core of Odin's vision quest for magical wisdom is distilled in the following lines:

> I know that I hung on the windswept tree for nine full nights,
> wounded with a spear and pledged to Odin,
> offered, myself to myself;
> The wisest know not from whence spring
> the roots of that ancient tree.

> They did not comfort me with bread,
> and not with the drinking horn;
> I peered downward,
> I grasped the 'runes', screaming I grasped them;
> I fell back from there.

> Nine powerful spells I learned
> from the famous son of Bolthor,
> father of Bestla,
> and I got a draught of the precious mead,
> poured from magic Odrerir.

> Learned I grew then, lore-wise,
> grew and prospered well:
> Word from word gave words to me,
> Deed from deed gave deeds to me.

Each of these lines refers to a whole world of symbol and significance, but the bare outlines are generally agreed by scholars: in the myth Odin climbed into a sacred tree, and stayed there for nine days and nights without food or water. Under these conditions of privation and intense focus, he entered states of consciousness in which the tree changed into an enormous white, eight-legged horse (who we shall revisit in a later chapter on guardian animals), on which Odin rode through the sky to the Upperworld and down to the Lowerworld, visiting the nine Otherworlds of Knowledge.

During this journey he met, at a magical spring bubbling up by the root of the World Tree, a wisdom giant called Mimir who yielded incantations and powers to help Odin in his quest. He then journeyed to far-off realms where he had to fight, using his wits, trickery, shapeshifting and other powers from Mimir to acquire the source of sacred inspiration which was stored in three vast cauldrons of mead hidden in a cave in the centre of a mountain. It was guarded by fearsome giants, and Odin nearly died in the mountain. But triumphantly he fulfilled his quest, and brought back to his fellow gods, and the human inhabitants of Middle-earth, the secrets of life contained in the mead of wisdom.

At the centre of his visionary journey was the tree. In Norse legend it is called Yggdrasil. This name is a compound of two words: the stem of *yggr* is *ygg-*, the 'frightening' or 'awe-inspiring one', which was one of Odin's nicknames; *drasill* is a literary word meaning 'horse'. So the name identifies the tree as the means of Odin's 'ride' to the spirit world, his transportation for the quest. I believe that the name Ygg is Odin's identity *before* he undertook his initiation in the World Tree. The name Odin is so close to the root meaning of the word 'shaman' that I suspect that Odin is a *title* acknowledging his new status.

> I know that I hung on the windswept tree . . .
> The wisest know not from whence spring
> the roots of that ancient tree.

These lines conjure an evocative image of a mysterious tree. Such images serve as a kind of springboard for the imagination. They lie at the heart of all shamanic visionary activity, and Odin's journey on the World Tree echoes an apparently universal experience of shamans in all cultures, and all times. In tribal cultures whose traditions have survived into modern times, anthropologists have described how apprentice shamans acquire their helping spirits, those 'beings' which advise, give healing powers and assist in journeys to worlds of knowledge. To journey there, they carry out highly ritualized, sacralized and impeccably executed retreats into remote areas of the wilderness. These ventures into the 'untamed' landscape are well beyond the normalizing and secure bounds of human society.

In all traditional cultures, there were sacred places which were favourable for such first encounters with the spirits. These were places which existed in the material world but which had extraordinary significance as entry points to another world. They were literally and metaphorically doorways into the spirit realm.

The physical nature of that special place depended of course on the terrain in which the tribal culture lived. It could variously be in the vast lake areas of Siberia, the mountains of the East, the desert plains of western United States, the snow plains of the Sami or the rainforests of South America. For the apprentice shamans of early north-western Europe, it may have been a hilltop, perhaps on an ancient burial mound left by previous civilizations. But it seemed preferably to be high in a tree selected for the ritual.

The initiate wizard entered an altered state of consciousness and plunged into the imaginal depths of the collective unconscious. This state of mind could be likened to 'dreaming with open eyes'. Nevertheless, the sacred process was framed within the material world: the physical, for shamanic inspiration is largely the sacralization of the familiar, rather than merely an escape into some 'other' reality. Seeing the familiar with new eyes is the gift of the shamanic journey, rather than simply an 'escape' into some other reality. So if ancient initiation practices were carried out in the same way as more recent traditions suggest, then the shaman climbed a 'real' tree in order to undergo a journey of the imagination as colourful and intense as possible. It engendered the arrival of spirit forces which would come upon the shaman in the guise of visions, sounds and the material form of animals.

In an example from a recent tribal culture, a Siberian shaman thought of the World Tree as represented by a birch. He explains that in preparation for the initiation ritual, or 'on the way to the ancestral shaman', the master shamans arrived with him at a tree believed to be possessed of powerful life-force. The initiate shaman rested at the foot of the special tree and examined the individual markings placed by various shamans over the years. By carving his name into the tree and vividly calling to mind the names of his shamanic ancestors, the newly inititated shaman shared the sacredness of the tree and acquired additional knowledge. Many recent tribal cultures believe that sacred objects like a tree are part of a cosmos which is structured in a manner we would call 'holographically'. In this view, every individual tree is considered to represent the essence, the centre, the World Tree. I turned and looked again at the remarkable spirit-features of the ancient yew. It is easy to imagine how such trees could have been treated as, in our modern terms, a metaphor for a journey from one realm into another.

Today we would tend to conceive of the Otherworld journeys as being located in our psyche, perhaps deep in the unconscious. The imaginal structure of the World Tree, and Odin's process of imagining journeying on the Tree as it transforms into a magical horse, would be tools and techniques for entering and accessing areas of the unconscious which might otherwise be closed to us except in the most deeply symbolic dreams.

But for the peoples of ancient Europe, the imaginal was a realm not physically bounded by the body, and not conceived of as 'only' an internal event, as we shall see throughout this book. For them, the significance of the imaginal was that it allowed humans to encompass realms outside even the physical plane of the material world. For our ancestors the everyday, logical, analytical, material world was a tiny microcosm of the magnificent, boundless imaginal world. Shamans were expected to be able to journey to this world, and act there on behalf of the community.

Odin's vision, as described by Snorri Sturluson, appeared as a giant ash tree called Yggdrasil. It was so vast that 'its branches spread out over the whole world and reach up over heaven'. Featured around the tree were three gigantic discs set one above the other, with a space in between each. These were the three realms which made up the cosmos. They were the Upperworld, Middle-earth and Lowerworld. Suspended among these three realms were nine worlds.

In the Upperworld branches of the World Tree lived gods and goddesses. There were two worlds of gods. Asgard was the world of a tribe of gods known as the Aesir, living in great halls; they were warrior gods representing aspects of the old sky god called Allfather, who was eventually replaced by Odin. Also in the Upperworld were the fertility gods known as the Vanir. There were twenty-seven gods and goddesses in all. Finally the Upperworld featured a third world of knowledge, the land of the light elves, magical creatures who expressed the spirit of nature.

The second level, around the lower branches and trunk of the World Tree was called Middle-earth. It is in this realm that human life unfolded. However, Middle-earth does not refer merely to the material world of everyday existence. Rather it is the spiritual world of humankind. It was surrounded by a vast ocean, and Jormungand, the immense world serpent, lay in this ocean. He was so long that he encircled Middle-earth and bit on his own tail. He 'bound' the energy of the realm. Without him it would have exploded in a raging chaos.

Another world witnessed by Odin in his visionary journey was at the outer edge of the Middle-earth disc, and lay 'over the ocean'. This was the world of the giants, or ents, called Jotunheim. The giants were the beings who established the Earth. They were huge elemental forces, brutishly strong but short on intellect. Also in this Middle realm, in the north, lived the dwarves. They dwelt underground in a world called Nidavellir (dark home), a 'subterranean' world of darkness where shapes are forged. And there was another world called Svartalfheim (land of the dark elves). No clear distinction though can be drawn between the dwarves and dark elves; they appear to have been interchangable.

Odin saw that the Upperworld and the Middle World were connected by a bridge of fire, a flaming rainbow bridge, called Bifrost (Trembling Way). This can sometimes be glimpsed from within every-day states of consciousness. Snorri Sturluson says: 'You will have seen it but maybe you call it the rainbow. It has three colours and is very strong, and made with more skill and cunning than other structures.' The Trembling Way bridge transported the wizard from the world of mundane reality to the Otherworld, the transcended states of consciousness.

Deep in the roots of the tree lay the third realm. This was the Underworld or Lowerworld comprising Niflheim (the world of the dead), located nine days northwards and downwards from Midgard. Niflheim was a place of bitter cold and unending night. Its citadel was Hel, a place with towering walls and forbidding gates presided over by the hideous female monster, half white and half black, of the same name. However, the Lowerworld in ancient European cosmology is a realm which has to be completely re-visioned in order for us to understand its significance, for the word 'hel' carries negative connotations for western culture of the Christian Hell.

Certainly the Lowerworld of the European wizard could be dark and potent. But this world also held the wisdom of the dead. For wizards to journey to the Lowerworld was dangerous, but could reap great rewards of wisdom.

Snorri Sturluson says that Yggdrasil had three mighty roots, one each for the three realms of Upperworld, Middle-earth and Lowerworld. The first reached into Asgard, and nourishing this root was the Well of Wyrd, by the side of which lived the three Wyrd Sisters, makers of destiny. Each day the gods gathered here in council. The Wyrd Sisters (Norns in the Scandinavian versions) nurture the great tree. Sturluson writes, 'It is said further that the Norns who live near the spring of Urd draw water from the spring every day, and along with it the clay that lies around about the spring, and they besprinkle the ash so that its branches shall not wither or decay.'

The second root spread to Jotunheim, and under this root was the Spring of Mimir, the great, wise giant who taught wizards some of their most important spells.

The third root plunged into the Lowerworld. Under this root was the Spring of Hvergelmir, the source of eleven rivers and the lair of the dragon Nidhogg. The dragon, or serpent, Nidhogg sends challenges and riddles up the full length of the trunk of Yggdrasil, carried by a squirrel, to a great eagle whose claws grasp the highest branches.

This, then, is the wondrous vision that Odin experienced during his initiation. He saw it, and he created it. It was the 'sacred geography' of his spiritual journey with Sleipnir, his eight-legged horse. In poetic form, it reveals how the people of the real Middle-earth imagined the cosmos.

THE DOOM OF DRAGONS

5. Towers of Doom

The Anglo-Saxon invaders' first glimpse of the Roman villas in England must have set their hearts hammering. The stone columns stood tall, towering above the landscape, and the massive dimensions of the buildings probably felt intimidating. During the four centuries that the Romans had occupied and ruled over ancient England, they erected over a thousand such luxurious mansions for their colonial governors. The buildings, with their classical proportions, stone pillars, thick walls and gates, beautiful mosaics and gardens, their sophisticated comforts of underfloor heating and hot baths, efficient sewage systems and water drainage – these masterworks of architecture were a manifestation of an advanced engineering culture. And in AD 410, when the Roman garrisons pulled out of England, in the north and west, they left many prominent Romano-British governors in positions of power. Some of them spread their wings, and established small kingdoms for themselves. But in the south and east, where the Saxons invaded, things were different. Roman administrators left, presumably with their families, for we have little evidence of their massacre by the invading small groups of Saxons. And when they evacuated, they left many of these buildings deserted. What happened next provides an opportunity to contrast the nature-based ways of life of the indigenous Middle-earth peoples with that of the Romans. While this contrast is similar for Celts, Saxons and Norse, in this chapter we look mainly at the attitude of the Anglo-Saxons towards the world left behind by the retreating Roman Empire.

Monsters Torn From Their Slumber

Soon afterwards, invaders rowed their boats up rivers and penetrated the heart of England. They were looking for suitable settlement sites.

But they had come from wooded areas of Denmark, and northern Germany – a homeland of wood-framed houses clad in timber and thatch. The Roman constructions they saw in England must have looked as if from an alien world.

Even their first encounter with a dead-straight Roman road would have been a shock. They were constructed to such a high standard that today, 2,000 years later, these ancient roads still form the foundations of many modern highways. Stretching into the distance for miles, they cut straight through stands of trees, hills, bridged over streams and rivers – the Romans even built them right through ancient burial mounds. In Saxon belief the trees, hills and burial mounds swept aside by the heavy Roman construction must have churned into the air of Middle-earth multitudes of ancient spirits, ancestors and monsters torn from their slumber in the depths of the Lowerworld, the realm of the Otherworld.

Saxons believed crossroads where three ways meet to be liminal spaces between Middle-earth and the Lowerworld. Human-formed pathways were intersections between the geographical world and the spiritual realm. Places formed by natural movement of generations of people impressed their human spirit into the landscape. And Otherworld spirits of all kinds normally wended their way through the landscape, sometimes travelling along human tracks. But dead-straight Roman roads offered no natural diversions, bends, or obstructions. They were linear intrusions imposed on the landscape. This was not only brutal – it was dangerous. Spirits would scream along the straight paths like spectres of the criminal dead, completely out of control.

Perhaps the Saxons avoided these regimented roads like accursed rents in the landscape. But if they did dare travel along them, they could not have missed the Roman villas, jutting menacingly above the soft green landscape like towers of doom.

Ghost Villas

One such villa, built about nine miles north-west of Oxford, near the banks of the River Evenlode, was once the property of a Romano-British noble. It was first excavated in 1865. The archaeological digs revealed that, like many of the Roman grand houses, it originally had a beautifully coloured, mosaic tiled floor. Today, close to the excavated old foundations of the villa, there is a village called Fawler. But in ancient England this settlement was called Fag Flor, meaning the 'coloured, or painted floor'. So the village was almost certainly originally named with reference to the mosaic floor of the villa – still visible, presumably, along with the rest of the villa's construction, when the Saxons arrived. The question is, why did they not occupy the villa, ready-built and comfortable as it was, but choose instead to establish their own village a short distance away? And did they consider occupying the villa, discuss it, even argue about it? Were they afraid the Romans might come back to reclaim it? Or was there something so repellent to them about the impressive building that occupying it was totally out of the question?

The same thing happened all across the country. Many villas, farms and settlements were avoided. Some of the haunted buildings disappearing under the green comprised entire towns.

Caistor-by-Norwich, in the east of England, had been constructed by the Romans over an area of 35 acres, and completely enclosed by a protective wall – on the north side it still stands today to a height of 6 metres (20 feet). After the Romans had defeated the uprising of Boudicca, and decimated and enslaved the Iceni tribe, they made Caistor-by-Norwich into a Romanized community called Venta.

Seventeen hundred years ago, the town was a large, busy market community and a centre of area administration. Then the Romans pulled out, and the town emptied. Well, not quite – some Britons must have stayed behind and lived in it, for archaeological evidence has recovered sixteen bodies of Britons slaughtered, perhaps by Angles, who were the principle invaders in that part of the country. Apart from that event, it seems to have been abandoned. And when later Anglo-Saxon scouts first saw the haunting sight of these ghost towns – presumably from a safe distance – they were probably devoid of human activity. Eventually the scouts ventured inside the walls, either swaggering with bravado or tiptoeing in trepidation.

The deserted buildings would have been silent save for rustling mice and latchless doors blowing in the breeze. After some decades of neglect, nature would have begun to reclaim the giant constructions. The Saxons saw weeds – slippery, green invaders – creeping and gnawing, breaking through the exquisite mosaic floors, and cracking up the carefully-laid courtyards; ivy winding up the pillars like snakes, clinging to the stone and plaster, sucking it dry, and eating through ceilings into the rooms above. Eventually, the towns disappeared, slipping beneath layers of spreading vegetation and the smell of rotting timbers. Caistor-by-Norwich lay hidden for fifteen centuries, and was only recently rediscovered.

Exploring the deserted streets and corridors of the Roman ghost towns, the Anglo-Saxons saw grand dwellings of a level of material comfort unknown before in ancient Europe. The remarkable thing is – they decided not to live in them. What can this tell us about the collective mind of Middle-earth?

Return To The Dark Ages?

The question has an edge to it, for classical education would lead us to be appalled by the Saxons' rejection of the Roman buildings. After all, a common stereotype of the Saxons is of mercenary gangs of primitive barbarians, about to bring the 'dark ages' to a country shaped, organized and 'civilized' by the occupying Romans. The Roman Empire is today widely regarded as not only a culture of remarkable engineering, but also as a paragon of progressive government. Its legacy survives, for example, in the United States Senate, and many legal systems, and in the art and culture of modern western society. So not surprisingly, conventional attempts to explain the Saxons' avoidance of the Roman buildings start from the assumption that the Saxons were an inferior culture to the Romans. And the easy verdict of some historians is that the renewed culture of Middle-earth brought about by the incoming Saxons was a step backward to the primitive world of the Celts, before the Romans had invaded. One recent, otherwise well-informed historical account of the Anglo-Saxons and Romans concludes with a judgement which betrays such a perspective:

> . . . the civilization of the Roman Empire had been an urban one. The life of the early Middle Ages was primarily rural. This transition is implicitly a tale of decline, for urban life is more

complicated, more structured than rural life, and an urbanized society invariably is one that has transcended its high degree of direct dependence upon agriculture and pastoral activity.

In other words, the Saxons' choosing to live outside these abandoned settlements was an aberration. The linear development of western civilization was supposed to be towards the ultimate destiny of living in cities. And yet today the proposal that urban life is more 'civilized' because it is more 'complicated' would hardly convince residents of our troubled cities, paralyzed by choking traffic and beset with street crime. There are many positive features to modern city living, but a change from rural to an urban lifestyle is not an inevitable march of progress from the primitive to the civilized.

Perhaps we value the Roman culture because in many ways it seems more modern than does that of the Anglo-Saxons. The Roman culture was remarkably rational for its time – and we tend to assume rationality to be a civilizing dimension. A strong element of imagination, as in the Anglo-Saxon more 'magical' world, seems to us less connected with the realities of life. These modern assumptions about the relative values of modes of thinking have been the greatest barrier to our understanding of people's lives in Middle-earth. As we shall see, our ancestors possessed a richness of imagination which sometimes afforded them inspired insights into the nature of life.

Awe, Giants, or Revenge?

We can certainly set aside some of the conventional explanations for the settlement pattern of the Saxon incomers. Some historians have suggested that the Saxons were afraid to enter the abandoned Roman villas because they were overawed by buildings whose construction revealed sophisticated techniques far in advance of their own native skills. However, this is unlikely to have been a decisive factor. Some of the timber Great Halls of the Saxon warrior-kings on the continent were impressive constructions, probably on the scale of the Anglo-Saxon hall at Yeavering in Yorkshire. This was revealed in archaeological research to have been about ninety feet long, surrounded by many smaller buildings and even a sports arena or event space with a grandstand.

In the poem 'The Ruin', one anonymous Anglo-Saxon poet, whom I quote at greater length later in the chapter, referred to the large Roman constructions as 'The old work of giants'. From this appellation some writers have assumed that the invaders did not know the origins of their construction. But communications were good in Europe – after all, trade had flourished across the continent for centuries – and the incoming settlers to England would have known the villas to have been built and then abandoned by the retreating Romans.

What about the impetus of sheer hostility towards the Romans? On the continent, their spreading empire had led to some bloody battles with the continental cousins of the Anglo-Saxon incomers. Perhaps hatred of the Romans as a rapacious military machine led to destruction of their abandoned centres of power and prestige? But avoidance of the Roman buildings did not seem to have risen from seething enmity, either. Archaeological excavations of the abandoned settlements rarely show signs of fire or other destruction.

The answer seems to be much more positive. We know much about the military, economic, even domestic circumstances of the Anglo-Saxons in England. But the influence of a more subtle dimension inspired the sensibilities of these peoples. And when we begin to explore this, we find that the Saxons' avoidance of the Roman villas and towns was to do with their intimate interconnection with their natural environment – especially the forests.

On the continent, the forests of the early Germanic peoples north of the Rhine were even more plentiful and dense than those of ancient England. And in the early years of the first millennium, the Romans pushed their military Empire north through Germany and there encountered the peoples whose descendents would later invade England. These tribespeoples, Saxons and others, successfully resisted the Roman expansion. The Rhine effectively became the northern border of their influence. However, the Romans were fascinated by these peoples.

Tacitus was a Roman official charged with documenting the customs of the 'natives' and, in his account called *Germania*, written in the year AD 98, he tells us a lot about the way they lived. His observations were impressionistic – really those of a war correspondent – but they offer nevertheless a startling perspective on how these people thought. For example, he reports that they 'have not even learned to use quarry-stone or tiles'. And as we saw, later in England, when presented with empty and beautiful villas constructed of such heavy and durable materials, they steered clear of them. Perhaps the material felt alien and 'hard', rather like our being asked to live in a house constructed entirely of glass.

Tacitus also tells us that 'None of the German tribes live in walled cities.' He writes that their houses were not even contiguous with each other, let alone joined in streets and terraces in the ordered and compact Roman style of early urban housing. 'They live separated and scattered, according as spring-water, meadow or grove appeals to each man . . . Everyone keeps a clear space around his house.'

Such clearly expressed styles of living preferences suggest that the Saxons in England may have avoided Roman towns for their own positive reasons. Rather than insulating themselves from the environment in engineered comfort, they felt more naturally at home in houses of wood, constructed with their own traditional woodworking skills developed over many generations. As well as sticking with familiar crafts, it seems that the Saxons liked the freedom to construct their houses in the timbered landscape and natural architecture of the forest, rivers, hills and valleys.

This was more than a simple aesthetic preference. For the Saxons, the natural environment was imbued with the presence of spirits, a parallel universe of sacred power. Their homesteads were constructed from the very materials of nature around them – the provisions, just like crops, provided for them by the spirits.

The Spirit of Mother Earth

Tacitus goes further in explaining the basis of the strong connection with the Earth. He describes the Angli and other tribes living along the west coast of the Baltic, in what is today southern Denmark and northern Germany, participating in '. . . the common worship of Nerthus, that is Mother Earth'. With the entrance of the spirit of

Mother Earth, we begin to get closer to the deeper reason for the Anglo-Saxons' intimacy with nature.

For nearly two thousand years, a peat bog in western Denmark held the clue to one of the most remarkable rituals of ancient Europe. Unearthed from the bog, where they had lain preserved for all that time, were a pair of beautiful and intricately carved two-seater carts. These small, lightweight, wooden carriages were widely used by the ancient Celts – most famously by Boudicca, who in AD 61 fought the Romans to free her people from their slavery. Boudicca fought in the thick of the battle from the back of her cart, pulled by charging ponies.

However, the carts recovered from the Danish bog were more delicate than battle vehicles. They had four slender wooden wheels, and a frame covered with figures and symbols expertly carved in the solid wood. Also recovered from the warm, womb-like protection of the peat bog was a small alder-wood stool, which was the seat for the person riding in one of the carriages. Except that it was not a *person* riding in the carriage; rather, the wagons were occupied by a spirit – the Earth Goddess. Women's tools like clay vessels and a loom-piece were buried with the sacred carts. Similar carved and decorated wagons from ancient times have been discovered in locations all over Europe.

Tacitus's *Germania* provides the fullest account of the early use of the symbolically carved wagons. Writing in AD 98 he tells us about the tribes living along the west coast of the Baltic and northern Germany:

> After the Langobardi come the Reudigni, Auiones, Anglii, Varini, Eudoses, Suarines and Nuithones all well guarded by rivers and forests. There is nothing remarkable about any of these tribes unless it be the common worship of Nerthus, that is Mother Earth. They believe she is interested in men's affairs and drives about among them. On an island in the Ocean sea there is a sacred grove wherein waits a holy wagon covered by a drape. One priest only is allowed to touch it. He can feel the presence of the goddess when she is there in her sanctuary.

This escort accompanies the wagon 'with great reverence' when at the appointed time of the year it is drawn from the island and pulled by oxen around the tribal lands.

So the people believed that the spirit of Nerthus was in some way present, hidden in the wagon, and the role of the 'priest', more likely a figure we would recognize today as a wizard or druid, was to interpret her messages to the communities being visited. The spirit was feted wherever she went: 'It is a time of festive holiday-making in whatever place she deigns to honour with her advent and stay.' Clearly Nerthus brought peace, wherever the wagon was pulled. 'No one goes to war, no one takes up arms, in fact every weapon is put away: only at that time are peace and quiet known and prized until the goddess, having had enough of people's company, is at last restored by the same priest to her temple.'

From Tacitus's commentary it sounds as if the goddess's stays in any one location were for a substantial period; certainly more than hours, more probably days or weeks, since 'no one goes to war' during her stay.

It is only when she is 'present' that the fighting stops. 'No one . . . takes up arms, in fact every weapon is put away . . .' says Tacitus. It sounds so complete that it was more than just a suspension of intertribal skirmishing. Rather, it was a change of mind, of heart, from the usual. It is the only time that 'peace and quiet are prized', says Tacitus. Mother Earth seems to have allowed light into darkness. And although Nerthus is treated with 'reverence' by the escorting priest, the advent of the 'peace' is greatly welcomed; it is not a po-faced occasion; Tacitus says that is is a time of 'festive holiday making' wherever Nerthus deigns to stay.

The sight of these carved and draped wagons being wheeled about, from village to village, must have been common all over western Europe, presumably on days or seasons especially appointed for the ritual. We know that the Earth Goddess ceremony thrived in at least seven major tribal groups, and that the Celtic tribes of East Anglia in the early centuries used wagons for war as did Boudicca. St Martin in the fourth century AD tells of Cybele's image – she was the Syrian goddess of fruitfulness – covered with white curtains and carried round the fields in ancient Gaul. So Nerthus and her corresponding spirits and deities transcended not only tribal groups, but also entire peoples. These goddess figures predated many of the later well-known gods and goddesses of the real Middle-earth, developed and elaborated in the Norse culture of early medieval times.

For these people of Middle-earth, the ultimate power was the presence of Mother Earth. And this was so in England, where we know that the Anglo-Saxons did indeed worship Mother Earth. In the Lacnunga manuscript, the charm for restoring fertility to the fields reads: 'Hail to thee, Earth, mother of men! Be fruitful in God's embrace, filled with food for the use of men . . .'

So what do we make of this image of an invisible spirit on a sacred 'round', accompanied by a priest serving her needs, and bringing peace and celebrations wherever she stayed? First of all, she contrasts dramatically with the Roman deities. They were depicted in human form in massive statues in the grounds of villas and temples of garrison towns, and they tended to be men. These dominating icons seemed to rule over nature – rather like their political systems which were all-pervasive and hierarchial. For example, the Roman temple at Colchester has been revealed in its dimensions during successive archaeological digs starting in 1919 and continuing right through the 1960s. Calculations made from the surviving walls and piers suggest that the temple itself measured some 150 feet by 80 feet, that it was surrounded by a colonnade, with columns 35 feet high and more than 3 feet in diameter, and fronted by a sweeping flight of steps where there would have been a series of statues. A reconstruction at the Castle Museum, Colchester, shows a building of gleaming white, with ostentatious red, blue and golden ornamentation; Roman eagles and a triumphant statue of the Emperor Claudius at the front steps. Tacitus called this temple a 'blatant stronghold of alien rule'.

For the people of Middle-earth, the gods were nature itself. In the early part of Britain's history, connections with the sacred were through spirits based in trees, streams, rocks and other features of the natural landscape. Gods seemed more connected with the agricultural year, along with the sun and moon. Even in the more elaborated pantheon of gods written up in Scandinavia in the thirteenth century, when they had been reified to more prominent positions (some say in response to the presence of the Christian god brought in by missionaries) many of the gods still had nature or landscape references. Thor (Thunor in England) was the thunder god, and Freya and her later masculinized version called Frey were nature fertility gods.

The people of the historical Middle-earth believed that it violated the sacred presence of spirit to separate it from the natural world within masonry walls, or to erect artificial likenesses of the

Otherworld beings as if to somehow 'capture' their presence. The real connection with divine forces for these people was with more intimate spirit beings which were indivisible from natural phenomena like great oaks, running streams and wild animals. This is why the engineered environment of the Romans was rejected in favour of their own traditional timber buildings.

There is nothing unnatural about stone, tile and the other building materials of the Romans per se, but the way they were structured made for massive houses which cut off the inhabitants from nature. In a way, this was intentional – distance from the effects of the environment is equated, as in our culture today, with creature comforts. But to divorce oneself from nature would have been, for the people of real Middle-earth, to divorce oneself from the spirits.

We may now be getting closer to the true reasons for the Saxons' preference for building their own settlements. However, there is another perspective we have not yet touched on. Their avoidance of the Roman villas and towns was also due to the feeling that the buildings violated the deepest beliefs and taboos of Middle-earth.

Wyrd and Wisdom

Ammianus Marcellinus, a Roman historian of the fourth-century Empire, said of the Anglo-Saxon peoples that 'the towns themselves they avoid as if they were tombs surrounded by nets'. Tombs surrounded by nets! What an image – as if to live in the towns would have trapped the occupants like fish in a net, unable to escape, incarcerated until death.

This doom-laden view of a town is expressed in a poem written by an Anglo-Saxon. The poem, its original manuscript in a damaged condition, is included in a collection called the *Exeter Book*, so-named because it was given by Leofric, Bishop of Devon and Cornwall, and Chancellor to Edward the Confessor, to Exeter Cathedral. The lines are believed to refer to the Roman town of Bath, where the foundations of the once impressive public baths have survived until today, and can be seen along with ruins of the associated buildings. Such structures must have been emblematic of all that was Roman in ancient Britain, but falling into ruin at the time of the poem's composition. The lines of the poem, translated into modern English, no longer have poetic cadence, but the meaning is clear:

> Bright were the castle dwellings, many the bath-houses, lofty the host of pinnacles, great the tumult of men, many a mead hall full of the joys of men, till Wyrd the mighty overturned that. The wide walls fell; days of pestilence came; death swept away all the bravery of men, their fortresses became waste places; the city fell to ruin.

These lines reflect appreciation, even admiration, not only for the Roman buildings, 'bright castles, many bath houses, lofty pinnacles', but also for the human life imagined within them – 'great tumult', and mead halls 'full of the joys' of life. When the poet wrote of such imagined splendid occasions in the ruins of Roman houses, he was surely identifying with the Romans not as alien beings, but as people who loved the same pleasures as he enjoyed in the Saxon timber halls. But there is also recognition here of something far greater, far more powerful – 'Wyrd the mighty overturned that' – the lines reflect the fact that something went terribly wrong with it all, and the civilization died.

The term 'Wyrd' in Anglo-Saxon is the origin of the modern 'weird'. Today it means 'strange' or the 'unexplainable'. It meant the same then, but with a far greater significance. In ancient England the unexplainable was the flowing of life's complexities beyond the ability of words to comprehend. It was not a belief in simple fate, in which whatever happened was destined to happen, and humans simply had to accept it. It was not a fixed future, either. Rather it was a natural outcome of the forces of life as they are presently flowing. Wyrd was the inexorable, deeply embedded evolution of the world within which human affairs ebbed and flowed. It was an intelligence beyond human ken but integral to everything, perhaps most like the Great Tao of Eastern philosophy of the same period, and it flowed like a European form of Chinese chi. We shall come back to it in a later chapter. But the judgement of destiny which Wyrd wrought meant that when 'Wyrd overturned that', it ended it all. The 'wide walls' fell, men were no longer brave, and the civilization which produced the town disintegrated into ruin.

Wyrd was sensitive to human affairs. Such a destiny for Rome and its abandoned buildings cast a long shadow. The people of ancient Middle-earth seemed to say that the material achievements of the Romans could be admired, but that seeking to emulate it was fraught with danger. To be faced with the deserted buildings, magnificent though they were, of a civilization that had fallen into ruin, was enough to warn them away from the sites of a disastrous destiny. They believed that even abandoned and ruined buildings still carried the ghostly presence of their former occupants.

Underlying this judgement about destiny was an understanding of the impermanance and delicate balance of life. For the people of the real Middle-earth, bearing in mind their views about nature, the Romans' bringing of the judgement of Wyrd on themselves in this way meant that they had violated the honour of Mother Earth, ravaging her landscape with stone buildings and straight roads and setting up false gods in the form of statues. No matter how superb the stonemasonry, the icons were barbaric compared with real nature. The Romans had failed to live well with the spirits. The Anglo-Saxons' avoidance of Roman buildings opens the way to our understanding of many of the major elements of the imagination-imbued world view of people in ancient England.

In sum, nature itself was a palpable presence in people's spiritual lives as well as their practical environment. Many of their ways of living, and decisions about how to live, were inspired by a desire to harmonize their lives with the spirit of Mother Earth. The woodlands in particular shaped their sensibilities, and provided a setting in which people felt comfortable physically and imaginatively.

Also, in order to understand the ramifications of the Middle-earth mind, we need to overcome the prejudices of our conventional histories, in which the Roman occupation of Britain was a beacon of light in an otherwise primitive and ignorable period of a thousand years. The Romans were remarkably advanced in many ways, but beyond that, we can see that the Celts, Anglo-Saxons and Norse had their own sophisticated views, and different values.

And yet, the Anglo-Saxons' sense of the 'doom' of the Roman civilization, trapped in its empty buildings, went a stage further even than this. More than a vague altercation with the spirit world, the Romans had fallen foul of an eternal rhythm in human affairs – one which we have since forgotten. It was an understanding of currents in the ebb and flow of history – and what happens over time to civilizations – when people dishonour the wealth offered up by Mother Earth and when greed overcomes wisdom. In ancient Europe, greed often concerned the acquisition and hoarding of gold. This aspect of destiny was distilled and dynamically expressed in the lives of people in the historical Middle-earth through a being of great power: the dragon. And understanding the dragon, in the next chapter, will help us to realize how the historical destiny of the Dark Ages was dependent not only on the crude forces of politics and battles, but also on those people's sense of how eternal life unfolded.

6. The Dragon's Lair

In the historical Middle-earth, the evidence shows that dragons were more than merely creatures of stories. Scaly, fire-breathing monsters, they occupied the shadowy world between waking and sleep, day and night, life and death. They could be heard booming under the ground or high on the hills. Their sour smell drifted across the countryside on the morning mist. Sometimes their scaly hide could be heard slithering and crackling in the dark of night. Even if people had never come face to face with a dragon, they knew that one day, without warning, their worst nightmare could come true.

Of course today, the notion of dragons being real seems a fanciful idea more appropriate to childhood – our process of growing up requires that we gradually fetter our fantasies, and replace them with an adult perspective relentlessly based on reality. So were the Anglo-Saxons childlike dreamers? On the contrary, they had to be intensely practical, for times were hard. Unreliable crops could lead to sudden famine. Disease could rage through villages unchecked by an understanding of sanitation hazards and spreading infection. And the lawless feuding of rival warlords sometimes flared up, leaving innocent victims dead in their wake. So was their belief that dragons were real a sign of primitive thought? A groping for order amid the chaos of quixotic and cruel events? A symptom of the degradation of human spirit during the Dark Ages? Being able to distinguish between reality and fantasy even determines today our distinction between sanity and madness. So did the people of Middle-earth live in a kind of collective delusional world?

These conventional interpretations of Middle-earth magical thinking miss an important ingredient. What distinguished their civilization was a sense that beyond the pragmatics of survival, the meaning of life lay in another, separate kind of reality – in the Otherworld of spirits, beings and greater forces. The practical matters of everyday life were best solved through common sense and logic. But answers to the deeper issues of what life is about lay not in rational thinking, but in the realms of imagination. Even in our scientifically-oriented culture, we realize that imagination is often the state of mind from which we connect with profound insights: from the extra-logical leaps of new paradigm thinking, to the creation of great art, and even to ways of knowing God. And for the people of Middle-earth, the dragon brought insights to people's understanding of life's vicissitudes, as we shall see.

But it also spread dread. The people of Middle-earth lived with a constant awareness of the perennial presence of this terrifying creature. The dragon's hidden realm was the Lowerworld, reserved for the spirits of the dead. The dragon's lairs, as entrances to the realm of the dead, were supercharged points of contact between the everyday, surface world of Middle-earth activity, and the timeless, subterranean layers of the Lowerworld – caves, burial mounds, crossroads and streams. And there, in the deepest darkness, lurked the dragons – apparently sleeping. But through eye-slits glowing red with internal combustion, these fire-breathers controlled the creation and destruction of whole civilizations. Perhaps stemming from a folk-memory of dinosaurs, embedded deep in human memory – even beyond the handing down of stories through thousands of generations they became a kind of instinctive adversary, rather like people's inborn aversion to snakes, presumably an evolutionarily-evolved protection from poisonous snakes which in early times may have been more numerous and therefore a constant threat to well-being.

To understand the significance of the dragon, let us begin with the dread.

Finding the Dragon's Lair

In the real landscape of ancient England there were hundreds of such 'dragon-lairs'. There hid these monstrous creatures, like fireballs waiting to explode. Their lairs were mapped meticulously, like ancient minefields. The nature and naming of dragons' lairs illustrates how, for the people of the Real Middle-earth, the natural landscape was an extension of their minds. Threads of the imagination were cast over the objective features of the physical world like a magical net, pulling together the hills, trees, streams and hollows within the deeper dimensions of inner experience. Tolkien used this perspective in *The Hobbit*, where the dwarf Thorin pored over an ancient map. In all the places marked there, he remembered well the most important landmarks – including the Withered Heath which, he said, used to be a breeding ground for dragons.

Today, a millennium later, we can still visit the original location of some of the most famous dragon lairs from the real Middle-earth. They can be identified through their ancient place-names, many of which have survived through a thousand years of history. Beneath their prosaic presence on a modern map of England lies the hidden terrain through which dragons dragged their scaly hides.

Anglo-Saxon land charters were legal documents which detailed the boundaries of pieces of property. Often prominent features of the landscape were used as markers – large and ancient trees, spreading their presence on the countryside for scores of generations; or man-made features constructed specifically as boundary markers, like fences, ditches and gates.

But the charters also stamped the landscape with mythological footprints. On 10 April 739, Aethelheard, King of the West Saxons, inked his signature to a vellum document granting land at Crediton, Devon to the Bishop of Sherborne for the purpose of building a monastery. This place survives as a town near Exeter, just north-east of the Dartmoor National Park. The extent of the land for the monastery was marked out precisely in the document as '. . . from the boundary ridge to Luha's tree, from Luha's tree to the enclosure gate, from the enclosure gate to Dodda's ridge, from Dodda's ridge to Grendel's pit . . .' But Grendel was no ordinary natural feature. He was a legendary man-eating monster. Dragons, as we shall see, had particular significance and meaning for the people of Middle-earth, but also in those times the creatures of the earth were not categorized so precisely as now, with our Linnaean system and certainly dragons belonged to the more general genre of monsters. It will help us understand people's relations with dragons to consider first how they dealt with the monster, Grendel, immortalized in the great Anglo-Saxon poem *Beowulf*. This poem is reckoned by historians to have been composed sometime between the middle of the seventh and the

end of the tenth century, and written in Anglo-Saxon. The language
is archaic now, and has to be translated into modern English. It was
written in England, and the events it describes are in a 'once upon
a time' but quasi-real historical period, and set in Scandinavia.
Undoubtedly, the poem was performed orally in the mead halls of
England, especially those of East Anglia, where scholars reckon the
poem to have originated. It is likely that the story developed
gradually, perhaps by more than one storyteller, before it was finally
written down. Here, Grendel is described in snatches, for he was
glimpsed only in the flickering firelight of night, before he carried
out his destruction.

And Grendel was an experience the people of Middle-earth
would have preferred to do without. He loomed up out of the night,
and melted back like a phantom into darkness. But we know from
other beliefs of these times that for the people of Middle-earth
listening to this story, he was not an apparition. The name Grendel
is connected with an Old Norse term meaning 'to bellow' – a
booming growl of a large creature – and the word eventually came
into the later Middle-English as 'grindel', meaning angry. Grendel
entered the mead halls silently at night, smashed brave warriors to
pieces, and carried their corpses back into the wilderness from
whence he came. In his rage, he drowned out the screams of his
victims, and left the smell of fear and blood. The Anglo-Saxon
audience would have accepted these monsters as monsters, not as
abstract symbols of evil, plague or war. Such creatures had a kind of
material reality, as well as an Otherworld identity.

Grendel and his kind menaced people's lives in all areas of the
country, and in various parts of the landscape. The monster was
particularly associated with low-lying, watery places, echoed in the
cognate old East Anglian dialect word grindle, meaning 'drain' or
'ditch'. In AD 931, King Athelstan of Wessex issued a charter in
which a certain lake in Wiltshire is identified as a grendles mere.
Other place-names mentioned in old charters, Grindles bec and
Grendeles pyt, were likewise places that were lairs of the beast.

The Beowulf poet describes the habitat of the monster as an
intimate, familiar landscape, surrounding the mead-halls where the
lines of the poem were being performed orally: 'It is not far from
here, measured in miles', says the poet, 'that the mere stands over

which frosty thickets hang – a wood firm of root covers over the water . . .'. Marshland and bogs had special significance as liminal areas of the landscape. They hovered between the known and unknown. They were neither dry land nor water. Seemingly fordable, they could, without warning, suck animals or people down into the darkness of the Lowerworld, the land of the dead.

The Lowerworld was a place of wisdom for wizards. In an oral culture, people who died took with them a lifetime of knowledge, of experience. So this place underneath the everyday world was packed with potential words to the wise – tips, techniques and spells. Wizards could risk journeys there, conjure conversations with the dead, and then return. But for the ordinary person, to be sucked into its dark depths was the end.

The *Beowulf* poet describes Grendel's liquid lair as no ordinary feature of the landscape: 'At night there, something uncanny happens: the water burns'. Even animals would rather die rather than plunge in: 'On its bank, the heather-stepper halts: the hart in flight from pursuing hounds will turn to face them with firm-set horns and die in the wood rather than dive beneath its surface. That is no good place.' The 'Grendel's Pits' of Middle-earth maps were unwelcome landmarks. The presence of these beasts must have issued from the land like a menacing mist rising from a swamp, threatening to manifest as a monster.

Grendel was not a dragon, but his character helps us to understand theirs. They were separate species, but similarly prescient beasts. Dragons lurked in the landscape, ready to erupt at cataclysmic moments in the aeons of time. And everyone knew where they were – their lairs were hidden, but always known, and named. By the end of the eighth century, most of the villages in England had already been formed. Many still survive today with their original names, or close derivations, or can be identified in early forms in ancient land charters, or the Domesday Book. And these place-names suggest that hundreds of sites may have been originally identified as dragon-lairs.

Drakes

The people of Anglo-Saxon England would have had no doubt about the appearance of dragons. They knew their size and shape. How they moved and walked. How they sounded. Their flight paths. Dragons who could fly, they called drakes, and those that were confined to reptilian slithering across the ground, wyrms.

Flying dragons must have got around, for many place-names are based on the word drake. Sometimes they were sited at dramatic promontories, on hills topped by trees, like visual antennae to the fire-breathers that coursed below. So Drakenage (Drake's edge) Farm, in Warwickshire, adds to 'drake' the word 'edge', which in Old English denoted the crest of a narrow ridge. It undulated above the landscape like the spiny back of an enormous, half-hidden dragon, sleeping – until disturbed, of course. Not a peaceful thought. Especially since 'edge' also connoted the power to cut with the sharpened edge of a heavy sword – or in this case, ripping talons and tearing teeth.

People in those days would have travelled on foot – a speed at which features of the landscape stay in your view for far longer than when speeding past in a car or train. A spiny ridge would make a menacing horizon – especially if you believed that it was gazing back at you through hidden, slitted eyes. Conceptions which hang between material reality and the power of our imaginations are the most haunting. And for those people who sometimes had to walk across such ridges as winter footpaths, to avoid the wet valleys, walking lightly on one's feet must have been the norm, if there was a possibility that, when disturbed, the whole ridge could erupt into an enraged dragon.

Nearby, on today's A442 road running west of Stourbridge, lies the town of Drakelow. In Anglo-Saxon times this road was a track, the town a village. And the name reveals the brooding presence of a resident dragon. The ancient word 'low' was directly connected to dragons, for it originally meant both to 'live under the ground, lying dead and buried', as in a burial mound, and also 'to flame, to blaze, and to be on fire with passion'. Dragons may have slept 'like the dead' for generations, but they were hardly cold-blooded reptiles.

Their internal flames flickered perpetually, ready to spit fire. Was the 'low' of this dragon lair a natural hill, visited once by a dragon flying in for a reconnoitre? Or was it occupied long-term, perhaps as a burial mound?

Dragley Beck, in Lancashire, was also the haunt of a fire-breather. In ancient times a 'beck' referred to a rugged, coursed stream with an especially stony bed. These streams twisted through the landscape like the ominous, bony spine of a serpent-dragon lying hidden beneath the water. Were these streams avoided, like the death-bogs of a Grendel monster? Or did people fish from them, very carefully? Did they fish from the bank, or dare to enter the water and stand on the dragon's backbone – perhaps slipping an offering into the water to appease the monster?

So the derivations of place-names not only reveal the locations of the lairs, they also tell us something about the nature of the dragons who hid there. The ancient lair names show the drake as huge, snaky, spiny-backed and fire breathing, sunk in deep holes, stony streams, or high on ridges and ancient burial mounds where it lay sleeping, as if dead and buried. Until disturbed.

Then, terrifyingly, the dragon emerged from such deep hiding places, its screaming roar booming across the countryside. The people of Middle-earth knew what dragons sounded like. We know they were loud from the place-name of Drakeholes, in Nottinghamshire. In Old English 'hole' had two meanings; a burrow dug into the ground by an animal, and a yell or scream, as in the modern-day word to 'holler'. So Drakeholes was named after the underground lair of a dragon, from which the beast was heard to make its scream. Perhaps a roar, but higher pitched than a Grendel. In the Celtic legend of 'Lludd and Llefelys', we hear of a terrifying scream which echoed every May Eve over every hearth in Britain. It left all animals and trees and the earth and the waters barren. It was found to be the scream of a dragon in combat with an invading dragon, the battle taking place in the Lowerworld in a lair beneath the mid-point of the country.

One of the danger places was at crossroads. Drake's Cross, just south of Birmingham, marks the lair of one such dragon. From Drakelow it is barely twenty miles as the crow – or dragon – flies; perhaps it was an alternative nesting site of the same dragon. In ancient England, crossroads were not only places where human

pathways intersected, but were also entrances – or exit-places connected to the realm of the dead. Spirits travelled along trackways
made by people, by animals, by nature. And criminals were hung on
crosses at crossroads, because the location would speed their souls'
journey down into the Lowerworld, avoiding the unpleasant possibility that their souls would hang around among the world of the
living, haunting them with evil intent. Crossroads were unsuitable
places to linger in the days of Middle-earth.

Wyrms

Not all dragons flew. There were also long, slithering wingless dragons
who crawled over the landscape like huge reptiles. In Old English
they were called 'worms', although clearly a different order of creature
from the small, friendly garden worm of today. The word derives
from the Scandinavian 'orm', which means 'snake'. Even the largest
snakes bear little relation to dragons, of course. For how big were
these crawling, or flying, fiery creatures? Ancient descriptions range
from dragons about as large as alligators, to the 50-foot dragon in
the epic Anglo-Saxon poem *Beowulf*, all the way to Jormungand, the
world-serpent of later Norse legend which wound itself completely
around the world, and grasped its own tail in its fangs.

These wyrm-dragons were related to monsters like the killer
creature Grendel. Place-names for their lairs include Wormwood, in
the Peak District National Park, at a place just outside the village of
Hassop, and South Ormsby in Lincolnshire – 'orm' names which
came when the Norse invaded eastern England in the eighth century.

Tolkien's dragon Smaug, who dominated *The Hobbit*, was a
combination of these two types of Anglo-Saxon dragon – the drake
and the wyrm. In Tolkien's own illustrations, his dragon has the
curious upturned nose that is the consistent facial feature of dragons
from the Viking north-west, although it exists in no real reptiles
except the crocodilians. And Tolkien explained in a letter that the
name is the past tense *smaug* of a Germanic verb *smugan*, 'to squeeze
through a hole'. So Smaug, while able to fly, also had the serpent-
like body of a 'worm' dragon. Perhaps the different kinds of dragons
could interbreed!

While many would consider that the language of dragons is too fanciful to use today, more at home in children's story-books than in adult discourse, we could nevertheless concede that there is a role for a more esoteric and poetic language in describing the qualities of a site in the landscape. Such imagery can be more appropriate than our supposedly more credible scientific terms. In painting, for instance, the terms movement, rhythm, tone and texture have a different meaning from the same terms in music and are certainly different from their meaning in physics. In any area where human perception, consciousness and emotions interact with non-human factors, simple scientific descriptions in the physical sense are inadequate. Intuitive language and imaginative images can better describe a myriad of subtle factors. For our ancestors, the imagination was the doorway from the everyday to the Otherworld. And there was a constant flowing of the imagination into the material world. The sense of reality in Middle-earth was more an awareness of realities, in the plural.

Many ancient cultures have had a similar sensitivity to dragon lairs in the landscape. For example, the aesthetic science known to the Chinese as the geomantic system of 'feng-shui', that is, 'wind and water', studies the currents of subtle energy which permeate all landscapes with their hills, rocks, trees and rivers. Traditional Chinese landscape artists followed this principle, treating the landscape like the physiognomy of Mother Earth, and trying to imbue their art with a deep sense of 'dragon veins' running through the landscape. In their eyes, every part of the landscape is animated by dragon's breath.

And for the Chinese, the dragon is the animating principle of every place. It represented the living spirit of trees and rocks, of pools, rivers, mountains and seas, of bridges and buildings, of men and women and children.

For the people of the historical Middle-earth, the dragon was not a totally negative creature. A fearsome beast, yes, but one whose presence fired the landscape with magical power, and who embodied the fate of whole civilizations. And in the real Middle-earth, as we shall see in the next chapter, the dragon's hoard of treasure influenced the fate of entire civilizations.

7. A Hoard of Treasure

In the rolling countryside of Wiltshire rises a large mound called Dragon Hill. The view from the top of the mound is breathtakingly beautiful. In one direction sprawls the immense figure of a creature, carved aeons ago into the chalk which lies just beneath the grassland. The etched outline is that of the White Horse of Uffington, more than 350 feet from head to tail – possibly a depiction of Epona, an ancient Celtic horse goddess. In the opposite direction, open countryside undulates to the distant horizon where, in the soft light of dawn or dusk, the swell of the hills fades into the sky. Long ago the landscape below Dragon Hill, unbroken by buildings, roads and fields, would have been interspersed by the deep green treetops of extensive stands of woodland. In one of the ancient legends, this beautiful vista was the last sight to fill the serpentine eye-slits of the dragon before it was slain by St George.

The image of St George, a Christian knight astride his white horse, slaying the dragon with sword or spike, features in scores of now famous paintings and woodcuts produced over the centuries. In medieval Christian art the dragon came to represent the power of evil and darkness – the very pagan beliefs that the Christian missionaries, introducing the new religion from Rome, had to try to defeat. This was a difficult task, for the dragon was ubiquitous. And anyway, battles with dragons had an ancient tradition and a deeper meaning than this Christian version of the perpetual battles between religions.

The Dragon's Hoard

In pre-Christian times the legends of the historical Middle-earth relate how dragons would discover treasure hidden in hoards by humans, often interred with their chiefs and kings in their burial mounds. The fiery beast would take possession of the whole mound. They heaped up the treasure and slept on it. In ancient England 'wyrm-bed' became a standard kenning or slang for gold.

Tolkien's Smaug, *Beowulf*'s dragon, the *Nibelung* cycle's Fafnir – poetic dragons all – were depicted as guarding a hoard of treasure. Generations of literary scholars assumed that such hoards were figments of fantasy by ancient authors and oral poets – just like the dragon itself. That was before the real treasure hoard was discovered – complete with a resident dragon.

Just south of Woodbridge, Suffolk, at a place called Sutton Hoo (Sutton being Anglo-Saxon for a settlement, and Hoo meaning 'hill' or mound – often denoting a burial mound), lies a famous burial mound reckoned by most experts to be that of King Redwald. Interred in 623 by the Anglii tribe, they buried with this chief's body an entire 90 foot-long ship. And amidships, a treasure chest was packed with wondrous objects of gold, silver and gems to accompany him to the Otherworld, where he would thus be equally in glory. The glittering hoard included a solid gold buckle decorated with a rich ornament in an intricate interlace pattern, a gold lid for a purse, mounted with garnets; a gold and garnet sword pommel and mounts for a sword harness, a pair of gold shoulder clasps for gripping together a cloak, small gold and garnet strap ends, buckles and fittings, a superb Byzantine silver dish, a set of ten silver bowls, parts of a lyre, a large and magnificent decorated shield, an ornamental sceptre, bronze hanging bowls, cauldrons, drinking horn mounts and drinking vessels, coins, and a gilt bronze war helmet which is now the most famous icon of Dark Age Britain – the 'Sutton Hoo helmet'.

This fabulous hoard was discovered in 1939 by an archaeologist called Basil Brown who was engaged by the landowner, Edith May Pretty to investigate the mounds which then lay hidden by weeds and rabbit warrens. Basil Brown was a self-taught archaeologist. One of his contemporaries, Richard Dumbreck, described him as

> ... a character; his pointed features gave him the, not inappropriate, appearance of a ferret and were invariably topped with a rather disreputable trilby hat, while a somewhat moist and bubbling pipe protruded dead ahead from his mouth. He had ...

gravitated to archaeology without any real training thanks to a quite remarkable flair for smelling out antiquities.

In May 1939 he uncovered a mound in which a King's treasure had lain hidden for 1300 years, the main mound of Redwald. It confirmed that burial mound treasure was not merely a fancy of poets' pens. It was material as well as symbolic gold.

And guarding this treasure from Sutton Hoo was a dragon. Exquisitely created in miniature by a goldsmith, like a dragon's calling card, it was formed in gilt-bronze, and was mounted squatting across the front of the king's great shield. This seventh-century dragon has a long snout and large mouth, huge, fierce-looking fangs, and bright eyes set far back in the head. It has four legs to power it across land, and two sets of wings folded back against the body. The body is covered in scales, detailed by the Middle-earth artist in tightly interwoven, finely drawn, curling strands of metal.

In the material world the hoards were sometimes real enough, as in the Sutton Hoo burial mound. But the dragon's hoard of treasure often represented something much more important than mere grave goods. It was the pivotal point for understanding the fate of entire civilizations.

The King's Treasure

Treasure was central to an understanding of the mind of Middle-earth. Gold, in particular, was used as a mark of the success of a kingdom, whether it was gained as war booty, as tribute from subservient kingdoms, or through trade. But this level of success dealt with a deeper dimension than mere material wealth. For a person's degree of success was a result of that individual's luck, or personal charisma, or mana. It was a fundamental characteristic of life rather like fertility – and the luck of a chieftain could mark the fate of a whole tribe. In Snorri Sturluson's account of the Battle of Stamford Bridge in 1066, King Harold of England interprets the fall of King Harald Sigurdsson from his horse as a loss of the royal luck; 'Do you know the stout man who fell from his horse, with the blue cloak and the beautiful helmet?' the English king asked. 'That is the king himself,' they answered. 'A great man,' said King Harold, 'and of stately appearance is he, but I think his luck has left him.' The defeat of the Norwegian king and his people ensued.

But this luck is more than we would mean by it. The Anglo-Saxon terms 'eadig' and 'saelig' are used to mean both 'lucky' and 'rich', and wealth is taken as a token of that quality on which the gods shower their blessings. The king was the charismatic holder of the tribal 'luck'. When bad harvests continued in Sweden under the Ynglingar King Domaldi, in spite of rich sacrifices by the ruler, he was killed. The early Germanic king was, consequently, not a god and not all-powerful, but he was filled with a power on which his tribe depended for its well-being.

So hoards of treasure representing a tribe's success were kept by the king in trust for his people – a quantifiable measure of his luck. And when the king gave a gift of an arm-ring, or a sword, from the hoard to a warrior or favoured servant – a common event in the mead-hall – it carried with it an obligation. It was a kind of debt.

Historians have suggested that all gifts from the king were accepted with a sense of this deeper dimension. The gifts were 'on loan' in a way, for they came from the king but on behalf of the tribe. Such a gift had a soul of its own. It would seek to return to the hoard through a reciprocal gift. Accepting a gift therefore implied an obligation. The honouring of gift obligations inspired some of the best dragon stories of the people of Middle-earth.

Fighting the Dragon

Great, bone-crunching and bloody accounts of battles with dragons were dramatized in the mead-halls by oral poets. Some of them – probably a small proportion – were written down and have survived until today. One of the most famous of all these accounts is the Anglo-Saxon poetic epic, *Beowulf*. In written form, it totals over three thousand lines.

The manuscript of the poem dates from about the year AD 1000. The first we hear of its existence was when it came into the hands of Lawrence Nowell, a sixteenth-century pioneer in Anglo-Saxon studies. He wrote his name on the manuscript and the date 1563. Of its

earlier history we know nothing. In the seventeenth century the
manusript found its way into the collection formed by Sir Robert
Cotton. Today it is in the British Library. Historians reckon that the
oral composition of the epic took place several hundred years before
it was written down – perhaps in the seventh century. It tells the
story of a man, Beowulf, who in youth achieved glory in a foreign
land by fighting and killing first a monster called Grendel. The beast
had been terrorizing the people of a kingdom ruled by Hrothgar,
creeping into their mead-halls at night and ripping the warriors to
pieces. After his heroic victory, Beowulf eventually became king and
ruled his country well for fifty years. In his old age, he fought one
more great battle, challenging a ferocious dragon who was attacking
and destroying his people.

Michael Alexander's inspired translation of Beowulf into modern
English relates how, for an age, the dragon lay sleeping. He was
guarding a treasure hoard, hidden in a burial mound raised high
above the moor, on the sea coast. The ancient burial mound could
be seen looming high on the clifftop, but no one knew of a way into
it. But then one day a slave, on the run from a flogging and looking
for shelter, stumbled upon the entrance. Finding his way inside, he
came upon an enormous sleeping dragon. At first he was too terrified
to move, in case the dragon woke up. But he was also overwhelmed
by the sight of the tremendous store of treasure.

Tolkien retold this story in *The Hobbit*, as Bilbo stealing from
under the dragon Smaug's sleeping nose a magnificent gold two-
handled cup. He wrote that although dragons cannot spend their
treasure, they know it intimately, and realize immediately if any of it
is missing. The dragon in *Beowulf* had been guarding his treasure for
a very long time. 'There were heaps of hoard-things in this hall
underground which once in gone days gleamed and rang; the treasure
of a race rusting derelict.' The slave succumbed to temptation, stole
a golden goblet, and made his escape.

When the dragon awoke, he realized the theft at once. Simmering
and seething, he waited for nightfall to exact his terrifying revenge.
As darkness fell, the dragon 'issued forth flaming, armed with fire',
and flew around the kingdom vomiting flames and setting alight the
timber halls and buildings, 'the blazing rose skyward and men were
afraid: the flying scourge did not mean to leave one living thing'.

Beowulf, the great but aged king, resolved to fight the dragon. In preparation he had a special shield made of iron, for he knew that the traditional linden-wood shield would turn to ashes against the dragon's fire. Gathering together a posse of twelve of his bravest warriors, he had them led by the hapless slave who stole the goblet, to find the entrance to the burial mound. The account of the battle is hair-raising, even now after 1,000 years and many changes in the tradition of story-telling.

Clad in his mail-shirt and gripping his iron shield, Beowulf peered up from the rocky foot of the cliff. He saw in the cliff-face a stone archway. The king bellowed as loudly as he was able. When the dragon heard the human voice, his hot breath billowed from the rock and 'the ground boomed'.

Beowulf unsheathed his famous sword, a mighty heirloom, which had cut down many with its sharp edge. The dragon burst from the burial mound, surging, flaming and coiling. Fire swept around Beowulf's shield, and he knew he could not stand his ground very long. He struck a violent blow to the dragon's head with his huge sword. The famous blade bit into the dragons' scales and, meeting the bone, it blunted. 'The blow made the dragon savagely angry, and it reared back and spat death-fire. The sparks of their battle blazed out over the sea. Fire enclosed Beowulf; he felt bitter pain.'

Seeing their leader engulfed in flame, the brave band of hand-picked warriors turned on their heels and fled. All except one: Wiglaf. Gripping his sword and wooden shield, he stood by Beowulf. The dragon roared again, and Wiglaf's wooden shield was withered back to the boss by the billow of fire. Beowulf, recovered a little from the shock of the dragon's first attack, swung his huge sword again with all his strength; it struck into the dragon's head, but this time the blade snapped.

The dragon flew forward and grasped Beowulf's neck between his fangs. Streams of blood from Beowulf covered them both. Wiglaf jumped forward, his hand burning in the flames, and struck his sword not at the dragon's head but in the softer throat. The sword went in, the dragon's fire immediately spluttered and abated. The huge jaws slackened and dropped Beowulf. Gravely injured, Beowulf staggered up, pulled out a stabbing knife and struck it deep into the serpent's body. The huge dragon lay still, mortally wounded. Scorched by its own flames, the dragon's blackened body stretched 50 feet along the ground. But the wounds the dragon had inflicted on Beowulf began to burn and swell, and he could feel the poison the dragon had injected into him boiling in his chest. Beowulf was dying. He staggered back, fell and lay dead.

Beowulf's grieving people threw the body of the dragon into the sea. They then built in tribute to Beowulf, a stronghold near the dragon's lair, high on the headland. They cremated their great king on a funeral pyre, and his ashes, along with all the hoard of jewellery and gold, was placed in the stronghold and sealed up for ever.

The Dragon's Taboos

This powerful poem echoes deep elements of the minds of the people of Middle-earth, and what the dragon meant to them. Lines of the poem speak of times when the treasure was first interred in the burial mound, long before the battle between Beowulf and the dragon. 'In another age', an unknown man, 'brows bent' in sadness and despair, walked along a deserted beach. He was dragging sacks heavy with treasure. He struggled down to an area of flat moorland which rose from the headland. There, through a narrow fissure in the rock, he prepared a new burial chamber, a barrow in which to bury the gold hoard. 'Hold, ground, the gold of earls!' he exclaimed. 'Men could not. Cowards they were not who took it from thee once, but war-death took them.' In other words, man had once taken the gold from the ground, but the great, rich kingdom had fallen in battles, lost its grandeur and ended. This man was the last survivor of an ancient clan, commending his people's treasure to the earth with the curse that it must destroy whoever removes it.

It was the end of a cycle of history. The man guarded the gold until his own death. And at that point, the dragon arrived, 'swimming through the gloom enfolded in flame', to 'guard for an age' the gold hoard. The dragon is the guardian of the aeon, the natural time in which a civilization rises, prising gold and wealth from the ground, and then falls, and eventually returns it there. It is a never-ending cycle. The past and the future coil around the present like the Norse

World Serpent – the biggest dragon of all, chewing on its own tail, its body never-ending.

In an age of exchange of wealth through gifts, largesse, tribute and dowry, the handling of wealth was a delicate and elaborate issue carrying moral and ethical overtones. The presence of the dragon pointed to the potency and consequences of negative, acquisitive and selfish aspects of hoarding and breach of trust. The *Beowulf* story was always told in verse, like the casting of a spell, set apart from the everyday pragmatic use of language. Verse was more than entertainment – it carried with it the force of 'galdor', or singing of magic charms.

The story of Beowulf suggests that in the Old English tradition, gold itself seems to have been animate, charged with a power capable of killing. Interfering with its natural condition could bring wealth but also risked destruction. And this is what happens in *Beowulf*, where the dragon is there at the beginning of a civilization, guarding the treasure left by the last. As long as the taboo against disturbing the natural balance of events was not violated, then the civilization could continue. But if someone tried to interfere with the ordained balance – as by stealing the treasure – then destruction came.

The dragon's role as guardian 'for an age' of hoards is central to the nature of life. Note that the dragon does not guard 'for ever'. Only 'for an age'. Ages, and dragons, come and go. And come again. *Aion* is a Greek word that denotes the sap of life, and hence a life-span; later it came to mean an epoch, or an 'age'.

The Cycles of Time

At the heart of the dragon stories lies the fact that the peoples of the real Middle-earth had a conception of time different from our own. They did not believe in linear, unfolding time, beginning from some point distant in the past and disappearing into the future. Rather they experienced time as a constant. History, the past, was always with them in their daily lives, affecting the present.

In the ancient Norse legends, the story was told of perpetual battles between the god Thor, and the World Serpent. It was

prophesied that at the end of time, called Ragnarok, Thor would slay
the world serpent. But he would only manage to stagger back nine
paces before he died of its poison, like Beowulf. The dying dragon
killed the heroes too, at the end of an age.

The dragon is first and foremost a snake, which rejuvenates each
time it sloughs its skin. It dies and is reborn. The inevitability of the
dragon's return lies at the heart of the Middle-earth understanding
of life. Everything was in perpetual cycle. Dawn to dawn, summer
to summer and aeon to aeon. The dragon was the animating force
behind all of death and rebirth. And beyond the material creation
of treasure by humans, this sense of cyclic time points the way to
the nature of the dragon's real treasure. The gold and silver of the
dragon's hoard were the symbols of eternal circling time: the sun and
the moon. These perpetual orbs in the sky were the dragon's most
precious wish-fulfilling jewel, reborn every day and night no matter
however many times they died and sank beneath the horizon.

In Tolkien's story *The Hobbit*, the dragon Smaug was slain by an
arrow fired from a bow. But as psychologist Daniel Noel points out,
this incident was more than a simple execution to rid the town of a
monster. A deeper story powers the action. The man who killed the
dragon Smaug was called Bard. He was a man who had three gifts:
firstly, the gift of prophecy, that caused him to anticipate the dragon's
coming and warn the people of Lake-town. Secondly, an 'unfailing
arrow', which was an heirloom. It had been passed from father to son
down a line descended from Girion, Lord of Dale, whose realm had
been destroyed by the dragon when it entered the region one hundred
and seventy-one years before. And thirdly, the understanding of
birds. This inherited understanding allowed him to learn the dragon's
weak point from an old thrush that had listened to Bilbo and the
dwarves. So Bard was no ordinary bowman. He had special gifts of
the kind we associate with shamans or spiritual warriors. When Bard
slayed Smaug, he was carrying out a sacred act which lies deep at the
heart of the beliefs of Middle-earth. The dying of the dragon marked
a new age, the beginning of a new civilization.

So the Anglo-Saxons regarded the dragon's hoard as a sign of a
people's luck. But it carried with it deep responsibilities. If people
behaved dishonourably, and did not acknowledge their obligations as
receivers of gifts, then the dragon would become enraged. He was

the wyrd of an epoch – an age coming to an end. In the annals of a thousand years ago, *The Anglo-Saxon Chronicle* recorded sightings of drakes flying high and leaving trails of fire. The entry for AD 793 says:

> This year came dreadful fore-warnings over the land of the Northumbrians, terrifying the people most woefully: these were immense sheets of light rushing through the air, and whirlwinds, and fiery dragons flying across the firmament. These tremendous tokens were soon followed by a great famine: and not long after, on the sixth day before the ides of January in the same year, the harrowing inroads of heathen men made lamentable havoc in the church of God in Holy-island, by rapine and slaughter.

And 300 years earlier, when the Saxons had landed to settle in England, and saw the deserted Roman towns, with 'bright castles, many bath houses, lofty pinnacles', brought down by the Wyrd destiny of civilizations, they knew what had happened. Forces greater than the politics of Rome had driven them out. The Roman age was over. And the corollary was that the Anglo-Saxons thought themselves 'chosen' as the next civilization. Just so long as they did it right. And that meant, for starters, steering clear of the Roman ruins of Fag Flor, Caister-by-Norwich, and Bath. They built their own homes in the 'good' places, populated by the spirits. This was the deeper dimension of their history – an abiding sense of destiny. If they lived in accordance with the wishes of Mother Earth, and the precepts of the dragon and its treasure, then they were destined to thrive in their new homeland.

THE ENCHANTED EARTH

8. Elves' Arrows

Around AD 1030, a beautifully handwritten, leather-bound manuscript was carefully packed for a long journey. Monks set out from Utrecht, and carried it across the flatlands of what is now Holland, by boat across the English Channel, and eventually delivered it to the monastery of Christ Church, in Canterbury. It was a book of psalms, from which Christian worshippers recited during their services. This particular book of psalms had originally been created in Rheims, a town in modern Belgium, during the ninth century AD. Now, 200 years later, the precious book was being sent to Canterbury so that English monks could make a copy of it. This labour-intensive process was, of course, how multiple copies of manuscripts were laboriously, and exquisitely reproduced. The Canterbury copy of the *Utrecht Psalter*, as the manuscript is known, is now in the British Library.

Books of psalms were widespread in monasteries and churches across the now-Christian Europe, towards the end of the Middle-earth period. But the *Utrecht Psalter* had an unusual feature – it was illustrated well beyond the ornate opening letters common in medieval manuscripts. The scribes had been joined by an artist, who prefaced each of the 150 psalms with a vivid pen drawing illustrating one of its lines, or themes. And at Christ Church, as the monks bent over their exacting work in the scriptorium, they must have been charmed by these drawings; they not only copied the monochrome outlines, but also filled them in with colour.

Most of the drawings represented conventional Christian themes – with one exception. This dynamic and arresting sketch provides us with an image of one of the most fascinating features of Middle-earth magic. The ninth-century artist has drawn a male Christian worshipper writhing in distress, and uttering desperate cries for deliverance from his tormenters. Piercing right through his arms and legs are five full-length arrows, complete with feathered flights and sharp iron heads. Such wounds would be catastrophic under any circumstances – but these are no ordinary arrows. Historians concur on the identity of his tormenters – he had been shot by the arrows of elves.

Elves of Beauty

Elves? In the more recent popular imagination of Victorian England, elves were small, slightly mischievous creatures who perched on flower petals, and flew around on summery days. Like most fragments of folklore, this image is a much reduced remnant of a more powerful original. In the real Middle-earth, people went about their daily activities with an awareness of elves as Otherworld beings who ghosted in and out of their lives like wraiths of pure life-force. They seemed to emanate from familiar features of the landscape – woods, streams, rocks and fields, and also lived in human-built burial mounds. These aspects of the environment took on an elf-presence imbuing them with a kind of consciousness. And while elves may have been difficult to see in the normal run of daily events, they were much more than a vague association of 'spirit' with landscape. They were beings with a vivid identity, imagined as creatures in human-like form.

The Old English word 'aelf', the linguistic origin of 'elf', has cognate words in Norwegian and in Old High German. Because it occurs in such ancient forms of these languages, we know that belief in these beings goes back to very ancient times, when the ancestors of the English, Germans and Norwegians still spoke the same language. In fact, the term 'elves' was widely used when referring to 'spirits' among ancient Germanic peoples in general, and it may have served as a cover-all term for Otherworldly creatures.

Despite the picture of destructive elves' arrows in the Christian manuscript, they were a positive presence in people's lives throughout much of the real Middle-earth period. The elves were often described as beautiful. A considerable compliment for a woman was to compare her appearance with an elf. An Anglo-Saxon poem – found in the same manuscript which contained the epic *Beowulf* – refers to its heroine as 'Judith, wise in thought, a woman as brightly beautiful as an elf. . . .'. The beauty was more than mere physical attractiveness. It was of an iridescent quality – a radiant, pale brightness. This glow is reflected in the Anglo-Saxon word 'aelf', which is cognate with the Latin 'albus', meaning 'white and shining'. The name of the Alps, peaks shining with snow, is based on the word for elf, and the Anglo-Saxon word for swan is 'ylfetu', the ylf referring to 'elf-white'. The radiance, and whiteness of elf-beautiful seems to refect a pureness that washes out hues and leaves the 'original', the shining, like a bright moon.

Tolkien revealed in a letter that in *The Lord of the Rings*, his fantasy version of these creatures drew on the elves from the real Middle-earth. His elves, too, shine with goodness. He said they were beings of the Otherworld, the realm of spirit. In appearance, Tolkien depicted the elves as the most beautiful of all earthly creatures – 6 feet tall, slender, graceful and strong.

In the historical Middle-earth, people perceived elves as possessing special qualities of mind. King Alfred, the first Saxon king to rule over the whole country of England, has the word aelf or 'elf' as the first element in his name: 'Aelf-red' means 'possessing the wisdom of an elf'. This sort of wisdom extends further than book-learning. It is more than worldly information. It seems to have had connotations with what we could call supernatural wisdom – uncanny knowledge, extending beyond the five senses. Tolkien expressed this by endowing his elves with a keener sense of sight and hearing, and greater aesthetic and creative qualities than people. They also had special ways of using their minds, talking directly from mind to mind without words.

Seeing the Elves

So where were these bright, beautiful and wise creatures in the original Middle-earth? Were they visible perched on rocks, flitting between trees – or even prowling in the undergrowth with an armed bow, ready to fire an arrow into human bodies and souls? And how did people communicate with them? The medieval Danish writer Saxo reports in his *History of the Danes*, written in 1182–1210, that in the ancient Norse culture, in order to see a being of the

Otherworld (in this case, a 'wargod'), you had to go to a 'gifted person'. In all cultures, through all times, gifted people were believed to be chosen by the spirits to serve the community as mediators between the everyday material world, and the world of spirit. These were often people who, early in their life, had experienced powerful dreams which seemed prophetic, or had visions that others could not see.

Sometimes these people went through an initiatory sickness – a serious illness which plunged them into hallucinatory fevers, and seemed to mark a 'death' of their human person. They were 'reborn' as beings with the ability to have one foot in the mundane human world, and the other foot in the unseen Otherworlds. They were uncanny. In western parlance, before the recent adoption of the term 'shamans' from anthropologists' observations of the Siberian tradition, they were called wizards. In Anglo-Saxon the term was 'wicce', which referred both to witches and wizards. They were the Gandalfs of the real Middle-earth, and the villages of Anglo-Saxon England had such people – men and women who could glimpse the spirits.

Under the direction of one of these gifted people, reports Saxo, one had to prepare one's eyes by 'hallowing' them. This was in order not only to see the supernatural being, but also to be safe in its presence. Saxo quotes the instructions from the wizard as 'You must first hallow your eyes with the sign of victory to recognise the wargod safely face-to-face'. For a similar exercise in seeing the elves, people must have visualized an image like the 'sign of victory' but which was appropriate for bringing oneself into the presence of the elves.

Saxo explains that these 'gifted' people would then help the ordinary mortal to glimpse the spirits by a guided form of viewing: 'Bring your gaze nearer and look through my arm akimbo,' says Saxo. This suggests that the wizard stood upright, with hands on hips, elbows sticking out to the side. A person seeking a glimpse of these Otherworld beings crouched down and looked through the space between the arms and the body of the wizard.

Was this magical vision available to anyone? Or did the wizards reserve such crossings-between-the-worlds for apprentices? By the time Saxo was writing, several centuries had passed since the high point of Middle-earth. Powerful incantations, secret signs, magical practices may by then have become debased, open to everyone, shorn of their original potency by a disapproving Christian orthodoxy.

If a person successfully petitioned a wizard for such a special vision, what would they have seen? When they were glimpsed, reports Saxo, the Otherworld creatures would 'appear' as 'apparitions marked by a false pallor whose momentary corporeal substance was borrowed from insubstantial air'. So they looked unnaturally pale, and although they had a 'solid' presence, it was only temporary, and conjured from the ephemeral, the very 'thin air'. Was this an enhanced ability to see forces beyond our understanding? Did the elves manifest in a world we would call the 'paranormal' – which says nothing except that what one sees is beyond the normal. Did the Anglo-Saxons think of the elves as 'normal', but usually invisible?

People certainly experienced the elves as being ever-present. They had a tangible presence, an aura, an energy with which people felt connected. They were spirit-beings in their own right in the light and shadows of Middle-earth. They did not exist simply as reflections of human problems, issues or needs. They lived by their own rules. And so people had to bridge the gap, to befriend the elves on their own terms.

Feasting With The Elves

The country landscape of England today swells with small hills, rises and knolls. Many are natural undulations in the ground. Some are man-made mounds, with earth heaped over the consecrated remains of a person in a burial barrow. I am sitting on one in Sussex, a short distance north of Lewes, reputed to be an elf-mound. It has, as far as we know, no history as a burial site, but its natural features are evocative. Perched atop the Sussex Downs (so-named from the Anglo-Saxon world 'dun', whose original form has survived most closely in the term 'sand dunes', meaning hills), it rises high above the valley of the Ouse river. Grass-covered, still warm from the afternoon sun, it smells sweet, feels soft, and whispers timeless secrets as the wind rustles its surface.

In Middle-earth times, the elves often seemed to be associated with these places. There they were left offerings of milk and meat, and people asked the elves for help in overcoming difficulties or illness. Far from being blatant bribes, or pragmatic payment for services rendered, the process, called 'blot', was seen as magical. In the Norse *Cormac's Saga*, a woman called Thordis instructed: 'There is a knoll a little way from here where the Elves dwell; thou shalt take thither the ox that Cormac slew, and sprinkle the blood of the ox on the outside of the knoll, and give the Elves a banquet of the meat; and thou shalt be healed.'

People built a fire at the site, spit-roasted the meat, and offered it for the spirits. Toasts were drunk in honour of the elves. Sprinkling the blood of an ox – his spirit energy – and to leave for the elves a 'banquet of the meat' was clearly a serious offering. Ox-meat was the sort of meat available only at particular times of the year, and the elves were being offered a real feast.

Sometimes there were larger community ceremonies where people could gather to show their respect, and even love for them. In Sweden an annual offering was made to the elves in the interest of future harvests. It was called *alfablot* – literally 'sacrifice to the elves', and this phrase makes clear the sort of relation people sought to have with them. Honouring the elves in this way is a different process from religious worship. The elves were not remote greater powers to whom people offered obeisance. Rather, they were spirits with whom people wanted to be friends. But being friends with them entailed such gifts – the elves were not automatically beneficent.

The Celtic tradition placed the elves – or *sidh-folk* (creatures of the burial mounds) – clearly in connection with ancestors. They were considered immortal, and able to pass from Middle-earth to the Upperworld at will. They were not considered human, but they lived their lives close to those of humans, regarded by people as a race who required a great deal of respect.

Furious Clergy

Towards the end of the Middle-earth millennium when the Church became more powerful, the elf ceremonies were denounced by the Christian priests. From pulpits all over England, priests denigrated elves as demons, antipathetic with the world of God. They preached against belief in them, and abhorred their popularity. Such creatures, connected directly with nature, were outside the jurisdiction of the Church, and were therefore a hindrance to the centuries-long task of converting the populace to Christianity. In fact, some historians think the arrows piercing the holy man in the *Utrecht Psalter* may have been Christian propaganda, intended to depict the elves as negative forces.

Aelfric, a teacher in the monastery school in Cerne Abbas in the late 900s, thundered from the pulpit:

> Some men are so blinded that they bring their offerings to an earth-fast stone, and also to trees, and to well-springs, even as witches teach, and will not understand how foolishly they act, or how the dead stone or the dumb tree can help them, or give them health, when they themselves never stir from the place.

In the Christian view, elements of nature are 'fixed' and so cannot go to help people. They have no 'intelligence', no way of transportation (the 'earth-fast stone'), no way of speaking (the 'dumb tree'). This sounds remarkably rational at first glance – like a modern, secular view that a dynamic connection between rocks, trees and health is unlikely. But for the early Church, it was not so much a clear rejection of the possible influence of 'unseen forces'. Treating elements of the landscape as spiritual forces went against the idea of the Christian God as the sole source of spiritual and heavenly intervention. It was the elvish spirits of these natural features which people honoured. Presumably elves were not 'fixed', ignorant or dumb.

In addition, Aelfric's anger is partly due to the fact that, not only were people participating in these ungodly rituals, but they were also heeding the advice of indigenous wizards ('even as witches teach'). The Anglo-Saxon word he uses is 'wiccan' which then referred to both male and female wizards. These people seemed to use a magic outside the control of the Church. The Christian clergy were attempting to undermine the magical perspective of the culture of Middle-earth, and replace it with a monotheistic religion.

But elvish conversations continued. Three centuries after Aelfric's denunciations, the early fourteenth century Icelandic Hausbok criticized 'women . . . so stupid as to take their food to stonepiles and into caves. They consecrate it to the land spirits and then eat it, believing that the landspirits would be friendly to them, and they will be more prosperous.'

Towards the end of the Middle-earth millennium, the elves became identified as gods and goddesses. The thirteenth-century literary traditions of Norse myths, as recorded by Snorri Sturluson, talked about two races of gods – the Aesir and the Vanir. The latter are fertility gods, and sometimes the texts talk of the two kinds of deities as 'gods and elves'. The most prominent god amongst the Vanir in Viking times was called Frey, and he is spoken of as living in 'elf-home'. It seems likely that the nature spirits, which were the medium by which most people made the imaginative leap from the pragmatic world into middle-earth, later became depicted as deities, perhaps in response to the advent of Christianity with its emphasis on an all-ruling God.

The early Christians, of course, subscribed to a more simple delineation of morality. Things were either good, or bad. They were polar opposites. And the spirits of Middle-earth, which existed in a domain beyond Christian dogma, were denounced by priests from the pulpit as demons, rather than gods!

In Tolkien's *The Lord of the Rings*, at first the Elves of Middle-earth welcomed men, but then the two races became estranged. This may have been the same in the original Middle-earth, too. The Christian authorities painted the elves as disease-demons.

The Elves Fire Their Arrows

How does the elves' 'goodness' reconcile with their propensity for firing multitudes of arrows into people? This is where Tolkien's image of the elves as all goodness differs from the everyday experience of them in Anglo-Saxon England.

'Elf-shot' was believed to be one of the causes of disease, in which the victim had been pierced by their arrows. The tiny spears were invisible to the naked eye, and had to be driven from the body by healers. They were malevolent powered barbs. The Anglo-Saxon magical manuscripts include wizard's herb conjurations that could be effective against these demons of disease. For example, the *Lacnunga* has a concoction 'for a salve against the race of elves'. It includes a large variety of plants: 'the female hop plant, wormwood, bishops's wort, lupine, vervain, henbane, harewort, viper's bugloss, sprouts of heathberry, leek, garlic, seeds of cleavers, cockle and fennel'. The spell-book then instructs the magical practitioner to 'put the herbs in a vessel', enchant them by singing incantations over them, boil the mixture in butter, strain it through a cloth, and smear the resulting salve on the face and painful areas of the body to release the patient from the illness caused by elves.

There is also a chanting cure – a 'charm' – for the wizard to intone magically: 'If you were shot in the skin, or you were shot in the flesh/ or were shot in the blood, or were shot in the bone/ or were shot in the limb, may your life never be threatened/ if it were the gods' shot, or it were the elves' shot,/ or it were the witches' shot, I will now help you.' Clearly the damage could be done by the gods, or by witches, as well as the elves. This implies that it was not an automatic hostility but something brought on in some way.

The cause of the pain in this charm is referred to as the 'pieces of iron' – the arrowheads. Supernatural the elves may have been, but their weapons made wounds in the pragmatic world.

The understanding of spirits in the magical world of Middle-earth was complex. They were not all good or all bad, and it does not therefore need a Christian twist to give them the negative dimension. Perhaps sometimes the elves were in no mood to listen. People tried to befriend them, and it did not always work. And then there was trouble. For just as nature can be cruel and seemingly unreliable, so could the elves. They were propitiated to keep them sweet. To alienate them might bring one down with the 'water-elf disease', for when the elves harmed people, usually it was by making people ill.

Magical Conceptions and Modern Medicine

These concepts of elves and elves' arrows bear an intriguing resemblance to our contemporary lay concepts of illness. For example, it is commonly assumed that illnesses are caused by bacteria or viruses which 'invade' our bodies. These micro-organisms are invisible to the naked eye, but are indeed visible to trained specialists who, in place of the 'spirit vision' of ancestral wizards, have microscopes to enhance their perceptual capacities. There is a strangely compelling parallel between the micro-organisms and the elves' arrows of Middle-earth.

Furthermore, our treatment for them resembles the magical medicine of our ancient past. When we are ill from these 'invasions', we go to a doctor, a person who, just like the shamanic healer of old, has indeed *seen* these invisible invaders. The doctor prescribes for us a medicine concocted out of our sight in the pharmacy, and containing substances which for the most part we as lay people do not know, indicated by an unreadable Latin name (it could even be an incantation!).

Even the rituals of taking medicine have some faint resemblance between the cultures. For example, to cure a neck-tumour, the *Lacnunga* manuscript instructs the healer to take neck-wort, wood-marche, wood-chervil, strawberry runners, boar-throat, cockle, ironhard gathered without iron, farthingwort, butchers' broom, broad-bishopwort and brown-wort.

> Let him collect all these plants, an equal amount of each, three nights before summer sets in, and make them with Welsh ale into a drink. And then, on the eve of the first day of summer, the man who intends to drink that drink must wake all night. And at first cock-crow let him take a drink once, at first dawn a second drink, at sunrise a third drink. And let him rest thereafter.

The admonition to begin the healing on 'the eve of the first day of summer' must apply to the spiritual forces of the plants rather than to their material qualities. But the form of the instructions, including 'At first cock-crow let him take a drink once . . .' sound wonderfully familiar, for when we receive the medicine, we are instructed to take it according to a detailed ritual: e.g. in a 5 ml spoon, three times a day, immediately after meals. Not so colourful as 'on the eve of the first day of summer' and 'at first cock-crow', but nevertheless perhaps possessing some ritual cachet in its very specificity.

But in our modern understanding, it is not only the fact that we have been 'invaded' by a disease-causing bacteria or virus, it is the fact that our immune system was unable to resist the debilitating powers of that invading force. When we are strong, 'hale and hearty' to coin an Anglo-Saxon phrase, then we are better able to withstand attempts to invade our boundaries.

And who embodied fertility energy? Frey, the elf-god. And that is why when we lose touch with his favours, when the elves fall away from us, they rob us of the immune powers against invasions. The elves arrows are not a Christian invention to denigrate these spirit beings – rather, they are the shadow side of having a mana-giving force. This is the nature of magic.

9. Plant Magic

In the real Middle-earth all plants had powers beyond their biological qualities. They contained a vital life force, which could be released like a spirit. It cauterized, healed, mended and repelled invading malignant forces. Today, in low-lying wild fields of England, Wales and Ireland, some of these Middle-earth 'power-plants' species can still be found.

Vervain

The Anglo-Saxon herbal books often feature vervain, or verbena, among the healing concoctions and salves. Today this herb still thrives, growing up to two feet tall, with toothed leaves. From July to September, bees buzz and forage for nectar amongst the lilac, five-petalled flowers. The Old English translation of the *Herbarium* of Apuleius Platonicus, a compendium of Latin texts, recorded that vervain drove away all poisons and was 'said to be used by sorcerers'. And in the *Lacnunga* collection of magical medical remedies, along with rue, dill, periwinkle, mugwort, betony and other powerful herbs, vervain was an ingredient in a healing salve against the 'demons of disease'. This somewhat general pharmaceutical indication makes it sound endearingly like the cure-all quack medicines of the old American Wild West, sold from the back of a wagon. But in fact, ancient European herbal practice used many plants which have today achieved recognition as having therapeutic qualities, and from which some modern medicines are prepared. For example, to cure a cough, the *Lacnunga* manuscript calls for: '. . . honey droppings and marche seed and dill seed. Pound the seeds small, mix into the droppings to thickness, and pepper well. Take three spoonfuls after the night's fast.' Today we would recognize this as an effective intervention for breaking up congestion.

Enchantment Of Plants

Herbal medicines were applied to patients directly. But another ingredient was often added: magic. Herbs were 'enchanted' with incantations and rituals before they were prepared for use as medicines, or as they were being administered to the patient. Even today, a popular name for vervain in Wales is 'enchantment herb', or 'wizards' herb'!

Tolkien included Anglo-Saxon magical plant medicine in *The Lord of the Rings*. When Frodo had been wounded by a dagger cut, the Strider lifted the blade of the offending knife and it disappeared like smoke in the air. It had evil magic. Aragorn grasped the remaining dagger hilt, and sang over it slowly and in an alien language to counter its force. Then he pulled some long leaves of a plant from the pouch at his belt. He called it Athelas, explaining that he had to journey a long distance to find it, locating it by its strong aroma. He boiled the leaves, and bathed Frodo's wounded shoulder.

In ancient Europe, the Church authorities preached and legislated against the practice of using plants in a magical way, for it seemed to draw on an Otherworldly power that was outside the church's jurisdiction; 'Let no one enchant herbs!' said St Eligius in AD 640. His plea fell on deaf ears, for the practice of magical medicine seemed to thrive. But certainly the Christian concern about the enchantment of healing plants being somehow a threat to their missionary activity was well-founded. For in the times of Middle-earth, a person's health was considered to be, literally, a blessing.

Life-Force and Healing

The notion of a person's well-being centred on the idea of wholeness. We can see this in the etymological relationship, still preserved in modern English, between the words heal, whole, health and holy. These concepts were still actively and intimately related for the Anglo-Saxons. A person's physical health was linked with their psychological and spiritual vitality. This is how the intervention of ritual and 'magic' was thought to add to the immediate biological properties of a plant remedy. The Anglo-Saxon word 'haelu' meant good fortune, material prosperity, and health, along with spiritual blessing. From it is derived our word 'heal'. This power could be passed on to a person through anyone with Otherworldly 'connections' – like a king granting wealth, a wizard or, later, a priest offering blessings, or it could be granted by an object of 'power' – like a magic ring or rune-carved necklace. When a person was ill, it meant that they had lost this general life-force of haelu, and may even be afflicted by a malevolent force of anti-haelu.

Haelu was like a generalized life-force. It was similar to more recently identified notions of 'mana' among some indigenous peoples – a kind of personal power and 'good luck' which kept a person safe and granted them various abilities, including the capacity to heal others.

Life-force was the source of all vitality. In a person it was believed to be generated in the head, and flowed like a stream of light into the marrow of the spine and from there into the limbs and crevices of the body. Power-plants help to control the channels through which the energy flowed. Since life-force was believed to emanate from the head, the experience of fevers must have felt like an upsurge in its production, in an attempt to guard against invading malevolent spirits, or elves' arrows. The increase in life-force made the head feel hot, even to others. If the spirits continued their attack, life-force flowed down the spine like molten metal in a smith's crucible and the entire body became hot.

But the possession of life-force was not restricted to people. The Anglo-Saxons believed in a generalized spirit force suffusing their cosmos. This view of a vital presence in the environment is today labelled 'animism'. It implies a belief in a level of life that in our culture we reserve for human, or animal species only. It is a label redolent of the 'primitive' views documented by anthropologists among the indigenous cultures of the world. And yet in the recent resurgence of interest in complementary medicine, we are once again recognizing that the natural plant world has healing resources that might yield up more secrets if we pose the right questions.

Research projects are underway at Oxford University and other major medical centres into healing properties of plants used by indigenous healers in the Amazon, Africa and Australia. And explorations into the psychology of healing has shown how the state of mind of a person has a remarkable impact on their ability to resist infection by affecting the strength of the body's immune response, and also in the recovery from serious and life-threatening illnesses. At New York University, a hospital-based study run by Professor of Nursing Dolores Kreiger, initiated a body of research which indicates that massaging a person's 'energy field' which extends a few inches beyond the body, without physically touching them, resulted in both faster healing protocols than ordinary massage, and an increased haemoglobin level in the blood when compared to conventional massage techniques. And controlled trials at Stanford Research Institute demonstrated how jars containing seedlings, when touched daily by a spiritual healer, grew faster than identical jars of seeds touched only by a laboratory assistant. This dash of twenty-first century science shows that some of the features of Middle-earth magic are still thriving deep within the paradigms of a world view we assume to be on the opposite pole of rationality. They knew nothing of such studies a thousand years ago, but their experience convinced them that life-force permeated everything.

Mugwort and the Battle for Magic

The second half of the Middle-earth millennium saw a battle waged between the indigenous wizards and Christian missionaries to control magic. The Christians believed in much of it – their objection to its use was that it gained its powers from sources outside the blessings of the Church. For the missionaries this was both sacrilegious, and undermined politically their influence with the people of Old England.

We can see this power struggle as it focused on particular magical plants – like mugwort. It grows wild still in clumps 3–4 feet high, by roadsides and along the bottom of old hedges throughout lowland Britain. It has tiny red-brown flowers which appear in July and August. As well as being a plant for wizards and healers, it was used as protection by the general populace. This custom continued towards the end of Middle-earth, when it was incorporated into Christian practice – people picked, purified and strengthened it in the smoke of ritual bonfires on St John's Eve, and then made it into garlands and hung it over doors to keep off, we are told, 'all the powers of evil, including the spells of sorcerers'.

But earlier in Anglo-Saxon England, before the advent of Christianity, the plant had special significance not as a superstitious protection *against* sorcerers, but as a plant used on behalf of the populace *by wizards* in order to counteract malevolent spells made by other spellcasters. In the *Lacnunga* manuscript an entry called the 'Lay of the Nine Herbs' begins with an incantation to the powers of Mugwort:

> Have in mind, Mugwort, what you made known,
> What you laid down, at the great denouncing.
> Una your name is, oldest of herbs, of might against thirty, and
>   against three,
> Of might against venom and the onflying,
> Of might against the vile She who fares through the land.

In the lore of incantations, the number three and its multiples were traditionally employed to construct word magic, to weave a spell. Mugwort was believed to be able to counter such attempts to send malevolent magic. We can see from the way in which the herb was addressed by 'incantations' that its life-force or 'spirit power' was being addressed, while the onflying, the 'She', refers to the elves, who were sometimes depicted as agents of the Wyrd Sisters, the forces who determined fate.

Certainly the 'spirit power' of these 'enchantments' was recognized by the early Christian authorities, and they developed invocations for disarming the plants of their powers. For example, St Hildegard, a nun who lived from 1098 to 1179, came from Bingen, near the present town of Mainz, feared the power of the plant mandrake, and wrote:

> When it is dug out of the earth, at once let it be put into running water for a day and a night, and thus all ill and evil humour which is in it is expelled, so that it is thus no longer of value for magical purposes. But when it is uprooted from the ground, if then it is laid down with the earth adhering to it which has not been removed ... then it is an evil agent for much hurtful magic.

This hostile Christian view pictures the plant mandrake as retaining its healing power only while still in contact with the earth. But since it was the indigenous healers and wizards who employed this power, rather than Christian monks, it was depicted as 'hurtful magic' by Hildegard.

Christian Hallowing of Plants

Sometimes where the Christian authorities could not successfully outlaw a magical practice, they adopted it into Christian custom. Celandine is a common perennial, a member of the poppy family. It grows 1–2½ feet high, with yellow, four-petalled flowers. It is easily identified by the drop of poisonous, deep orange latex which is exuded if a stem is broken. This was once used as a cure for warts, and was also believed to be a cure for sore eyes. In the *Lacnunga* healing manuscript, the plant gatherer is instructed to: 'Dig round a clump of celandine root, and take with thy two hands turned upwards, and sing thereover nine Paternosters; at the ninth, at "Deliver us from evil", wrench it up; and take from that shoot and from others to make a little cup full, and then saturate them, and let him be fomented by a warm fire; he will soon be better.'

The spell seems to indicate that the stems be broken and the juice milked until a small cupful is obtained, and then the stems saturated, or covered with water. The patient takes the concoction and sits by the warmth of a fire. This incantation as written is obviously Christianized. Originally, it would have almost certainly involved the enchantment of the plants by singing incantations nine times (a number sacred to the Middle-earth heathens) over the plant before digging it up. St Eligius would have winced.

Similarly, vervain was Christianized, as in a prayer which made it a plant of Calvary: 'Hallowed be thou, Vervain, as thou growest in the ground, For in the mount of Calvary there thou was first found. Thou healedst our Saviour Jesus Christ, and stanchedst his bleeding wound; In the name of the Father, the Son, and the holy Ghost, I take thee from the ground.'

Clearly this is meant as a Christian prayer to be used by people (perhaps as a step in their conversion) as they picked the plant for 'magical medicine'. Further, the person who, a thousand years ago, recorded this remedy, wrote that the vervain was picked, crossed with the hand, and blessed with the charm, and then worn against 'blasts', a general category of illnesses caused by 'ill winds'. From the praising lines, the indication of the herb's power in staunching bleeding wounds, and in the making the sign of the cross over the herb and blessing it with 'the charm', we get some idea of the detailed process of enchantment.

Collecting Magical Plants

The indigenous peoples of Middle-earth collected their herbs and plants with very great care. They observed strictures concerning the location for collecting, the phase of the moon, and the particular individuals who were allowed to cut the plants from the ground.

The impeccably detailed rituals for collecting the plants, and the complexity and specificity of the preparations of them into salves and other concoctions, is evidence that the wizards saw plants as existing simultaneously on a physical and a spiritual level. Pliny, writing about the Celtic tribes in Britain several hundred years earlier, explains that the Celts gathered vervain at sunrise after a sacrifice to the earth 'as an expiation'. And the maladies for which vervain was used by the Celtic tribes were not always of an organic nature, but to do with psyche or spirit. Pliny says that they believed that 'When it was rubbed on the body all wishes were gratified; it dispelled fevers and other maladies; it was an antidote against serpents; and it conciliated hearts.'

There were various other procedures and taboos in collecting sacred plants, common to most ancient tribal groups. For example, the Roman writer Pliny, reporting on the Celts in Britain, also describes a herb which the Celts collected called selago which we cannot now identify. They believed it 'preserved one from accident, and its smoke when burned healed maladies of the eye'. He explains that they culled it without the use of iron, and after a sacrifice of bread and wine. The person gathering it wore a white robe and went with unshod feet after washing them.

Another plant, samolus, was placed in drinking troughs as a

remedy against disease in cattle. The person collecting the plant had to have fasted first. It could be pulled from the ground with the left hand only, and uprooted wholly. And the gatherer must not look behind him! Clearly, this ritual deals with life-force and magical powers well beyond any merely material qualities of the plant. In sum, collecting the above plants have included such ritual observances as fasting, washing and keeping the feet bare, wearing white, not using iron, using the left hand only, uprooting the whole plant, collecting at sunrise, not looking over the shoulder, maintaining silence, and sacrificing to the plant in 'expiation'.

Expiation to whom, or what? The plant? Many of these practices were, as I have said, later incorporated into Christian worship in order to render a new and alien religion familiar, user-friendly. The Middle-earth practice of giving thanks to the plant being picked or harvested was incorporated into the Christian ritual by prayer, in which thanks and praise were accorded to the plants and to the powers of the Earth: 'Ye (herbs) whom earth, parent of all, hath produced . . . this I pray, and beseech from you, be present here with your virtues, for she who created you hath herself promised that I may gather you with the goodwill of him on whom the art of medicine was bestowed, and grant for health's sake good medicine by grace of your powers.'

It is remarkable that in this prayer, the source of creation of the herb was credited to the Earth in her *feminine* aspect apparently, for it refers to the 'she who created you' rather than to the masculine God of Christianity. Further, the plant is addressed directly, as in a magical tradition, rather than addressing God and asking Him for his strength and blessing to be applied to the plant (as in another incantation turned into a prayer directed to God: 'Whatsoever herb thy power do(th) produce, give, I pray, with goodwill to all peoples to save them and grant me this my medicine'). The 'him whom the art of medicine was bestowed' was in this case the wizard about to collect the herb. The direction of his thought, and heart, is to the herb he is addressing; the sacred presence he is 'expiating' is the feminine aspect of Earth; Mother Earth.

10. Spirit Nights

The night sky must have seemed huge to the people of Middle-earth, compared with today. Then, on clear nights, the stars glittered and the moon hung bright, pouring silvery shadows across a landscape undimmed by the electric glare of cities. On cloudy nights, when the celestial sources sank out of sight, the world would have been plunged into darkness. In the houses and villages, people moved about by the soft and flickering light of fires, candles, burning torches and oil lamps.

Against this gentle glow, the prominent sight of the moon seems to have inspired people. They carried the monthly lunar rhythm close to their heart. They even told each other variations on legends in which night was dominant over day. One, Snorri Sturluson's collection of myths called *The Prose Edda*, told of a woman called Night, daughter of one of the original giants. She was dark-skinned and dusky-haired, like the family she came from. Then she married a god called Shining One – the Sun – and they had a son named Day. He took after his father's side being bright and beautiful. So Night was conceived of as the original state of the cosmos.

The story goes on to explain that Night and her son Day were given two horses and two chariots and they were put in the sky, so that they should ride around the world every twenty-four hours. Night rides first on a horse called Frosty-mane, and every morning he bedews the earth with the foam from his bit. Day's horse is called Shining-mane, and the whole earth and sky are illuminated by his mane.

The story gives the impression of a universal version of mind-rhythms, in which the nocturnal came first, a deep darkness in which 'external' images were no longer visible, and allowed the Earth's imagination to roam freely. In this dreamlike state, the realms of spirits were created. And then Day was born, and people awoke into a perception of what had been created.

Tacitus in his *Germania* says of the ancient Germans that 'they do not reckon time by days, as we do, but by nights. All their engagements and appointments are made on this system. Night is regarded as ushering in the day'. Longer time-spans, too, were calculated in 'moons'. But this counting by the moon was not simply a unit of time passed, metered out in equal durations of apparently arbitrary significance, like our relentlessly marching minutes, hours and days. Each stage of the moon had a presence which was palpable, and affected everything people did, and everything around them. We can see this in the way they approached the collecting of plants and crops.

Moon Cycles

In ancient Europe, people seemed to experience what we have largely forgotten – that moon cycles affect plants, animals and humans profoundly. The moon's gentle but persistent pull affected everything. For example, people believed the moon's presence to influence the growth rhythms of plants, just as strongly as it punctuated the lives of people. The position of the moon readied the plant's power. Expeditions for collecting the plants to be used in healing remedies had to be carried out according to the moon's phase. This cycle of influence was finely calibrated. The *Lacnunga* medical spellbook instructed that the wizard collecting periwinkle must pluck it 'when the moon is nine nights old, and eleven nights, and thirteen nights, and thirty nights, and when it is one night old'. The mulberry plant should be picked 'when to all men the moon is seventeen nights old, after the setting of the sun, ere the rising of the moon'. These timings are specific. They take the collecting of plants for magical medicine to a finely-tuned art.

The Anglo-Saxons' measurements of the power of plants at periods in the moon's cycle was partly the result of observation. The people of Middle-earth did not have our biological knowledge of plant life, but they had intimate and detailed experience of collecting wild plants at various stages in their life cycle. However, regardless of the extent of their practical knowledge of the plants' natural healing powers, their collecting rituals emphasized other forces. They were attuned not only to biological factors, but matters of spirit, too. In filling a plant-collecting sack, a wizard was keen to take into account the total balance of influences.

Not only was the particular point of the moon's cycle important, but the balance between sun and moon was also crucial. The ancient *Anglo-Saxon Herbal*, translated from the ancient herbarium of Apuleius Platonicus, listed 132 plants and added some more from classical sources. It incorporated classical injunctions into Old English usage, prescribing for sea-holly: 'And when thou shalt take up this wort with its roots, then beware that no sun shine upon it, lest its beauty and its might be spoiled through the brightness of the sun.'

Balance of Sun and Moon

The sun was not always cast in the role of spoiler. The farming people of ancient England were well aware of the seasons of the sun and its influence on growth of crops. But for them it was the alternation and balance between the energies of moon and sun, night and day, darkness and light, which determined the condition of a plant for use in medical remedies. The people of Middle-earth hallowed the moon and celebrated the life-force of the sun. These two great presences empowered all of life. They had to stay in balance; if not the result was chaos.

In another legend, an apocalyptic story from near the end of the Middle-earth times and reproduced in Snorri Sturluson's *Prose Edda*, the moon and sun are depicted as driving chariots through the sky. They are both being chased by powerful wolves who embody the primal energy of wildness, untamed forces, entropy and chaos. They come from the east of Middle-earth, in a forest called Iron Wood. There lives a giant troll. This aged giantess has given birth to many giant sons, all of them in the shape of wolves. One night one of the wolves will catch the moon and, in the words of the ancient poem, '. . . he will swallow the moon and bespatter the sky and all the air with blood. Because of this the sun will lose its brightness, and the winds will then become wild and rage on every side.' It is an image of the End. It is the time when people have lost their balanced attunement to the bright and dark sides of life – and are overwhelmed by the chaos that ensues.

For the people of Middle-earth, the way to avoid this scenario was through keen awareness of those places, times, events in life which were pitched right on the balance point between great forces.

Liminal Moments

In the historical Middle-earth, the dividing lines between the contrasting periods of time, whether night and day, first and second halves of months, or halves of the year, were charged by a special power. People were not surprised to feel the presence of spirits in these moments. Events could take a leap, and suddenly appear very differently from just before. These critical points of balance between the earth's forces, these liminal moments, were out of the ordinary, beyond understanding and explanation, because they were supercharged. Even the setting sun and the rising moon created a charged atmosphere in which remarkable events could transpire.

Liminal moments and spaces at sunrise and at sunset bestowed benefits. Wizards mixing healing herbal mixtures could add to their potency by stirring in fresh dew from the early morning. And in applying these medicinal potions along with a chanted healing spell, the powers of magic were at their height as the sun set on the dusk horizon.

Tolkien reflected this Anglo-Saxon belief in the power of such moments in *The Hobbit*. There, he described how Bilbo sat on a hill all day long, watching the glowing sun slide gradually across the treetops of the distant forest. As sunset came, the sun burned orange and drifted down towards the horizon, revealing another light in the sky: a thin new moon. Then, as the sun disappeared into a haze at the edge of the world, it shone a last red ray of light which illuminated the face of the rock behind Bilbo. Suddenly a piece of the rock cracked, fell off, and revealed a hidden door. It was the entrance to the secret pathway that the hobbits had been searching for. Then the sun disappeared, and the moon too. So the rock cracked and revealed a secret just as the sun set and the moon rose.

In the historical Middle-earth, supernatural power was thought to be present in its most potent form on November eve and May eve, the joints between the two great seasons of the year. These two eves (together with Midsummer's eve) were known as 'spirit nights', for they were marked by a dramatic increase in the presence of spirits from the Otherworld among the people and activities of Middle-earth.

Following the pattern of night and day, so the year in the real Middle-earth was divided into winter and summer. The year began on 31 October, celebrated with great festivals which have survived until today as Hallowe'en. Winter is the dark side of the year – Earth's night, the time when nature sleeps. 1 May brought in the summer, filled with outdoor activities, crop farming and animal husbandry, land clearing and building. These two festivals divided the year into two halves of six months each.

The Celts' Samhain festival, called by the Anglo-Saxons, Hallowe'en, and Christianized as All Saints' or All Souls' Day, was the great festival to mark the beginning of winter. It was also a festival of the dead. The bonfire and the lit brands carried into the fields were a fertility rite impregnating the earth with the seed of the dying sun, so that after a long winter of gestation vegetation would burst forth again in spring. The cattle too were driven through the fires, and people leaped over them, taking on themselves the potency of the magical flames.

As well as times of special power, there were also physical places which had a similar liminal capacity. We have few concepts today which compare with the Lowerworld. It was demonized by Christian missionaries as a bad realm, Hell, but is less prominent in modern discussions of that religion. But then, the Lowerworld was equivalent in power to the Upperworld concept of 'heaven' which characterizes Christianity and various other religions.

The Celtic peoples' image of these spirit worlds was very close to the everyday world. Enticing and yet threatening, it hung intangibly near, like a reflection in a deep, clear pool. Natural features of the landscape provided the dividing line between this world and that. They were also the points of juncture, the connections, the doorways into the Otherworld. So when a person from Middle-earth forded a river, the swirling waters felt like the very energy of the Otherworld, ready to sweep the person away at any moment. How the physical landscape intersected with the spiritual is evidenced in Celtic mythology, where the source of the Irish River Boyne, named after the goddess Boann, is described as 'a shining fountain, with five streams flowing out of it . . . Nine hazels . . . grew over the well. The purple hazels dropped their nuts into the fountain, and five salmon which were in the fountain severed them, and sent their husks floating down the streams.'

The streams leap by metaphor into spirit-world significance, where they are described as 'the five streams of the senses, through which knowledge is obtained. And no one will have knowledge who drinks not a draught out of the fountain itself and out of the streams.'

The experience must have been exhilarating, transcending, terrifying. Ridges of high hills similarly carried the traveller into a space between worlds, straddling Middle-earth and the mysteries of a different world. It did not even have to be natural features of the landscape only, for the people living in Middle-earth times infused the landscape with the spirit of their souls. Boundaries, or tribal markers between clans of people in early Middle-earth were charged with magical power. More than mundane territories of trespass, they were also points through which the mist of the Otherworld could seep into this world.

Liminal points were many. In the course of a year everyone would negotiate a number of times, places and events which made them feel poised between the worlds, one foot in the familiar Middle-earth, another in the half-hidden Otherworld. These points at which the material world and the Otherworld came close included psychological shifts between states of consciousness, moments of light shift at dawn and dusk, turning points in the periodic waxing and waning of the moon, New Year's Day, the summer and winter festivals, and the beginning and ending points of thunderstorms. All were occasions when the unseen powers from the Otherworld came very close, and were to be guarded against, unless one was preparing an intentional journey into those realms. At these times and in these places, powers from the Otherworld might disturb the expected unfolding of events.

On Samhain (Hallowe'en) the interpenetration was mutual and open for all who sought successfully, for it was the night of celebration of the unity of the material and spirit worlds.

Enchanting the Earth

The earth's fertility, the fecundity with which it had its 'babies', be they animal, human, crops, fruit and so on, was of prime importance in the subsistence economy of ancient England. Accordingly, sun and moon festivals took place at these high points in the calendar. In the spring, through dramatic metaphor, their rituals attuned to the heat of the sun and the cool of the moon in drawing sprouting seedlings from the ground. The *Lacnunga* details an account of a spiritual invocation for fertility of the fields. The entire ceremony began in the cool dark of night, before dawn, and reached its climax in the rays of the setting sun at the end of the day. The activities had three aims; relating to the sun and its power over the vitality of the grass fields; invocations in honour of Mother Earth to bless the crops, and protection of the crops from damage by hostile wizards or witches.

The *Lacnunga* explains: 'at night before daybreak take four sods from four sides of the land and mark how they stood before'. In the early hours of the morning, by the light of bright moonlight or fire torches, the wizards service the rural people of Anglo-Saxon England dug up chunks of earth at the four corners of a farm field. They placed markers carefully on the pieces of sod so that they could be restored later to the holes in their original positions. The ancient manuscript says that the wizard next takes 'oil and honey and yeast and milk of all the cattle that are on the land, and part of every kind of tree growing on the land, except hard trees, and part of every well-known herb, except burdock only, and pour moonglow dew on them, and then let it drip three times on the bottom of the sods'.

Collecting all these natural ingredients would have taken days of preparation. The list excludes hardwood trees like oak and beech. They are slow-growing and perhaps are not therefore appropriate for encouraging the fertility spirit of fast-growing crops.

Moonglow dew was revered as a sacred liquid. It sprinkled onto the Earth at night, the overflow from the moonlit watering of the mythological World Tree by The Wyrd Sisters, the three sacred beings who symbolized the birth of the cosmos. Oil, honey, yeast and milk were all catalysts used in cooking and fermentation; in other words, processes in which the bounty of the land was prepared and transformed for people to eat and drink. This spell itself is like a recipe, with tips for the ways in which the ingredients should be combined for maximum benefit.

The sods of earth and grass were then sprinkled three times with water and the wizard chanted: 'Grow, and multiply, and fill the Earth.' In the *Lacnunga* manuscript, written by Christians, the account of the ceremony has the sods being taken to a church and placed with their grassy sides facing towards the altar, while masses were sung. But it is likely that the mass is a later Christian substitution, or even just an interpolation by the Christian author of the manuscript. In the original ceremony, it is more likely that the sods would be taken to a sacred site, a forest sanctuary or stone circle, where they could be placed so that the first rays of the sun would strike upon the grass, and incantations would be sung rather than a mass.

The manuscript records some of the incantations used in this magical ceremony: 'I may through this magic spell, open from my teeth, through a thought firm-grasped; waken up the swelling crops for our worldly need; fill the fielded earth, and make the green fields beautiful.' After this enchantment, the wizard turned about three times 'sunwise', then stretched full length along the ground, chanting for the fields to be green for the benefit of the owner of the land and all those who were subject to him.

The people of ancient England lived in a way which reflected their perceptions of the sun and moon, day and night. They maintained a balance between the brightness of 'sun thinking' and the imagination of 'moon thinking'. The objective days were when they could 'see what is there' and 'get things done'. But their lives were also informed by the intelligence of night, the power of the imaginal, the states of mind that manifest when the constraints of a visible, material world are lifted. In the real Middle-earth, the interplay of the sun and moon created many a shimmering pathway into the Otherworld. The sun, moon and stars were essential to the magic and mystery of life.

Celestial Powers

The seeing of a connection between celestial and earthly events attracted the frustration of Bishop Wulfstan near the end of the Middle-earth period, when he was Archbishop of York from 1002 to 1023. He composed a large body of directives which railed against the traditions which had been current all through the millennium, and still thrived. He said deprecatingly of the non-Christian people of Middle-earth: '. . . they took it as wisdom to worship the sun and moon as gods on account of their shining brightness . . . Some men also said that the shining stars were gods and began to worship them earnestly; and some believed in the earth because it nourished all things.' He contrasted these beliefs with the truth according to the Gospels: 'But they might have readily discerned, if they had the power of reason, that he is the true God who created all things for the enjoyment and use of us men, which he granted mankind because of his great goodness.'

For many today Wulfstan's words have an ominous ring. In a time of ecological reawakening, Wulfstan's early Christian view of man in all his goodness being granted dominion over the earth presages many centuries in which we progressively lost touch with an intimate connection with nature. But it certainly highlights clear differences between magical perceptions of Middle-earth in which the great forces of life are located in the natural features of this and the Otherworld; and the Christianity of the medieval period which asserted the primacy of humans. And Wulfstan's claim that it was the 'brightness' of sun, moon and stars that attracted people as objects of magic and mystery is a caricature of their beliefs.

11. Wells of Wisdom

In the spring, the roadside banks and hedgerows in Cornwall are dotted with the delicate-stemmed flowers of the wild violet, yellow stars of celandine, and nodding clusters of early bluebells – colours coaxed from their hiding places by the warm sun in this most southwestern tip of Britain. Down one of these winding country lanes near Penzance lies the ancient site of Sancreed Well. Many wells like this one have survived from the time of Middle-earth. A survey conducted in the 1950s identified over twelve hundred in Wales alone.

The path to the well runs from the lane and past an old church, which was probably built in the vicinity of the well, like many churches in those times, to discourage people from seeking spirits at enchanted spots of the landscape in favour of worshipping at the altars of the new religion of Christianity. The path past the church is well trodden, worn hard over the centuries by people who have continued to come here to visit the waters.

Throughout the thousand years of Middle-earth, people came to these wells and sat in their presence in silence, or danced, sang, left offerings and dipped ritual objects into the waters. They used the wells as a way of connecting with the powers of the spirit world.

The first glimpse of the Sancreed Well is not of the well itself but the thorn trees which stand next to it. When I visited one May, their branches were heavy with white blossom, like aromatic snow. And hanging from the branches were scores of coloured ribbons, rags, pieces of material, tied and knotted into place by streams of visitors over the previous months, or even years. Small banners spun in the wind, longer ones draped over the branches and rocked back and forth, a few tied low down dragged onto the ground. Some were quite new and still brightly coloured; most were faded with exposure to the weather, a few very tattered and breaking up with age. The effect is stunning and even eerie. Even now, a thousand years and more since the end of the time of Middle-earth, these tokens carried with them the human need for connection with greater forces, for help, for blessing. Other wells across the country are similarly festooned; the spirit trees are often thorns, but also old 'blasted oaks', beech trees and others.

The entrance to the Sancreed Well is a low stone archway, cut into a large mound formed of earth covered with turf. The interior of the entrance glows with soft sunlight slanting through the arch. Inside, stone steps descend steeply into darkness. Stepping carefully down the worn steps, I saw that the interior of the well was lined with stones reaching to a ceiling above. The walls glistened with beads of moisture, and at the bottom of the steps the water sat still and clear as crystal, as it had for centuries.

As I reached the bottom step, the outside world seemed to disappear, and I was cocooned in a timeless space. It was so quiet in the well, so peaceful, so conducive to the floating of images in the mind, to plumbing the depths of one's fears and wishes. I felt protected in the well's cool, sparkling, softly-lit embrace. I crouched by the water, and gazed into its depths.

Not only the Celts, but also the later Anglo-Saxons used wells for connecting with the Otherworld. Even where the wells are no longer visible, surviving place-names mark their original presence. The village of Fritwell lies a few miles north of Oxford in the Cherwell Valley, alongside the M40 motorway. In the time of Middle-earth, it was a site of divination. The Anglo-Saxon word 'friht' and its derivative words referred to diviners – people who foresaw the future by consulting the oracles or supernatural powers, whereas 'wella' is a wellspring. And so Fritwell denotes a place where divination took place at a spring. These divinatory wells were anathema to the Christian church. The eleventh century Laws of the Northumbrian Priests assert that 'If a sanctuary be on someone's land around a stone or tree or well or any superstition of that kind then let him who made it pay "law-slight", half to Christ, half to the landowner.' The place-name 'frihtwella' must have been in use before such practices were outlawed.

Roman Wells

The Romans are counterpointed elsewhere in this book as lacking some of the imaginative sensitivities of Middle-earth culture. However, they also honoured wells. One well dating back to prehistoric times was rediscovered in 1876. Excavations showed that it had originally been built by the Celts and had subsequently been taken over by the occupying Romans. Displacing the indigenous Celts, or at least setting up military overlordship, they built a fort at the well right on the northern border of England, called Brocolita, now named Carrawbrough. Artefacts recovered at the well show that it was dedicated to Coventina, almost certainly a local Celtic goddess who was adopted by the Romans. The Celts presumably told the Romans about her – the soldiers may even have witnessed ceremonies at the well.

It is often said that for the Celts, Romans and later Anglo-Saxons, the wells represented fertility. But this word no longer captures the depth of meaning that it did in those distant times. Today, in the high-tech Western world, we are far more distanced from the sources of our sustenance, and do not therefore feel so attuned to its precious regeneration.

What did fertility mean for the Roman warrior? In the earliest times of the Empire, he was a man living in a remote garrison a thousand miles from the delights of Rome and the comforts of home, often distant from his family and loved ones. Or later in the Roman occupation, which lasted perhaps twenty generations – he may have been born in England, with his family living in a garrison town. But he was an enforcer of the overlordship of an indigenous culture in which resentment and rebellion were ever present dangers. And the posting at Brocolita was not a lonely one. In summer, the land on this northernmost edge of England is beautiful. But the fort was dangerously hard up against the frontier with the Picts, whom the Romans never successfully subjugated. In winter, the dreary desolation and boredom of a remote outpost would have dragged time into tedium. So perhaps Coventina's special presence connected the centurion with distant loved ones, allayed fears of their health and well-being and vouched for their vitality, reassured against the

constant threat of destruction by rampaging Picts suddenly attacking
the fort. Perhaps in the summer, there were crops grown nearby
which afforded fresh food, rather than the monotonous winter
rations. Coventina could be thanked for that. And fertility was a
kind of life-force, which sustained each person in body, mind and
spirit. So she could respond to a visit by strengthening resolve,
resistance, and hope.

It is doubtful that the Romans used Celtic wizards or priestesses
to plumb the secret messages of the ancient well of Coventina. Did
they use their own divination techniques at such a site? We cannot
tell, but the excavations showed that during the time it had been in
use, they had gone to the site and celebrated and communed with
the goddess. At the very least, in the harsh winters they probably
ducked down out of the wind, murmured or even voiced their
thoughts, fears and desires, and cast offerings into the deep waters in
exchange for a blessing, and perhaps a glimpse of their personal
futures.

And not just occasionally, either. When the well was explored in
the nineteenth century, the offerings recovered included twenty-four
altars, and over fourteen thousand coins, glass, pottery and bronze
figures, dating up to the fourth century AD, when the Romans
abandoned the fort. The archaeological evidence shows that the well
and associated altars may have been attacked around then. The
Romans, now Christian, still honoured the wisdom of the wells, but
may have been forced to abandon the fort in rapid retreat. Perhaps
the Picts scaled their walls. Perhaps, as Christians, the Roman soldiers
felt less attuned to Coventina – and therefore no longer under her
protection.

Water and the Source

Wells, or natural springs, are formed by underground water trapped
between two layers of impervious rock. The water is forced up out of
the ground by the build-up of pressure and released through a small
gap in the top layer of rock. Such a point of escape can occur
naturally, or be engineered by digging or drilling a releasing shaft

through the rock. These water phenomena, which we now under-stand in modern geological terms, were accorded special status among the people of ancient England. Sometimes, in thinking back to the times of Middle-earth, when less was known about the mechanics of springs, it might seem that those people's precious regard for wells was based on ignorance of these laws of nature. We might imagine that when they came across such attractive features of nature, they were overcome with simple wonder at the sight of water flowing 'miraculously' from the ground.

But today in the technologically developed countries of the west, we take water for granted. It is piped into our houses, and we use it with barely a second thought for drinking, cooking, washing, bathing, showering, flushing waste, cleaning cars, watering lawns and swim-ming. Waterfountains spray attractively in our town squares, and fish swim hypnotically in the bubbling water of their tanks as palliatives in the dentist's waiting room. Our everyday encounters with water are frequent, but not mindful.

However, the pulse of life beat more deeply for the people of Middle-earth than it does for us. Water was more than just a biological feature of life, to be used pragmatically. Every spring, every woodland brook, every river in glen or valley, even lakes were imbued with the presence of spirit. It was not the wide-eyed marvelling at the appearance of a spring which directed such sacred thoughts, but rather the sense of connection with a realm more encompassing, transcending and deeply imaginative. Waters were, for the people of Middle-earth, flowing from the very source of life.

Early goddesses like Coventina were not the all-encompassing major deities who as arose later in Middle-earth, possibly to counter-act the incoming Christianity, with its single sky-god. Local goddesses were spirits, similar to elves. Such Otherworld presences at sources of water existed because the outpouring of this liquid from the earth was blessed, magical and powerful, and therefore emanated from and was protected by the spirit. Many of them had individually named spirit beings to whom blessings were offered.

Of course, the people of the real Middle-earth knew that water fell from the sky, drained into streams and rivers, and flowed to the ocean. But this pragmatic account of a geological and meteorological process was not enough. It described the mechanics of how, but not the why of origins. Water was more important than that – it was invested with spirit. And so any person in Middle-earth using water did so with an additional, parallel account of the flow of waters in mind and heart, a vision which dipped into their deep well of imagination.

Many of the main sources of rivers in western Europe were dedicated as sanctuaries, especially at their source. The spirits of these water sources had a strong presence and appearance. Most often people thought of them as beautiful female spirits who were associated, and represented the larger awareness of the Earth Mother.

The cosmological geography of the real Middle-earth's Upperworld was of a land having twenty-seven great rivers flowing through it, unabated, and perpetually. Seven more great rivers connected the Upperworld with Middle-earth, the land of people. Snorri Sturluson names flowing rivers as called, 'Slow, broad, cool, battle-defiant, loud-bubbling, forward-rushing, old, spear-teeming', and a further list includes 'frothing, greedy, strong, way-knowing, sweeping-people-away'. These were magical rivers, connecting and nourishing the heavens with the green landscape of Middle-earth.

Many names of rivers refer to the goddesses or spirits who embodied the life-force of the river. In England today, some rivers still bear their ancient names – the River Glen in Lincolnshire, and another River Glen in Northumberland, derive their name for a British Celtic root *glanos*, which means 'clean, holy, beautiful'.

On the continent, too, the River Seine is named from Sequana, who was the beautiful goddess of its source for the Celtic peoples of ancient France. And again, the occupying Roman soldiers sustained their souls amid empire-building by taking over the honouring of a Celtic spirit. The archaeological excavations in 1964 at the head of the River Seine revealed nearly two hundred pieces of wood carving, including many of complete figures, the features of which confirmed that it had been the site of a healing centre in the Roman period during the early part of the first millennium.

The Wyrd Sisters and Water

The three Wyrd Sisters dwelled directly beneath one of the three massive roots of the World Tree in a cave by the side of the Well of Wyrd, a pool of great wisdom. And every night, under the glow of the moon, the sisters took water from the pool and, mixing it with clay from the banks, pasted the World Tree's root to keep it moist. Snorri Sturluson describes it this way:

> There stands an Ash
> called Yggdrasil, I know,
> a soaring tree with
> white clay sprinkled;
> dews drip from it
> and fall into the dales:
> it stands ever green
> by the spring of Wyrd.

Through this nightly task the three were the nurturers of creation, with the water in the Well of Wyrd coming from the beginning of time. This water flowed into all wells, which therefore contained the essence of life.

Water as Vital Energy

The people of ancient Europe thought of the water in the Well of Wyrd as a vital energy which permeated all aspects of the cosmos. Iceland's medieval historian Snorri Sturluson says that they believed the water in the well to be 'so holy that all things which dip into the well become white as the film which lies within the shell of an egg'.

This precious vibrancy of water was expressed by Tolkien in *The Lord of the Rings*, where the elf Queen Galadriel prepared a small crystal phial. It had special properties, with a special, glittering light. She told Frodo that the phial contained waters from her fountain, which carried within it the light from a distant star. It would glow in the dark and light its way at night.

In addition to the flowing rivers, the people of Anglo-Saxon

England saw another way that the waters flowed to the Earth. At night, when the Wyrd Sisters watered the World Tree, their splashing and sprinkling fell all the way to Middle-earth, and sparkled as dewdrops in the early morning mist. The water poured onto the World Tree by the Wyrd Sisters came to Middle-earth as dew and rain, and then returned to their pool. By this notion the water we drink today is this same original water from the beginning of time, eternally recycled.

Birth

Childbirth was an enormously important aspect of life in tribal culture, and women made pilgrimages to wells, drank or bathed in the waters, wore some clothing which had been dipped in it, and implored the spirit of the well, in order to have an easy delivery or abundance of milk for breast-feeding the child. The Bride's Well near Corgarff in Grampian was visited by the bride on the evening before her marriage. She would bathe her feet and upper body in well water to ensure that she would have children, and she placed a little bread and cheese in the well so that they would never go hungry.

The rituals carried out by the women in order to gain the favour of the well continued in some cases right up until recent times. In the late 1860s two men were by chance able secretly to watch a fertility ritual being practised at the sacred well of Melshach in the parish of Kennethmont in Grampian. They wrote this account:

> On the first Sunday in May, a keeper, accompanied by an expert from Aberdeen, set out for the moors to investigate grouse disease then prevalent. From a distance they spied a group of women round the well. With the aid of a field-glass, the men watched their movements. The women, with garments fastened right up under their arms and with hands joined, were dancing in a circle around the well. An aged crone sat in their midst, and dipping a small vessel into the water, kept sprinkling them. They were married women who had proved childless and had to come to the well to experience its fertilizing virtues. No doubt words had been repeated, but the two observers were too far off

to hear . . . the remarkable thing is that the custom lingered so
late.

All over the world, wells have long been associated with women.
Mythologist Joseph Campbell suggests that this link of women's
mysteries with water is essentially a connection between the waters
of birth and that of the cosmos; the amniotic fluid is precisely
comparable to the water that in many mythologies represents the
elementary substance of all things. In early Europe, wells represented
secret entrances to the body of the Earth Mother, the Underworld,
all leading back to the Well of Wyrd. And because the life-force of
water came from the Wyrd Sisters it was particularly associated with
the mysteries of women. This bond between women and water is
common to almost all traditional cultures.

At St Helen's Well, Rudgate, there is a legend that the original
spirit of the well used to accept offerings from young girls in the form
of pieces of their clothing hung on the nearby tree. This is obviously
an early example of the ritual of cloth ripping and hanging as seen
on the Sancreed Well. In the legend, the spirit of St Helen's Well,
having received the offering, would then reveal to the girl, in a
dream, the identity and image of her future husband. The Church
rededicated the well to St Helen about eight hundred years ago, so
this story refers to a period at least that old.

A similar legend attaches to Pin Well at Brayton, near Selby. A
young girl going to the well for the same purpose would be turned
into a fairy-sized being by the spirits of the place. In exchange for
pins dropped into the well, to be used by the elves for 'elf-shot', the
spirits agreed to reveal a vision of the girl's 'true love'. The local
clergy exorcised the well and rededicated it as the Well of Our Lady.

Oracles

Tolkien applied the Celtic and Anglo-Saxon magic of waters to
his character Galadriel in *The Lord of the Rings*. She had powers
of magic and sorcery. 'Galadriel clear' are the waters of your well,
sang Gandalf, when Wormtongue accused him of being in league
with that sorceress. Tolkien's descriptions of her were remiscent of

Coventina and other spirits of water sources. She worked her magic with water. She entered an enclosed garden, and descended a long flight of steps, which led into a grassy hollow. Through it ran a stream bubbling from a spring further up the hill. At the bottom of the hollow sat a wide, shallow basin, and a silver pitcher. Galadriel filled the basin with water from the stream, and breathed on it. When it had settled, she explained to Frodo that it was her 'mirror', and she invited him to look into it. She explained that he would be able to see in it things which were beyond everyday sight.

In the historical Middle-earth, wells joined people to the spirit-world, and helped wizards to foresee events, to be 'far-seers', to gain a glimpse into the future. As well as being sites of special significance at which one could pray, meditate, make offerings, the wells were also oracles. They answered whatever questions a wizard held in mind, through a number of signs. The manner in which the water flowed from the well, or the height of the water level in the well, whether bubbles appeared on the surface of the water when an offering was dropped into the well, whether objects dropped in sank or floated; and especially the visions that could be seen in the reflection of the well water: all these clues formed the nature of the well's response, and provided answers to the questions being posed.

In the earliest time the questions were posed, and answers interpreted only by the wizards. One such wizard was Lodfaffir who features in one of the ancient Norse stories. Gazing into a well for information and insight, he declared: 'I've stood and stared into the Well of Wyrd, stared in silence, wondered and pondered. For a long while I listened at the door of the High One's hall. This is what I heard.' He then recited the words of advice on life which Odin gave to him. Listening '. . . at the door of the High One's hall' meant that gazing into the water gave Lodfaffir the ability to eavesdrop on the god Odin. Lodfaffir was in Middle-earth, but the well connected him with a totally other realm: the Upperworld. This reflects the essential sweep of Middle-earth imagination: wells were precious sites, as were all sources of waters, but their potency rested on their own ultimate source – the huge parallel spirit world which existed alongside the preoccupations of everyday life.

By the end of the Middle-earth period, when Snorri Sturluson was writing the Icelandic sagas, Odin had been reified to the status

of an all-round deity in Norse mythology, as a rival to the Christian
God. But earlier in the millennium, his chief presence was as mentor
to all wizards. Odin knew how to cast runes, how to ask questions
about the origins of the cosmos, how to shape-shift, and to journey
from his home in the Upperworld to Middle-earth, and to the
Lowerworld. So for a wizard like Lodfaffir gaining knowledge and
wisdom from Odin, the crystal-clear waters of a well served rather
like the crystal ball of later legend.

We can understand today how meditation on a problem or
question can be refocused by a psychological projection. The use of
signals from the water, as from any such device like a pendulum or
cards, can trigger an otherwise unconscious insight from deep inside
our mind. The people of ancient England saw their minds reflected
in water. It was a medium which provided a language for understanding themselves.

Voice of the Water

Much of the inner language of the waters has remained with us. We
say, for example, that we have a stream of consciousness, that we will
brook no opposition, and we will pool our resources. Secrets leak out,
and we plunge into things new. Or, at least, we dip our toe in the
water. A wide-ranging alteration in a point of view is a sea-change.
When we see an aesthetically pleasing aspect we drink it in, people
are shallow or deep, and you cannot buck the tide. In fact, in dealing
with life's issues, it never rains but it pours, and problems come in
waves. We fish for a compliment, and throw the baby out with the
bathwater. We overflow with emotion, and boil with rage. And, in
going to a party, we hope to make a splash! Through these images
we are seeing ourselves at least metaphorically as being at one with
water.

Water seems especially to be the medium par excellence of the
unconscious. Our conscious awareness of water is perhaps meant
literally to be only the 'tip of the iceberg'; all that below the surface
represents the depths of the unconscious – deep images, flowing
receptive, swirling, still and calm, raging and torrential. It is hardly
surprising that this language comes naturally to us, for our own bodies

consist largely of water. Looking into water is like looking at our-selves.

However, the people of ancient Europe saw in their water not only the reflection of their own faces, but also the essence of their souls. Water washed, purified and connected them with profound forces of life. And they thought of water as having special properties beyond a template upon which people could project intuitive knowl-edge. A glimpse of this perspective can be seen in the research by engineer Theodor Schwenk in the 1970s which discovered one path to understanding such communicative properties of water. It reveals that the surfaces of water function like receptors, made especially sensitive by the presence there of complex wave patterns that turn them into structures with some of the properties of living membranes. The water's sensitivity may be as great as that of the human ear. A gentle breeze blowing over the surface of water immediately creases it into the tiniest capillary waves, and it passes this impression on rhythmically to its whole mass.

Christian Well Magic

Celebration of the life-force inherent in the waters of the well was recognized early by the Christian authorities. They were concerned to wrest control of such important sacred rituals from the indigenous wizards. They wanted instead to invest the powers of water in the Christian God, and in their own intervention as His earthly represen-tatives. They preached and made proclamations against 'magical' activity at wells, banning them from use until they had been blessed by a bishop and placed under the auspices of a saint: the twenty-sixth canon of Anselm, written in 1102, says, 'Let no one attribute reverence or sanctity to a fountain, without the bishop's authority.'

The Christians did not deny the power of the well. Rather, they appropriated the connection with that power, and the wells were systematically changed in name to associate each of them with an Anglo-Saxon or Celtic saint. In some areas of activity, the Church seemed to accommodate indigenous Middle-earth practices even where it would wish not to. It allowed them to continue while claiming that they fell under the guise of Christianity. But in the case of wells, the priests seemed to honour them just as much, so long as they were under their jurisdiction. Many wells still bear the names of saints, and today, 1,500 years later, the belief in the health-giving life-force of sacred wells persists, as for example at Lourdes in France, now under the control of the Catholic Church.

A surviving example of Christian-sanctioned honouring of wells is the tradition of well-dressing. This practice was widespread at one time, and is still celebrated in the counties of Derbyshire and Staffordshire. In the nineteenth century the 'Halliwell (Holy Well) Wakes' at Rorrington, a hamlet near Chirbury on the Shropshire/Wales border, saw on Ascension Day the local people meeting at the well. It had been decorated with 'a bower of green boughs, rushes and flowers' and a maypole erected. The people 'used to walk round the hill with fife, drum and fiddle, dancing and frolicking as they went'. This was followed by feasting, dancing and drinking. They drank the well water – and also ale which was specially brewed for the occasion. They also threw pins into the well, and they ate special flat spiced buns marked with a cross. When the man who brewed the ale died in the 1830s, the wake was no longer held.

The sacred, indeed magical, nature of rivers and wells seems to transcend religious conventions and restrictions. In medieval times, when people were making the gradual transition from the old ways of Middle-earth and taking up the new, official king's religion of Christianity, many of them went on pilgrimages. When they arrived at their destination, they were awarded badges indicating that they had been there. But many of these pilgrims' badges have been found in English rivers and streams, especially near towns. Beneath what had once been a ferry crossing over the Thames, over 250 of these badges from medieval times have been recovered from the river bed. So these people, devout enough about their new faith to go on a pilgrimage, had nevertheless on their homecoming committed their badge to the river, in a ritual long predating Christianity. They must have still believed in the magical powers of the water to grant them health, good fortune, protection from misadventure, perhaps glimpses of the future and so on. Our essential human relationship to the great forces beyond the ken of our everyday minds is magic. Religions are a temporary wrap giving context to that primeval act.

I leaned once again over the water in the Sancreed Well. The water glows in that soft light, and seems to fill with images of the future. I made a wish, and dipped my piece of cloth in the water, sending ripples shimmering across the surface. Then I turned from the Otherworld silence of the well, mounted the steps, and came out into the light of a spring day in England. Birds chattered and flitted from branch to branch. I knotted my cloth to the tree, as people have done since the days of Middle-earth.

MAGICAL BEASTS

12. The Raven's Omen

On the coast of Northumberland, the grey sea waters lap at long, wet beaches. Above, rocky outcrops and small cliffs border the land and snake down the north-east of England past the city of York. Black crows wheel above the beaches, and nest in the rocks. Other birds inhabit these coastal skies, and inland too, but the crows are special. In the days of Middle-earth, they were believed to communicate with wizards, and were ominous harbingers of danger and doom.

Even today, the seven distinct but closely related members of the crow family that live in Britain are regarded as unusual. They are among the most intelligent of birds. The magpie and larger jackdaw are drawn by the glint of bright objects, and will 'thieve' from people's window ledges shiny trivia and jewellery for their nests. But their hunting habits have brought them into real conflict with humans – most crows can still legally be shot all the year round in Britain. Rooks and carrion crows upset the farmer by pecking at seed; jays, crows and magpies take young birds as prey; and ravens – largest of the crows and often over 2 feet from bill tip to tail – will even hunt weakling lambs.

In the real Middle-earth, crows were known as carrion birds. They were observed picking and tearing at the flesh of corpses on battlefields, and this gave them a dark reputation. 'The raven screamed aloft, black and greedy for corpses . . . The raven rejoiced in the work,' says the Anglo-Saxon poem 'Elene', and another called 'Judith' speaks of 'the dark raven, the bird greedy for slaughter'. *The Anglo-Saxon Chronicle* entry for the year 937 records the victory of King Athelstan at the battle of Brunanburgh and reports that the carrion eaters on the battlefield were ravens (Corvus corax) and white-tailed sea eagles (Haliætus albicilla). And in Celtic mythology, the goddesses of war, Babd and Morrigu, transformed themselves into crows and ravens when they followed the march of armies or hovered over a battlefield.

But ravens and crows were equally known as magical messengers. The triple 'kaah, kaah, kaah' of the carrion crow has sounded a warning for people for centuries – even today, folklore says the sightings of magpies have a messenger significance, with 'one for sorrow, two for joy'.

During much of the thousand years of Middle-earth, the weather was warmer than it is now in Britain, with drier summers. Birds which today migrate south to avoid the cold, stayed on the island through the winter. And since a small human population of between only one and two million interfered little with the natural order of things compared with today, those times must have been idyllic for wildlife. As a result, the bird population was more varied than now, and probably huge in numbers. And they played a dynamic part in Middle-earth magic – especially as messengers.

Language of the Birds

In the historical Middle-earth, wizards were believed to understand the language of birds. A Celtic folk story from the Scottish Highlands tells of a youth called Alasdair, who was sent to the Isle of Birds to learn the language of the birds. To know their 'speech' was evidence that the boy had acquired magical knowledge from the spirit world. After three years' tuition, the boy's parents were not much impressed by his riddling interpretation of birds' language, especially when he interpreted for them the message of a chaffinch which prophesied that Alasdair's father and mother would humble themselves to their son. The father ordered the boy's death, but he escaped to the Isle of Birds and took the drastic step of quickly killing and eating the birds, the faster to assimilate what they had to tell him.

Gregory of Tours, writing in the sixth century of the early Germanic tribes, refers to observation of birds for prophetic signs as a custom of the Franks. They apparently watched their flight patterns, noted whether they appeared alone or in a flock, on the ground or in a tree, and at what point in the sun, moon, or seasonal cycle they arrived.

Judging from the popularity of amulets for protection of persons and property, and the dire warnings in The Anglo-Saxon Chronicle about the meanings of storms and lightning, it seems that omens frightened the ordinary people of ancient Europe. They believed them to be the predictions of events that were bound to happen. But the wizards appear to have had a more complex point of view. They read omens as pattern-pointers in the flow of events. They likened the sequential unfolding of events to the flowing of a stream, with ripples from each event. No event was repeated in exactly the same way. The wizard could open up to the pattern of the flow of events by observing the ripples. When he heard birdsong, or saw the flight pattern of birds, he believed he could follow the ripples into future time and foresee events yet to happen.

In ancient Norse legend, Odin, god of the wizards, had two ravens. They were named Huginn and Muninn, which means 'thought' and 'memory'. They perched on his shoulders, and according to Snorri Sturluson, 'They whisper into his ears every scrap of news which they see or hear tell of. At crack of dawn he pushes them off to flap all around the world and they return in time for second breakfast. This is the source of much of his information, and the reason why men call him the Raven god.' Tolkien used this idea in The Lord of the Rings, when Gandalf sends an eagle, called Gwahir the Windlord, to watch the river and gather information and news which he can being back to him. And in The Hobbit Balin explained that the ravens are special, because they used to be close friends of the people of Thror, and often imparted news which otherwise was secret.

In the real Middle-earth such birds were believed to bring important messages from the spirit world to those who could understand them. And one such crow became a central character in the destiny of a famous seventh-century king. This story takes us back to Northumbria.

King Edwin Converts

Inland from the Northumbrian coast lies the site of a fabulous Anglo-Saxon timber castle called Yeavering, nestling in a valley to the

north of the Cheviot Hills, near the present border with Scotland.
It was discovered by archaeologists in 1956, and the excavations
revealed an extraordinary array of buildings. The massive timber hall,
other unusual buildings and even a sports grandstand suggest that for
the people of those times, this may have been the most impressive
English castle of its day. The castle has been dated to the court of
Edwin, king of Northumbria from AD 617 until he was killed in battle
in 633. The story of this king encapsulates the power politics of
religions, and culminates in an act of magic with a messenger crow –
which seals the fate of the king.

Early in his kingship, Edwin's mentor, the powerful King Redwald
of East Anglia, died. Redwald's dominance had engendered subservi-
ence and resentment among other chieftains, but also a degree of
political stability in the country. His death resulted in a scramble of
negotiations as lesser kings sought alliances with others to consolidate
their positions. Edwin was as eager as anyone, and was pleased to
form an alliance with King Eadbald of Kent. He must have valued
this compact highly, for he confirmed it by marrying the Kentish
king's sister Aethelburgh, thus creating a family bond with his ally.

But this is where the subtext of Edwin's story begins to material-
ize. Edwin had not, like some kings, converted to the new religion of
Christianity. In fact, in religious terms, he had been committed to
the old ways – his first wife had been the sister of Penda, the heathen
king of Mercia. But his new ally, Eadbald of Kent, was Christian.
And so the terms of marriage to his sister Princess Aethelburgh
allowed her the freedom to practise her own religion, and to have
her own priest in her royal household in Northumbria. We do not
know the fate of Edwin's first wife. We do know that he still declined
to be baptized himself.

Aethelburgh took an Italian priest with her to Northumbria
Called Paulinus, he had been based in Canterbury as a missionary.
At that time he was probably in his fifties – an advanced age for
those times – and experienced in the politics of religion and kings.

Edwin's colourful life exploded into action again on Easter
Sunday of 626. An assassin sent by the West Saxon king Cuichelm
insinuated himself into Edwin's court. He loitered and lingered,
waiting for his opportunity – and then lunged at the king with a
poisoned knife. Lilla, one of the king's bodyguards, hurled himself in

1 & 2. The burial mounds at Sutton Hoo.

3. *Left*. Stane Street, a Roman road cutting straight through ancient countryside in the south of England.

4. *Below*. The Roman buildings at Bath dominated the original Celtic shrines with large and formal structures.

5. Ankerwyke yew, near Runnymede, estimated to be 2,500 years old.

6. The reconstructed Anglo-Saxon houses at West Stow.

7. Yggdrasil, The World Tree, with a stag browsing on its foliage, from the carving on the north wall of the eleventh-century church at Urnes, in Sogn, Norway.

8. A gold buckle from the Sutton Hoo treasure.

9. An Anglo-Saxon brooch from the ninth century.

10. A gold Anglo-Saxon buckle from the seventh century.

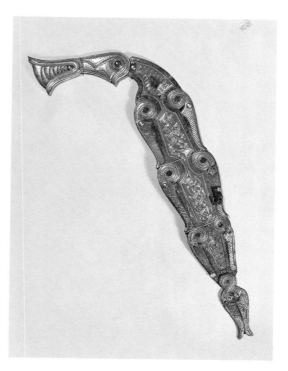

11. A dragon shield decoration from the Sutton Hoo treasure.

12. A carved dragon head from the Viking Age.

13. Even today, people leave tokens at Sancreed Well in Cornwall.

14. A statue of a Mother Goddess, from the Celtic well at Carrawburgh.

15. The figure of a giant, cut into the chalk hillside at Wilmington, Sussex.

16. Wayland's Smithy, an ancient stone site where magical smiths were believed to work in underground forges.

17. A dwarf-smith at work in his forge, depicted in a detail from the side of a twelfth-century baptismal font in Gotland, Sweden.

18. The dwarves, present at the creation of Middle-earth, supporting the four corners of the sky, carved into the side of a tomb in Heysham, Lancashire.

19. An illustration from the *Utrecht Psalter* shows a man being pierced with arrows shot by elves.

20. Odin, with his raven perched on his shoulder, tries to fight off the wolf Fenrir as chaos brings an end to Middle-earth.

21. Odin's eight-legged stallion Sleipnir, as shown on a gravestone from Tjängride, Gottland.

22. Warriors and other figures carved into a side of the Franks Casket, a box made from whalebone in eighth-century Northumbria.

23. A boar-crest on top of an Anglo-Saxon helmet from the burial mound at Benty Grange farm, Derbyshire.

24. The Earth Mother, Nerthus, represented between the two oxen who pulled her 'holy wagon', on a bronze cauldron from Rynkeby, Denmark.

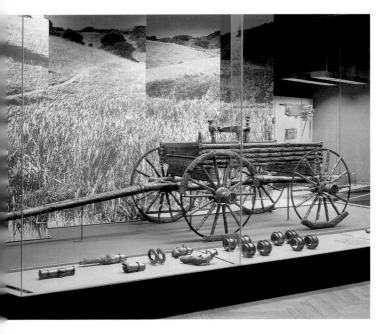

25. A Bronze Age wagon from Dejbjerg.

26. An Anglo-Saxon open boat, carved into rock from Häggeby, Upland, Sweden.

front of the knife, and was killed by the stabbing blade. Edwin was wounded by the assassin, but survived. Queen Aethelburgh, Edwin's pregnant wife, was so shocked by the bloody attack that she went into labour, and their daughter Eanfleada was born during the following night. Edwin gave thanks to his gods. Paulinus gave thanks to Christ, saying that it was through His intervention that the Queen's life had been spared during the sudden birth.

Edwin, as wily as Paulinus, resisted the moral pressure to convert to Christianity. But he added another hook. He said that he would seek revenge against King Cuichelm, and if the Christian God would gain victory for him, and also enable him to recover fully from his wound, he would agree to be baptized. Edwin led his army right to the south of England, and defeated his enemy.

Edwin's pride swelled. His position as king was strengthened by his military victory, for wealth began to flow into the kingdom as tribute from those for whom he was now overlord. He could dispense gold rings and expensive gifts to his greatest warriors and warlords. But still he stalled plans to take instruction, and be baptized. We do not know whether this was to avoid creating enemies of heathen kings such as Penda, or whether he was personally repelled by Christianity. But his reluctance caused alarm among the power brokers across Christian Europe. Pope Boniface in Rome sent Aethel-burgh gifts of a silver looking-glass and an ivory gilt comb, along with a letter urging her to continue to try to persuade her husband to become Christian.

Finally, Edwin agreed to convene a council to discuss the matter of Christian conversion. Famously reported by Bede, a debate was held in the King's council in the winter of 626–7 at which Paulinus made his case. At the conclusion, Edwin arranged to accept the Christian case, and his chief wizard of the Old Religion, Coifi, desecrated and destroyed his shrines by performing the symbolic act of throwing a spear into them. Edwin and his thegns agreed to accept Christianity.

Edwin and his court were baptized the following Easter Day AD 627, in a new wooden church at York. The populace of Northumbria were ordered to follow suit, and Paulinus carried out mass baptisms in the rivers. How seriously this was taken by the populace is doubtful, still steeped as they were in the magical world view of their ancestors. And as we shall see, the crow incident confirmed their scepticism.

Edwin replaced Coifi, his previous spiritual advisers and wizards, from his court. Christian priests were appointed by Paulinus who was, of course, committed to replacing the old ways of Middle-earth with his 'new' religion.

The Crow's Omen

In the *Life of St Gregory*, written between AD 680 and 714 by an anonymous monk of Whitby, and one of the very earliest pieces of literature in England, it is narrated that one Sunday, some time after converting to Christianity and dismissing his wizards, Edwin strode down the street to Church accompanied by Bishop Paulinus and his retinue. This may well have been down a street in seventh-century York, where he had hurriedly built a little church. Suddenly, reports the ancient manuscript, a crow landed in a tree nearby and 'sang with an evil omen'. The whole company stopped and stared at the bird, transfixed.

In Middle-earth belief, birds were sensitive to the ebb and flow of events, and could therefore be harbingers of the future. Crows and ravens, in particular, delivered messages which could be interpreted only by wizards who understood their language. Often they warned of impending death.

Edwin and his retinue, only recently baptized, must still have been saturated with these assumptions, traditions and beliefs. They would have been terrified by the ominous presence of a singing crow. After all, it was well known that when Hermigisel, King of the Warni (a tribe closely related to the Angles)in Germany, was out riding, he noticed a bird perched in a branch above his head. The king interpreted the croaking as a warning that he would die within forty days. Tantalizingly, we do not know whether the prophecy came true. We know only that on his deathbed, in around AD 500, he advised his son Radger to follow the custom of their ancestors and to marry Hermigisel's wife, Radger's stepmother.

The crows had significance for the Celts too, especially with regard to death. In Ireland, in a legend about the hero Cu Chulainn,

a goddess of war called Babd came in the form of a crow to the top
of the house where Cu Chulainn was staying and uttered the magic
words that were to lead the hero to his downfall. Then, when he
had fallen and she wanted to make sure he was really dead, she
approached the hero's corpse in the form of a crow, sweeping down
from the highest reaches of the heavens to utter three cries over him,
then settled in the foliage of a hawthorn opposite, so that thicket in
the plain of Muirthemne is known as the 'hawthorn of the crow'.

This crow-goddess also appeared in human form, her appearance
reflecting her bird-spirit. A description of her appears in the story of
'Da Choca's Hostel':

> Now when they were there they saw coming to them towards
> the hostel, a big-mouthed black swift sooty woman, lame and
> squinting with her left eye. She wore a threadbare dingy cloak.
> Dark as the back of a stag-beetle was every joint of her, from
> the top of her head to the ground. Her filleted grey hair fell
> back over her shoulder. She leant her shoulder against the door-
> post and began prophesying evil to the host, and to utter ill
> words . . . then the Badb went from them.

Edwin was faced with a singing crow, but no longer had a wizard to
interpret the message, and advise him how to profit from the bird's
warning. The bishop was galvanized into action by the petrified faces
of Edwin and his entourage. It was imperative that he regain control
of the situation. 'Shoot an arrow carefully into the bird' he ordered.
One of the king's bodyguards cocked his bow and fired. The arrow
pierced the crow and it fell dead from the tree. Grasping the arrow,
the bishop took the dead bird to the church hall, and there bran-
dished it in the air in front of a probably sceptical congregation who
had been ordered to show up for Christian instruction. Paulinus
proclaimed that this 'proved that they should know by so clear a sign
that the ancient evil of idolatry was worthless to anybody', since the
bird 'did not know that it sang of death for itself' and so could not
prophesy anything for those 'baptized in the image of God'. In other
words, a bird which could not even foretell its own imminent death
could not prophesy anything at all. Clearly Paulinus knew that the
congregation would believe that a crow or raven had the gift of

foretelling the future – it was one of the cursed 'idolatries' which he was trying to stamp out.

Of course, this is a Christian story, presumbly slanted by its monkish author to show the wonders of that faith, and illustrate how misguided the pagan beliefs were. But Middle-earth wizards would have reckoned the bishop to have made a serious mistake. He had assumed that if the crow had known it was going to be shot, it would have tried to save its life by flying away. But prophetic animals were not merely mortal creatures. This crow was a 'spirit messenger'. It would not, in Middle-earth belief, have been afraid of 'death' in the material world. So the intervention of the bishop probably did not convince the congregation. And certainly the crow's message was not interpreted for King Edwin.

Edwin perhaps took extra precautions, especially since he had already survived one assassination attempt. We do not know how long he survived after the crow incident, because we do not have a date for it. But when the end came, it was devastating. Edwin had been concentrating on the threats to his kingdom from various princely pretenders to the throne around whom ambitious warlords in the North were gathering. But instead, the fateful conclusion came from an alliance of the Mercian king Penda and the Welsh king Cadwallon. Penda was still a powerful and feared heathen warrior, brother of Edwin's first, pagan wife. They killed Edwin in battle in 633 in the fenlands at Hatfield, near Doncaster. Queen Aethelburgh fled back to Kent with her children, accompanied by Bishop Paulinus. The kingdom of Northumbria was ravaged and burned by the invaders.

Yeavering Castle was apparently abandoned after Edwin's death. Another site was established a short distance away at Millfield, where a new hall was built. Historians reckon it was abandoned because it had been damaged in Mercian raids, or because it was associated with a particular branch of the Northumbrian dynasty. Much more likely is that it was abandoned because the awesome unfolding of Wyrd had brought down Edwin's glorious sixteen-year reign – just as the Roman villas were avoided by the incoming Saxons 200 years earlier. He had been baptized a Christian for his own political ends, and paid the price. Could the crow have been warning him against Penda?

The Raven Banner

Germanic and Norse war leaders sometimes attempted to exert power over ravens and to accommodate their magical powers to their cause. Certainly for their opponents, the appearance of the ravens on the side of the enemy would have been terrifying, given their significance as messengers of death. In Celtic legend, a leader called Owein is described in *The Dream of Rhonabwy*, dating to the thirteenth century in its present form, but containing pagan elements which show that it had existed for centuries as an oral tale. Owein is playing a board game called 'wooden wisdom' with another leader called Arthur, when a squire approaches them and informs Owein that Arthur's men are attacking and molesting his ravens. Owein asks Arthur to call his men off the ravens. Arthur ignores his request and simply says, 'Play your game.' This happens three times, until the last message reports that the ravens are almost massacred, the most famous raven slain and the others so weak with loss of blood that they can barely rise into the air.

Owein commands the messenger to return to the scene of the conflict and raise aloft the raven banner. This is done, and immediately the birds are revived.

> Having recovered their strength and their magic powers, in rage and exaltation they straightway swooped upon the men who had earlier inflicted hurt and injury and loss upon them. Of some, they were carrying off the heads, of others the eyes, of others the ears and of others the arms; and they were raising them up in the air, and there was a great commotion in the air, what with the fluttering of the ravens and their croaking, and another great commotion what with the cries of the men being gashed.

So banners depicting the raven carried with them a magical power, a sense of indestructibility.

As ever, many of the bloody battles between warlords, chieftains and kings were over wealth, power and honour. Some were about rival religions, and involved the power of Rome and Europe-wide politics. Essentially it was a struggle for control of the magic. The wizards and seeresses practised with the blessings and energies of the enchanted landscape and the spirit world, whereas the Christian missionaries wanted those powers to be mediated exclusively through the Church. Most of them sincerely believed this was the way of truth, although some of it was undoubtedly a human need for power and prestige. This struggle for power, and the story of the crow, has an epilogue. It is in a chronicle written by William Ramsey in the twelfth century.

He recounts how, a hundred years earlier, the Earl of Northumbria, Siward the Stout, felt drawn to walk along his coastline. He was a famed and important supporter of King Cnut, Overlord of England. Siward's bodyguards were kept at a distance. The crows wheeled above the gleaming beach as the tide drew in. And there on the beach, he saw the cloaked figure of an old man. They met. The old man prophesied Siward's future, and gave him advice. Then he reached into his tunic, and pulled out a banner, called Ravenlandeye. It had on it the image of a raven – the emblem of Odin, god of the wizards, who had the ravens Huginn and Muninn as his messengers. Some historians reckon that the old man with the magical gift of prophecy and the raven-banner of Odin was the god himself, even though the twelfth-century Christian chronicler of Crowland who has given us this account did not know what underlay his tale.

The raven banner was given by the earl to the city of York where it was placed in St Mary's Church. The translation of Odin's banner into a venerated possession of Old St Mary's in York was one of the symbols of the passing of Middle-earth, and the beginning of the next thousand years, one of Christian and secular sentiments. But in the times of Middle-earth, people were aware of the passing of aeons, and the beginning of the new. The raven would also have known that at the end of that thousand years, another would begin – one in which the magic of Middle-earth would arise again.

13. Shapeshifters

In the real Middle-earth, it was believed that certain people could alter their shape and spirit from human to animal form. So that they appeared, sounded and behaved like animals. Some of these people were wizards and witches, who shapeshifted to acquire the knowledge, wisdom and guile of animals – as well as the ability to fly. Also, great warriors took on the shape of impressive animals in order to explode into combat with their fighting power. Manannan, a Celtic night-visiting god, is described in the *Book of Fernay* to have come to Middle-earth to claim his son, Mongan, and teach him the magic of the spirit-world. Mongan goes to the Otherworld, stays there until he is sixteen, learning the secrets of shapeshifting. Eventually he returns to his earthly family as a wizard. Manannan prophesies of his son:

> He will be a dragon before the host at the onset,
> He will be a wolf of every great forest.
> He will be a stag with horns of silver . . .
> He will be a speckled salmon in a full pool,
> He will be a seal, he will be a fair-white swan.
> He will be throughout long ages
> An hundred years in fair kingship . . .

Mongan transforms variously into animals of water, land and air, learning the qualities of each element – although he is destined to die in human form.

Such an attitude – that animals were possessed of such power that humans could seek to become like them, was very different from the Christian perspective being preached ever more frequently in ancient Europe. It was a distinctive tenet of the new religion that man (with a soul) was a creature quite separate and superior to animals:

And God blessed Noah and his sons, and said unto them, 'Be fruitful, and multiply, and replenish the earth. And the dear of you and the dread of you shall be upon every beast of the earth, and upon every fowl of the air, upon all that moveth upon the earth, and upon all the fishes of the sea; into your hand are they delivered. Every morning thing that liveth shall be meat for you; even as the green herb have I given you all things.

The animals were provided merely for people to exploit. But the indigenous people of Middle-earth had a more intimate perspective on animals. They hunted them for food, skins, bone handles for tools, and so on. But as we shall see they were seen as, in some respects, superior to humans.

Although the ability to transform into animals was accepted as possible, it was exceptional. Even so, 2,000 years ago, all people were naturally closer to, and more familiar with, wild animals. The Celts, Anglo-Saxons and Norse shared their lands with wild creatures of all shapes and sizes: brown bears; packs of silver-grey wolves; honey-hued deer on delicate, springy legs; mighty stags with rutting, raking antlers; scurrying hares; silent snakes, from harmless slow worms to adders with fangs which could deliver a bite so poisonous a person could die from it; rivers and streams crammed with fish; shrubs rustling with songbirds, skies dotted with eagles and smaller birds of prey like the silvery fast sparrowhawks; shuffling creatures of the undergrowth such as the hedgehog; scurrying spiders with their webbed world shimmering in the dewy morning sunlight. People worked outdoors, farming, collecting firewood, hunting, maintaining buildings and fences – and thousands of species of wild animal were their everyday companions.

We can understand that in an environment in which wild animals were ever-present, special relationships might develop between people and certain species of animal. The bear was one of the most special. It was the largest and probably supreme fighting animal of those times. But just as important were more subtle qualities which insinuated this impressive animal into the lives of humans.

Spirit of the Bear

In northern and western Europe, no other wild animal was so anthropomorphic. The bear rears up and walks like a human on two legs, with an erect gait and swinging arms. It sits down squarely on its haunches with its back resting against a tree. It eats omnivorously, as do humans. And it has a range of facial expressions which seem to express its emotions more than most animals. Also, unlike other animals, it walks on the soles of its feet with the heels touching the ground, leaving a footprint of a heel, toe and arch like that of a human being. Its head and ears – more rounded than those of most other animals – resemble human features. The mewling of cubs sounds remarkably like the crying of human infants; and the grown bear has an unusually wide range of vocalization, including a human-sounding high-pitched whine.

It had other qualities which were not human-like, but made it appear so special that it acquired a sacred status. Bears seem to live *inside* the earth. Their subterranean den is like an entrance to the Underworld; as if the bear is able to make a shaman-like passage from Middle-earth and down into the the realm of the dead. And its long winter hibernation suggests that the bear has died, but knows how to come back to life in the spring, when the green shoots lure it back from the womb of Mother Earth. To the people of ancient England, the bear seemed half human, and very spiritual.

The most widely admired warriors certainly found as many ways as possible to maximize their fighting powers. Tacitus, writing of the warriors of the Harii tribe, states that:

> not only are they superior in strength . . . but they minister to their savage instincts by trickery and timing. They blacken their shields and paint their bodies, and choose pitch dark nights for their battles. The shadowy, awe-inspiring appearance of such a ghoulish army inspires mortal panic. No enemy can endure a vision so strange and ghastly. Defeat in battle always begins with what the eyes see.

But berserker warriors went a stage further. They were reputed to literally have the spirit of bears. Sometimes they could even project that spirit out into the world as a fighting force. In ancient Denmark, Bothvar Bjarki, the celebrated champion warrior of King Hrolf Kraki, was famed for fighting in the form of a great bear in the ranks of the king's army, while his human form lay at home asleep. In one story, Bjarki (little bear) was 'sleeping' inside the hall while King Hrolf made his last, desperate stand against his enemies outside. But Bjarki was in a trance. And during his altered state of consciousness, out- side a huge bear suddenly appeared in the front of Hrolf's army, devastating the Dane's enemies. But soon after, when Bjarki was forcibly awakened, the bear ally outside disappeared at once, and the Danes soon lost the battle.

This strange and marvellous feat of acquiring an animal spirit and projecting it was considered to be a gift, and a sacred one at that, but still within the 'natural order of things'.

Bear-warriors were legendary in ancient England, too. The most famous Anglo-Saxon poem of all is named after its hero, a warrior called Beowulf. Scholars have done much work on the historical figures and other legends which might have been related to this poem, or even served as precursers to it. So far they have not identified a historical character on whom Beowulf himself is based – although as with all fiction, real people are often the inspiration for the spinning of a story about a fictional character, no matter how remarkable his qualities.

Beowulf's name means 'the wolf of bees' which, in turn, means 'that which attacks what belongs to the bees' – in other words, a 'honey-eater'. Bears love to eat honey and were a nuisance for the bee-keepers of ancient times. In the poem, Beowulf fought with bear- like power, snapping swords, tearing off the arms of his enemies, and in particular, killing with a bear hug. That is how he crushed the monster Grendel, and how he burst the heart and bones of Daegh- refn, the champion of the Frisians. Although Beowulf is not described as 'skin-changing' his appearance into a bear, he is a great warrior with the nature and strength of a bear.

In the historical Middle-earth, warriors like the legendary Bjarki and Beowulf who *became* bear-like and went into battle with height- ened ferocity, were called 'berserkers'. The original meaning of the word berserk was 'bear shirt', indicating not that they wore bearskins, but rather that they were 'clothed' with the 'spirit-skin' of the animal who inspired and protected them. It is also the forerunner of the modern phrase 'to go berserk', meaning to go 'out of control'. But the berserkers were 'controllably out of control'. They were 'shapechangers' who went a stage further, and purportedly took on animal form in order to acquire a more aggressive nature and physical strength.

Snorri Sturluson, in the *Ynglinga Saga*, one of the ancient stories from the historical Middle-earth, described how the berserkers '... fight without a mail shirt in battle and made it that they raged ... They would bite into their shields, and they were as strong as bears; they killed the men, but neither fire nor iron could injure them; this is what people called the berserker rage.'

It could go badly wrong, too. Saxo gives a vivid description of a person changing into a berserker. Unfortunately, he has been taunted about his chances of success in battle: 'Harthebn, processed by immediate transports of rage, took hard bites out of the rim of his shield, gulped down fiery coals into his entrails without a qualm, ran the gauntlet of crackling flames and finally went completely and savagely berserk . . .' – and apparently attacked both friends and foes!

It would certainly have been daunting to have been caught in battle in those times facing a veteran warrior made huge and powerful by his animal spirit, convinced of his invulnerability, wild-eyed and unable to feel pain or fear, and wielding a magical sword and spear. He would be terrifyingly ferocious and reckless in combat, this berserker.

Tolkien used this belief in men who could shapeshift into bears in *The Hobbit*. By day, his character called Beorn is a strong man with big arms, black hair and enormous beard. But by night he transforms into a huge black bear, and roams out of the oak wood and into the distant mountains, growling bear-language, afraid of no one or anything. The wizard Gandalf calls him a 'skin-changer'. In his skin-changed shape, Beorn is a ferocious warrior. He is in his element, fighting wildly as a bear alongside the dwarves in the Battle of The Five Armies. In a great roaring rage, he hurls wolves and goblins aside, immune to cuts and bites from them. A consummate user of language, Tolkien chose the perfect name for Beorn. In Old English, it means a 'heroic man'. It is also related to the name Bjorn, which in Danish, Swedish and Icelandic means 'bear'.

Shapeshifting

Today we assume that it is impossible to 'become an animal'. Rationally, we know that our material form is not subject to such radical, literal transformation. But in Middle-earth people believed differently. The Old Norse phrase 'eigi einhamr' means 'not having only one shape'. Concealed within our appearance were other possibilities, aspects of ourselves that if expressed physically, would look very different. So how can we understand the ways by which they transformed themselves into animal form?

The ingredients which made up the Middle-earth perspective on animal transformation include concepts to which we no longer subscribe. One was their notion of the 'hamr' or 'spirit skin', which determined a creature's shape and form in this life. Another was their emphasis on the importance of protecting the soul, as distinct from the physical body; and finally the idea of the guardian spirit, or 'fetch', a kind of shadow-self which looked after each person.

We can glimpse early forms of this constellation of beliefs and behaviours from the continental Germanic peoples documented by Tacitus. He reports that people often wore animal skins. This sounds unsurprising – for warmth and protection, skins were a common clothing material. But then Tacitus adds that these skins were often decorated with those of 'sea creatures'; and on the garments made from whole pelts, people sewed small fragments of other animal skins. This was almost certainly more than a Dark Ages fashion statement. Indigenous cultures which have survived until more recent times have strong connections with wild animals. And if their shamanic practices are similar to those of Middle-earth – an earlier indigenous people – these sewn decorations would have been like badges of identification between the human wearer and the animals whose skin was being added to their clothing.

We can imagine that wrapping themselves with the skins of animals and adding small pieces of pelts of other animals, literally placed the people of Middle-earth *inside* the animal's world, physically and symbolically. They believed that such close contact with those animals enabled them to share their knowledge, their power, and their spirit. The animals became their guardians, and people wore the talismanic symbols of their animal guardians. The spirits of these animals were believed to accompany the person throughout life, and could be called on for help.

Today we can empathize with this process on a symbolic level. But in Middle-earth, connecting with the powers of animal spirits went beyond the metaphor. It was an exchange of energies with the animal which transformed the person. We can see how this worked with the boar, or wild pig.

The boar was one of the most widely regarded wild creatures among the tribespeople of early Europe because it was so ferocious and fertile. The wild boar was a short and densely muscled beast. The weight of a slaughtered animal needed several of men to move it. Hunters trying to kill a boar for its meat knew how much injury it could inflict. A trapped boar would charge its tormenter – a quarter ton of fury which, at a spear's length distance away, could maim or kill.

Tacitus reports that among the tribes who wore it, the boar emblem was considered the best possible defence in battle. Helmets collected at various archaeological excavations show that in the period of the first millennium, many of them have images of boars attached. The magnificent helmet found at the Sutton Hoo treasure hoard had boars placed above the cheekguard. In battle, warriors slashed at the boar on the helmet, as in these poetic lines describing combat: 'When the hilt-bound blade, hammer-forged – the sword blood-shining, doughty of edge – shears away the swine from the opponent's helmet.'

Not only was the helmet attacked to injure the warrior physically – separating him from his boar emblem neutralized his defensive magic, and made him more vulnerable – but the boar emblem on the helmet was also an enemy in its own right. People believed that an animal which had lent its power to a warrior in this way could attack directly by launching itself as a spirit in battle, and savage the enemies of the wearer.

In the Norse story *Hrolf's Saga*, the boar spirit of Athils does just that: it suddenly materializes in the hall, a fierce opponent for Hrolf and his men. Significantly, Athils is not present when his boar appears. Hrolf's hound Gram subdues the boar in a dreamlike scene suggesting the battle of rival animal spirits. The moment the boar disappears, Athils returns to the hall – he has shapeshifted. He had sent his animal spirit out as a battle demon in its own right.

Protecting The Soul

The people of Middle-earth believed that the soul could travel outside the body. This was not a rare occurrence. For them, dreams came from outside the sleeper rather than being conjured in the brain – the concept of boundaries of the mind were far extended beyond our own. The Old Norse language uses a structure which translates as 'a dream came to me', rather than 'I dreamt', and also in Old English the phrase was 'to me came a dream'. Conversely, while sleeping, the person's soul was imagined to extend beyond the body and travel. When King Alfred translated into Anglo-Saxon the classical text of Boethius, *De consolatione Philosophiae* he edited some of the text, but retained the section on which he wrote of the 'soul' ranging away from the body while we slept: 'so also our spirit is faring very widely without our intention . . . while we sleep'.

A soul travelling away from its physical body was apparently considered to be vulnerable. It could be lost (causing illness or death), stolen, or separated from the body for an extended time in spite of the efforts of the spirit skin. This is why it needed to be guarded by animal spirits. The material helmet protected the warrior against physical blows to the head, and the boar crest performed the equally important task of warding off assaults upon the warrior's soul.

This guardian spirit was also known as the 'fylgia' in Old Norse, and the 'fetch' in ancient English. The term has its origins in the ancient word *fulga*, which meant a skin of an animal, like the totemic pieces sewn on to the clothing. The fetch was an aspect of our soul which could detach from the body, and travel vast distances like a shadow self. This could happen to any of us. Awakening at night with a start, and a falling sensation, was put down to our making a rapid re-entry into the physical body.

The soul travelling sometimes looked like the fetch protecting it – as in *The Hobbit*, in which Beorn looks like a bear. Sometimes these fetches could speak directly to people in visions or dreams, and manifest themselves physically. In an ancient Icelandic saga, for example, a man called Njal had the ability to receive communications from the fetch-world. One night he could not sleep because his mind was being 'visited' by visions of menacing shapes. They were the *fetches* of enemies who had massed in a nearby wood on their way to murder him. His visions were confirmed the next morning in the 'real' world, when a shepherd arrived who reported seeing men lurking in the wood.

The 'hamr' is a Norse word referring to a kind of 'spirit skin' for the soul when it was outside the body. In Old English 'hama' means 'home'. So when journeying from the body, the soul apparently was believed to keep its shape through this energy presence of the hamr. As a spirit skin it seems to have kept the soul's energies from being dispersed, much as the skin does the physical body. If the spirit skin or hamr maintained the travelling soul in the shape of the physical body, perhaps this is why in popular tradition ghosts look like the person who emanated them. However, just as each of us has a face unique to us, perhaps in Middle-earth the shape of each soul was different. Perhaps the spirit skin of one person could never fit the soul of another.

Soul Journeying

When wizards journeyed from Middle-earth to the Otherworld, in search of knowledge, they were helped in these journeys by their particularly powerful fetch, who 'lent' them their animal form. 'Odin could change himself,' wrote Snorri Sturluson of the god of the wizards. 'His body then lay as if sleeping or dead, but he became a bird or wild beast, a fish or a dragon, and he journeyed in the twinkling of an eye to far-off lands, on his own errands or those of other men.'

Today and in the recent past, indigenous cultures all over the world still believe that shamans can leave their physical body. Their 'soul' becomes at one with an animal 'fetch' or guardian, and in this form journeys to the Lowerworld or Upperworld, in search of wisdom and healing spells to bring back to their community. The process by which a shaman takes on the attributes of his spirit animal often begins with a ritual in which the shaman dresses in the skins of the animal whose spirit he wishes to contact, as for example when he puts on the hide and horns of a stag. The skins of the animal guardian are seen as agents of transformation.

The shaman then enters a entranced state of mind, often with the help of such techniques as fasting, going without sleep, rhythmic drumming and dancing, until the animal spirit becomes one with the shaman. It is not an act of 'possession', in which a person is controlled by a spirit, but rather a 'taking possession' of the helping spirits by the wizard. So it was with Beorn in *The Hobbit*, for Gandalf explained that his changing into bear-form was not the result of any enchantment or bewitchment except what he chose to exercise upon himself.

Of course, in Middle-earth, taking on the skins of an animal to acquire its power needed the animal's sanction. In the saga of the Volsungs, written in Iceland in the fourteenth century and telling stories placed several hundred years earlier, two men called Sigmund and Sinfjoth put on wolfskins, unaware that these were enchanted. The skins transformed the men into wolves, and they were trapped in that lupine state, unable to escape, until the tenth day when the spell was temporarily lifted. Greatly relieved, they hurriedly burned the skins and broke the spell. Shapeshifting was believed to be real and dangerous. To behave like a beast of prey was to cease to be merely a man, even when he was in his human form. To become an animal was a step into a special category of being.

The essence of the Middle-earth view is that the physical shape of a creature is only an aspect of it, and not its defining feature. Soul has fluency and energy which can be expressed in other forms. And there was an interflow between the soul forms of people and of other animals. This is the source of the intimate connections people felt with animals in Middle-earth.

14. The Wizard's Wild Ride

The Anglo-Saxon Chronicle has an entry for the year 1127, which reads: 'Let no one be surprised at what we are about to relate, for it was common gossip up and down the countryside that after February 6th many people saw and heard a whole pack of huntsmen in full cry.' This was no ordinary hunt for deer or boar, however, for these horses and huntsman were not of the material world. The document goes on: 'The huntsmen were black, huge and hideous, and straddled black horses and black he-goats, and their hounds were jet black with eyes staring like saucers, and horrible. This was seen in the very deer park of Peterborough town, and in all the woods stretching from that same spot as far as Stamford.' This hunt stretched beyond daylight: 'All through the night monks heard them sounding and winding their horns. Reliable witnesses who kept watch in the night declared that there might well have been twenty or even thirty of them winding their horns as near as they could tell.'

The Anglo-Saxons called this phenomenon The Wild Hunt. It was a generic name given to numerous folk tales associated with such chases, often led by a god, goddess or mythological figure accompanied by a cavalcade of souls of the dead. It was a streaming through the night of spirits liberated from the Lowerworld of the dead, and let loose through the woods of the living. To see or hear it was terrifying, for they seemed to have broken loose from the natural order of things. No one knew why the huntsmen were abroad at night, except perhaps to capture souls of the living and take them with them back down to the Lowerworld.

The belief in this Wild Hunt lived long and vividly, in Celtic lore as Gwyn ap Nudd, a wild huntsman who rides a demon horse and hunts in waste places at night with a pack of white-bodied and red-eared 'dogs of hell'. Cheering on his hell hounds in a fearful chase, he hunts souls.

More generally, beyond the specifics of this wild hunt, in the historical Middle-earth special horses were believed to be the means by which wizards journeyed between the everyday world and the Otherworld of magic and myth. These spirit horses could communicate with their owners or even understand human speech.

The horses were given mythical names, and sometimes the gods and goddesses could take on their form. Epona was one, a Celtic goddess whose name means 'divine horse'. Early images of her show her as a giant woman, dominating the horses on either side of her. At other times she is depicted with one or two foals. Today in the west country of England, the etched chalk outline of the fabulous White Horse of Uffington seems to be bounding across the hilltops. She is possibly a depiction of the Celtic horse goddess Epona. The appearance of Celtic horses could be spectacular. In the tale of the Death of Fergus, Esirt takes the poet Aedh to his own Otherworld country. They reach the sea and a horse comes galloping towards them over the waves 'of which horse the fashion was this: two fierce flashing eyes he had, an exquisite pure crimson mane, with four green legs and a long tail that floated in wavy curls. His colour was that of prime artificers gold work, and a gold-encrusted bridle he bore withal.' The magic horse takes both men on its back safely over the ocean to their destination.

Horses were also believed to ride through the sky to keep the days and nights turning. In one ancient Norse legend, the Allfather, the original sky-god, took Night and her son Day, and gave to each of them a horse and chariot and put them in the sky so that they should ride around the world every twenty-four hours. Night rides first on a horse called Hrimfaxi (Frosty mane), and showers of water droplets from the mane create the night dew on the surface of the Earth. Day's horse is called Skinfaxi (Shining mane) and the whole earth and sky are illumined by the glow from his mane.

In the real Middle-earth people believed horses to be in communication with the spirit world, and therefore capable of foretelling future events. Tacitus, commenting on the early Saxons, describes their breeding special white horses.

These horses are kept at public expense in the sacred woods and groves . . . they are pure white and undefiled by any toil in the service of man. The priest and the king, or the chief of the state, yoke them to a sacred chariot and walk beside them, taking note of their neighs and snorts. No kind of omen inspires greater trust, not only among the common people, but even among the nobles and priests, who think that they themselves are but servants of the gods, whereas the horses are privy to the gods' counsels.

Sometimes the wizards would consult the horses by laying spears on the ground and watching how the animals stepped over them. Some of these special horses were reserved for riding only by the king, or in legend, the gods, rather like Shadowfax who, before Gandalf chose him, could only be ridden by the Lord of the Mark.

The Norse mythical figure of Odin was a kind of template for all wizards, mystics and shamans, and Tolkien explained that he was his main inspiration for the appearance and character of Gandalf. Odin had a special horse, called Sleipnir (Slippery). The way he acquired the horse, and interacted with it, offers us a fascinating glimpse of the historical tradition behind the identity of Shadowfax. It begins with the massive trees of historical Middle-earth, which were the image which joined together all the realms of the Upperworld and Lowerworld.

Sleipnir

The ancient Norse legends describe how Odin came by his mystical knowledge in a visionary ordeal on a tree. He stayed in the tree for nine days and nine nights, without food or water. The images which came revealed to him the secrets of the runes, the structure of the cosmos, and gave him the necessary spells for him to go on a quest for the magic mead. Real wizards underwent these visions on trees. Each tree represented the cosmic tree which they believed held together all the lands and worlds of the cosmos. This great mythical tree was called Yggdrasil. The name is a compound of two words – the stem of 'ygg' is a nickname for Odin, meaning 'the awe-inspiring one'. 'Drasill' is a literary word meaning 'horse'. The name identifies the tree as the means of Odin's 'ride' to the spirit world, and his transportation for the quest.

So during the course of his nine-day fast on the tree, Odin's image of the tree transformed into that of a horse. In fact, the conception of a tree as a horse for journeys into the spirit world reached into all areas of life. In Anglo-Saxon England, when criminals were hanged, the gallows were also known poetically as a 'horse', upon which its victim 'rode' to their death, to the Lowerworld where reside the souls of the departed.

When the World Tree transformed into a horse, during Odin's vision quest, it became a magnificent white, eight-legged flying horse called Sleipnir. In *The Lord of the Rings*, Gandalf's Shadowfax seemed to come also from the dawning of time – Tolkien describes him as being a horse that might have been foaled in the morning of the world.

Sleipnir carried Odin on a visionary journey around the sacred cosmos to the nine worlds of knowledge. And Sleipnir, being eight-legged, had a leg for each of the worlds, with Odin the rider forming the centre point . . . the ninth world. For nine days and nine nights Odin rode Sleipnir to the Otherworlds.

Today we would probably conceive of these 'Other Worlds' as being located in our psyche, perhaps deep in the unconscious. The image of the World Tree as it transforms into a magical horse, would be a tool or technique for entering aspects of the unconscious which might otherwise be closed to us except in the most deeply symbolic dreams.

But for the peoples of ancient Europe, the imagination was a realm not physically bounded by the body, and not conceived of as *only* an internal event. For our ancestors the everyday, material world was a tiny microcosm of the boundless imaginal world. And for them, the magical horse Sleipnir enabled the archetypal wizard Odin to venture beyond the physical plane of the material world.

In the stories of historical Middle-earth, Odin's horse Sleipnir '. . . rode nine days and nine nights down ravines ever darker and deeper, meeting no one, until he came to the banks of the river Gjoll which he followed as far as the Gjoll Bridge; this bridge is roofed with burning gold'. The bridge was the fantastic bridge of fire known as the Rainbow Bridge; it was the transformational gateway to the realms of the Upperworld, and the Lowerworld.

Riding Sleipnir to the Otherworld

Odin soared from the World Tree and flew on Sleipnir to a fateful encounter with the Mimir, the wisdom giant. The legends of the historical Middle-earth do not provide a direct account of this ride, but there are several accounts of later journeys that give us a flavour of what this first journey must have been like.

One of the rides on Sleipnir was taken by the god Hermothr, whom some scholars think to be an alter ego of Odin. I shall therefore refer to Sleipnir's rider here directly as Odin. He was on this occasion riding from Asgard, in the Upperworld, down to Hel, the deepest realm of the Lowerworld in search of information about his brother Balder. He mounted his shamanic spirit-horse Sleipnir, its hooves kicking and sparking for the gallop through the heavens. He bent over the horse's neck and gripped with both hands hanks of the flowing mane as they shot off into the night sky. The flash of stars soon turned to a twinkle of dew as Sleipnir's hooves struck rock and they rode towards a mountainside, and the dark, looming entrance of an enormous cave.

The ancient sources describe how, to commence the journey, Odin had to get into a cave black as night, set among precipitous cliffs and ravines. This black cave was a magical entrance to the Lowerworld, but to get into the cave was an ordeal, because the entrance was guarded by a fearsome hound called Garmr. The huge dog had blood on his chest, which if the dog Cerberus from Greek mythology is a parallel, is the blood from the dead people who have tried to escape from Hel, the deepest level of the Lowerworld.

While the Lowerworld was a realm of wisdom, for it contained the collective knowledge of all people who have lived and died, it was important in the finely balanced web of forces that these 'spirits of the dead' remained in the Lowerworld, only seeping into the world of the living at liminal points in the year; Hallowe'en, Midwinter's Eve and so on. And in the mythology of the people of ancient Europe, the end of the world would be marked by setting the hound free, leaving the way out of Hel unguarded – the dead come roaring back into the world of the living.

Odin reined in Sleipnir by pulling at the mane, but the horse was already hopping sideways and slithering on the rocks to give Garmr a wide berth. Odin knew some binding charms, which he chanted over the baying hound, and the dog became constricted in its movements. It tried to bite at invisible bonds, then lost its footing, and was soon trussed up and helpless. Odin urged Sleipnir into the cave before the spell wore off and the dog could chase after them. It was like Gandalf's journey on Shadowfax, when he describes coming late one evening to a gate, which was like a great arch in a wall of rock. The gate was guarded, but the gatekeepers allowed him to ride under the arch. As soon as he had done so, he felt afraid, for no obvious reason.

In Odin's story, the high-roofed cave went deep into the mountain, and as they rode into the darkness even the glow of Sleipnir's coat faded like a dying candle. On they rode, until finally the cave opened out on the other side – a mere pinprick of light at first, getting larger – and then out into moonlight. The air smelled different; cooler, wetter; they were on their way to the Lowerworld.

'He rode nine days and nights down ravines ever darker and deeper, meeting no one,' the poem reads, descending until he was in the Lowerworld proper, the Realm of Shadows. 'Until he came to the banks of the river called Echoing.' This river was an important boundary, a great, open, echoing space blocking progress, testing one's will to cross. And there was only one way for Odin to cross the surging flow of Echoing space – over a bridge: 'this bridge is roofed with burning gold'. The bridge of burning gold is like other references to a magical bridge which links the Realms called Bifrost, which is also a bridge of fire and gold.

At the entrance to Echoing Bridge there was a mysterious maiden called Mothguthr who guarded the bridge. She asked him his name or lineage, saying that only the day before five droves of dead men had padded over the bridge, 'but the bridge echoed less under them than under thee'. The bridge of flaming gold stretched over the River Echo, and Odin, living but travelling in his spirit-form on Sleipnir, made more noise than droves of dead men. 'Anyway,' she said, realizing he was not dead but some sort of a shaman journeying in the realms of the dead, 'You haven't the pallor of a dead man; why are you riding down Helway?'

Odin told her the reason for his trance journey, explaining that

he was seeking the soul of a god called Balder. 'You don't happen to
have set eyes on Balder on the road to Hel?' He was in luck. She
replied that Balder had already ridden over the Echoing Bridge, and
'the road to Hel lies down still and to the north'.

Odin urged Sleipnir past the woman and thundered over the
bridge to the other side, the horse's eight hooves drumming on
the path Helway, and galloping on until they came to Hel Gate, an
enormous barrier. Odin slid off his spirit horse, and tightened the
girth. 'He mounted again and raked his spurs along the animal's ribs.
The stallion leapt so high there was plenty of twilight between him
and the bars.' From here the wizard rode on to the Hall where resided
the Queen of Hel. There he dismounted and went in to see 'his
brother Balder sitting on a throne'. He had completed his journey.

The story of Sleipnir shows that horses were not only seen as a
means of transport in the material world, but in the magic realms
also. And in the eight-legged horse of Odin, the animal was in itself
a representation of the entire cosmos.

WIZARDS OF WYRD

15. The Web of Destiny

At full moon, the landscape of Middle-earth was cast in a silver glow, right to the distant horizon. The brightness of the night, in a time before urban glow could diminish it, must have imparted a sense of the enormous scale of the spiritual cosmos. It stretched from the realm of the gods in Upperworld all the way through Middle-earth, and down among the spirits of the dead in the deep layers of the Lowerworld. This image, derived from some of the ancient Norse poetry, gives a framework through which people understood their lives to be woven by the forces of the Wyrd Sisters, as we shall see below.

Medieval accounts conjure a scene in which, in a wooden house amid a cluster making up the community, a baby is about to be born. The women of the village are gathered. The midwife is present. She is either a village elder, practised in the art and medicine of childbirth, or she is a witch, perhaps from another village. This is still the time when words like witch meant 'wise woman', before it was corrupted by an evangelical church intent on eliminating rival practitioners.

In fact the Anglo-Saxon 'hagtesse' may well have been the midwife present at such an event in ancient England. The terms suggested a woman of magic, probably connected with the powers of the elves, and skilled in the capacity to conduct magical ritual, along with the best plant medicine they had for a birthing woman. The word 'hag' today has been downgraded to refer disparagingly only to very old women. In those days, these women were powerful indeed, for they were believed to invoke the presence at the birth of the three Wyrd Sisters – and even the destiny of gods was subject to the divinations and rulings of these three female beings. The hagtesse, magical midwife, had spells to sing which would imbue the setting with the palpable presence of these dealers in destiny.

The potency of childbirth rituals is not surprising, for the gift of life must have been greatly prized. A sense of gratitude at the coming of life must have counterbalanced the ease with which it could be snatched away in those times. Hazards included famines caused by crops which failed or became diseased, plagues, war, or bandits. The evidence below confirms that tribal settlements then paid special attention to fertility and motherhood, and underlined the importance of this aspect of womanhood.

Dance of the Mothers

Becoming a mother was recognized, celebrated and even flaunted, as a woman's way of knowing, a woman's mystery. Its deeper dimensions were closed to men.

In Anglo-Saxon England, Frigg gave her name to Friday (Frigg's Day), suggesting that she was a goddess of importance before being suppressed in favour of the figure of Mary in the new Christian faith. It also suggests that Frigg was regarded as the equivalent of the Roman Venus, an Earth Mother, goddess of love and childbirth. And then, in the Germanic and Norse traditions of Middle-earth, a birth triggered a communal response from the women of the settlement. They ran wild. As soon as the baby arrived, all of the women, of all ages, danced and shouted their way to the house of the mother and, once assembled there, conducted some secret women's ceremonies. When these were complete, the women burst out of the house in a frantic race through the village; they ran all together, shouting and shrieking. In an account from the north of Schleswig, if they met any men they 'snatched off their hats and filled them with dung'. If they came across farm carts, implements of men's work, they broke them into pieces and set the horse at liberty. They went into houses and took all the food and drink they wanted, and if there were any men present, they compelled them to dance. This description is one of liberation, triumph, joy, freedom – and aggression.

The ceremonies from Schleswig, conducted by the women in the house of the new mother, have retained their secrecy over the centuries. However, an account from thirteenth-century Denmark provides a glimpse of what probably went on in similar form all over Middle-earth: '. . . the women gathered together in the house and sang and shouted while they made a manikin of straw which they called the Ox'. Two women danced with the Ox erotically, and sang secret songs. And then another woman began to sing in a deep, coarse voice, using 'terrible words' (the acronym is from the Christian reporter of the event, of course!).

For the childbearing woman, as well as the village women, this experience must have been liberating and empowering. The men presumably went along with it, cooperated, respected the outpouring of feminine energy. They must also have felt threatened. These were connections with Mother Earth which men do not have. It is a radical contrast with the twentieth century male-dominated world of obstetrics!

It represents, and reminds us, that motherhood is an expression, from within our own species, of a cosmological principle, in which birth of *everything* is a never-ending process. And while medical advances in childbirth are a boon, the formerly powerful role of Mother Earth, originally as Nerthus, later as the goddess Frigg, reminds us of the sense of gratitude at the miracle of birth that people must have felt in Middle-earth times.

The creation of life, especially in a time in which staying alive was more precarious than now, was a precious event, and could be a fraught one too. However, to the people of those times, it was also a prescient psychological and spiritual moment, for the moment of birth was when a child's destiny was laid out for the duration of his or her life on Earth. Character, outlook, luck, courage and intelligence would be crystallized at that moment.

The Wyrd Sisters

Figures of three female deities stretch back in prehistory for at least six thousand years. This is the dating of small clay figures depicting them, or images engraved on to rocks. And they are present in all the lands that gave birth to the Celtic, Germanic and Norse cultures. They were known as the 'mothers', and are reckoned by archaeologists to represent aspects of Mother Earth. Sometimes they were pictured alone, but usually in groups of two or three; they are shown standing, or seated on chairs or stools, sometimes with loose flowing hair, holding fruit or horns of plenty. They were still present hundreds of years later in Anglo-Saxon England; Bede mentions them when he tells us that the night before Christmas was called in heathen times Modraniht, 'the night of the mothers'.

By the beginning of the first millennium, and the approximate start of the thousand years of the culture of real Middle-earth, they were represented as three all-powerful female figures to whom even the gods and goddesses are subject. They were called the Wyrd Sisters in Anglo-Saxon England, Nornir in Norse lands, Parcae (meaning 'to bring forth') among the Romans. They were centrally involved in the Middle-earth understanding of childbirth and individual destiny. We know that the importance of these women survived all the way through the first millennium to the end of the Middle-earth culture because in the eleventh century Bishop Burchard of Worms rebuked women in general for their continued belief in three women known as the Parcae. He complained that it was a common custom (probably near the time of childbirth) to lay three places at the meal table for them!

Back in the village, beneath the moonlight, we can imagine the power of a child being born under the sanction of these three Sisters. *The Poetic Edda* helps us to understand how they were believed to be involved. One of its poems describes the Norse version of the Three Sisters, called the Norns. These three all-powerful women, to whom even gods are subject at the end of the Middle-earth period, are described arriving at a place called Bralund. It is a royal hall. They are attending a woman named Borghild who is giving birth to her child Helgi, a future king:

> Then was Helgi, the huge-hearted
> Born in Bralund to Borghild.
> Night had fallen when the Norns came,
> Those who appoint a prince's days:
> His fate, they foretold, was fame among men,
> to be thought the best of brave kings.
> There in Bralund's broad courts
> They spun the threads of his special destiny:

> They stretched out strings of gold,
> Fastened them under the hall of the moon.

The lines suggest that the people of Middle-earth saw their life's destiny laid out at birth as lacy, interwoven fibres, threads of gold stretching under the hall of the moon (the night sky). Perhaps the pattern, the weave, was stretched by the gravitational pull of the moon; just as it moves the great oceans in tidal cycles, so it moves the liquid of our brains, our bodies, our destiny.

Weaving Destiny

This vision sees the threads set the unfolding of each individual's life. In England, the Anglo-Saxon word 'gewaef' meant 'wove', and its cognate word 'gewif' referred to 'fortune'. Weaving and destiny, in the imagery of our ancestors, was one and the same thing. Our individual lives were structured by the spinning of subtle strings of fibres at our birth, their turning and twisting threads holding us to a course, weaving for us a life pattern.

But it was even more than this. For rather than weaving only the pattern of one life, the Sisters intertwined the individual with the pattern of all of life. Rather than lives being separate, linked to one another only by chance, the web of all life connected everything.

The interconnection with weaving and individual destiny suggests that for the people of Middle-earth, everything, from cosmic to individual level, was interconnected as if in the weaving of a great cosmic tapestry of which we are each a part. Each life was like a kind of knot in the threads, in which forces of energy were interlocked amid the shimmering, vibrating pattern of the entire web. The idea is based on the processes of spinning and weaving which were central to life in ancient Europe.

Of course, spinning and weaving are processes which have lost their impact for us as metaphors for the deeper realms of life. The making of our textiles is done almost exclusively by industrial machine, thus removing it from direct observation and participation. It is helpful therefore, in considering the images by which the people of Middle-earth understood their lives, to remind ourselves of the early techniques of spinning and weaving.

It started in the fields adjacent to Anglo-Saxon villages, where blue-flowered flax plants grew, reflecting the colour of the sky. When they were harvested, the stems of the plants provided fibres which were woven to produce a light coloured material still expressed in our contemporary language as in 'flaxen' coloured hair. It was linen, used for underwear and next-to-skin clothing.

The people of ancient Europe also wore clothes made from wool. The wool was sheared from the sheep which grazed – in large numbers, judging by sheep bones found in excavations – in fields next to most Anglo-Saxon villages. Early illustrations show the men shearing the sheep of their raw wool. Women then washed and combed it, and turned the fleece into yarn by drawing it into a thread with their fingers. The yarn was then attached to a weighted stick called a spindle, which they spun so that it twisted the yarn, giving it extra strength.

As well as spools and spindles, other familiar objects were the weaving looms, which wove the yarn into cloth. These were upright wooden frames on which the weighted threads of wool, called the warp, were hung down from the top bar. Alternate threads were attached to a wooden bar called the heddle. The heddle was moved back and forth on the loom, dipping between the hanging threads to weave the fabric.

Archaeological digs have unearthed thousands of examples of the tools used by the women in these tasks. Across Europe inscribed spindle-whorls have been found in innumerable neolithic sacrificial pits sacred to goddesses. It was as if in the prehistorical cultures of early Europe the Three Sisters were the 'original weavers of the universe'. Perhaps they were regarded in a manner similar to the Navajo peoples of North America where, for example, the women weavers believe they are directly inspired by the Great Spider Woman, the original weaver of the universe. Their woven blankets are valued as organic expressions of the special powers of the makers. Each blanket with its inspired design has a spiritual significance, and is thought of as giving power and protection to the person who wears it. In ancient textiles, a highly charged symbolic language was used to communicate story and myth.

Later, from Viking-age York, spindles were found – like sticks on the end of which was attached the yarn. Near the base was a weight to pull the yarn taut while it was being spun. Also found was a pair of metal shears for cutting the threads, and some loom weights – rings of baked clay – for keeping the spun threads tight in the loom. Even a piece of the finished material made from these tools was found – it had survived for a thousand years. Some of the tools are finely made and decorated, and must have lasted a lifetime. These objects are now displayed in the Jorvik museum in the city.

Tolkien used this powerful metaphor of weaving and destiny in *The Lord of the Rings*, where Eomer, one of The Riders, heard that Aragorn and his companions had been graced by the attentions of Lady Galadriel, Queen of the Elves. He was both impressed and alarmed. He reckoned that they might be net-weavers and sorcerers. Cloth for garments, blankets and wall-hanging tapestries, were the everyday, practical results of weaving. But 'net-weaving and sorcery' went far beyond the practicalities. And in *The Lord of the Rings*, when Gandalf proclaimed to Theoden, Aragorn and their companions that their fate 'hung on a thread', Tolkien meant it in a modern sense – that a small chance only could save them. But he was also referring to an ancient usage, for he knew that in the real Middle-earth, 'threads' were what patterned people's lives – the whole process of weaving was a metaphor for the meaning of life.

The practice of consulting the Norns lasted into medieval times, where the 'reading' of one's life pattern by the Norns was ritualized by people taking their young children to see women who were 'inspired' by the three Sisters of destiny. This had its disadvantages. Saxo Grammaticus reveals in his twelfth-century *Gesta Danorum* how in ancient Denmark, the 'Sisters' could become malevolent. He tells how a man called Fridlef took his baby Olaf to the temple for the 'Sisters' to make their ruling on the infant's fortunes.

Fridlef, having offered solemn vows,

> ... approached the goddesses' temple in prayer; here, peering into the shrine, he recognised the three maidens sitting in their respective seats. The first indulgently bestowed on the boy a handsome appearance and a plentiful share of men's good-will. The second presented him with abundant generosity. The third,

a woman of rather petulant and jealous disposition, spurned the unanimous favours of her sisters and, in a wish to mar their blessings, implanted the fault of meanness in the boy's future character. That was how Olaf, when the others' benefits had been vitiated by the mischief of a gloomier destiny, received a name from the two types of offering, niggardliness mixed with liberality. So it was that this blemish, conferred as part of the gift, upset the sweetness of the earlier kindnesses.

The Ending of Life

Through the centuries, stories about the three Sisters persisted. In England, they are mentioned by the medieval poet Chaucer, and famously a few centuries later by William Shakespeare in his play *Macbeth*. In the Norse culture, they were also known as the Daughters of the Night, and in the mythology written in medieval Iceland, they were described as living in sacred space in a cave, next to a pool with gushing water which gleamed white in the moonlight. The pool was at the base of the World Tree, where the Sisters spun at night by the light of the moon. They were spinning the same threads that formed the destinies of individuals; they were the threads of life.

The mythology also pictured the Norns as having sway over the creation, measuring and ending of individual life. The Greek version of the Three Sisters were depicted as having separate functions: one who spun, another who measured the strings, and a third who cut them to lengths. It is likely that the Sisters of Wyrd were believed to operate in the same way; one creating the golden strings, another laying them out in ways which reflected and determined the life unfolding, and a third who cut them off to length and so determined the life-span of each thread, and/or each life.

Among the Norse Nornir, one of the Sisters had the name Urdr, whose name is equivalent to the Old English 'Wyrd', meaning 'life unfolding'. Another was Verdandi, the present participle of the verb 'Verda', which means 'be' or 'become'. Being, perhaps. 'To be' is half of the famous question posed by Hamlet; 'To be or not to be . . . that is the question'. This phrase, its fame and recognition greater even than this celebrated play, seems to strike at the heart of an enduring human existential question; the very words, the posing of the polarities, has potency, even though supremely enigmatic. 'Being' in Wyrd was a state of life.

The third was named Skuld, which had the meaning of something owed, a debt to be settled, an obligation to be fulfilled. Sometimes these three great forces are represented in shorthand as Fate, Being and Necessity.

So while the Sisters were responsible for an individual's 'destiny' at birth, so also they had dominion over the ending of life. Sometimes they were depicted ruling over the fate of men in battle. The obligation, the debt, of Skuld could represent death – the cashing in of one's life debts at the time appointed for death. In a story called *Njal's Saga* written anonymously around 1280, and depicting events in Iceland several centuries earlier, there is reference to death as 'a debt that all must pay'. But a debt repayed to whom? The implication, and an intriguing one, is that life is a gift, or at least a 'loan', and it forms a debt to which we are subject, and which we eventually honour with our life – or rather, with our death. The givers of life are the Wyrd Sisters, and so it seems that the debt is repaid to them. And since the Wyrd Sisters represent forces of balance in the cosmos – the earth and the sky – it is to this principle that we 'owe our life'. The life we lead has with it a responsibility, as in something owed. To the earth?

This is a similar conception to that of the traditional Kogi tribes of Colombia, whose inspirational cosmology has survived to the present and has been widely publicized in recent years. In Kogi belief, the earth is a vast loom on which the sun weaves two pieces of cloth a year. The top bar of the loom is taken to signify the apparent path of the sun through the sky at the time of the midsummer solstice, whilst the bottom bar represents its path at the midwinter solstice. The crossing at the centre is the point of intersection of the diagonals of the solsticial sunrises and sets.

For our European ancestors, there seems to have existed a similar isomorphism between individual existence and the moving of the vast forces of the universe. The loom of life writ large was essentially the same as the loom of individual lives. The strings and strands of the sun and moon were intertwined inextricably with the strings and strands of our personal lives, forming our own unique patterns as our lives unfold. Each individual life-form is a kind of energy knot, or interlock, in the overall vibrating pattern.

Destiny and Free-Will

In Middle-earth, the interlocking threads which manifest the hidden forces of the universe were woven into patterns of destiny for our individual lives. But this is a very different concept from the notion of 'free will' which most of us unconsciously adopt in the western world, leaving us uncomfortable with a notion which sounds rather like determinism. So what do we make of the life-threads of our ancestors?

For the people of the real Middle-earth, life was a complex negotiation, an interaction between what is free and what is ordained. The unfolding of life patterns was subject to the intervention of magical practitioners, the many varieties of wizards and witches. This notion that the pattern of life designated at birth could be altered is carried in an Anglo-Saxon poem, *The Second Dialogue of Solomon and Saturn*, an anonymous manuscript preserved with the pages of *Beowulf*. It presents a dialogue purporting to be between the Biblical King Solomon and a prince named Saturn. Saturn asks which will be stronger, 'fated events or foresight', and Solomon explains that 'Fate is hard to alter . . . nevertheless an intelligent man can moderate all the things that fate causes, as long as he is clear in his mind and is prepared to seek help from his friends, and moreover enjoy the Holy Spirit.'

Nevertheless, the poetic imagery of spinning and weaving at the centre of so much of the ancient accounts and poems suggests that spell-casters were subject to the Wyrd Sisters. And the strong sense of 'woven' fabric as carrying the image of life-change means perhaps that when they did change aspects of people's lives, it was in harmony with their original life-design; the shape, colour, texture, pattern, theme and so on. It may have respected the integrity of a 'woven' design; the overall pattern of threads could be adapted, developed, re-arranged – so long as it honoured the basic theme with which it originated. So they were all, in a way, 'net-weavers'.

Certainly this concept of woven life was current in Anglo-Saxon

England, for *Beowulf* tells how 'to these men, the people of the Wederas, the Lord had granted that the web of their fate would be woven with victories'. And the special connection between the Anglo-Saxon concepts of weaving and the understanding of life is reflected by Tolkien in *The Lord of the Rings*. There, the Elves give Pippin and each of his companions a hood and cloak of the special cloth that the Elves have woven. It is a fine and lightweight material that shimmers different colours in the light. The leader of the Elves says that they do not call them magic, but that the web (meaning the weave of the cloth) is 'good'. He explains that everything that the Elves make has the love of everything they love put into it.

When babies were born in the historical Middle-earth, they came into the world supported by their webs of destiny, and their thread connections with all other people, creatures and spirits. This statement goes right to the heart of the vision of life in the real Middle-earth. It was woven. As each person encountered not only other people, but also animals, objects, ideas, feelings, events, dreams and nightmares – all were interlaced, folded in on each other, and inextricably linked as in a woven net. People did not experience life as being in a random universe, in which the events of the day, the year, a lifetime, unfolded without rhyme or reason. Nor did they see their lives as locked into inevitable cause-and-effect chains, in which one's actions had unavoidable consequences. Rather, it was the intricate linking between everything that was the very grounding of existence. A splendid crop, a safe childbirth, a happy event of love, and also the agonies of a plague, or the terrors of bandits and raids by competing warlords – all happened with 'reason'. Not human reason, stringing together causes and effects to understand 'why' something happened. Instead, it was a deep, unimaginably complex interaction of forces beyond our understanding – except by the sorcery of wizards and witches, and subject to the sanctions of the Wyrd Sisters.

16. The Seeress

The languages of Middle-earth teemed with terms for magic like Eskimo languages famously do for varieties of snow. Magic was a part of everyday life. Furthermore, this must have been the case throughout the period of the real Middle-earth, for the early Celts had numerous terms for magical practices, and as we have seen, the Vikings have left stories of shapeshifting, ghosts, and the conjuring of forces from beyond the material world.

In Anglo-Saxon alone, magic seems to have been so ubiquitious that it needed specialist terms to delineate fine distinctions between types of wizardry. From the limited corpus of Anglo-Saxon texts which have survived through the centuries, we have terms like 'scinn-lac', which meant magical action, and 'scinn-craeft' referred to magical skill. Both are derived from the word 'scinn', which connoted illusion and phantoms. 'Galdor-craeft' was the ability to use the secrets of chanting or singing to conjure the presence of spirit forces, or to cast a spell. It was literally, 'en-chanting'. Other terms such as 'wiccecraeft' translate directly into modern English as witchcraft, while 'wigle' and 'wiglung' were divination. 'Bealocraeft' was sorcery, and 'tungolcraeft' referred to skill in the reading of the stars. There were many more – other Anglo-Saxon words refer to such techniques of magic as speaking with the dead, making oneself invisible, casting runes and healing with power-plants.

This collection of words indicates that all these sorts of magic were known in Anglo-Saxon England and, probably, practised. However, translating these words today affords us a mere glimpse of their original impact. For people living amid these practices, terms delineating particular applications would bring also a rush of associations, induce many images, experiences, attitudes and prejudices, admiration and fear – even the names of known practitioners.

Germanic Seeresses

Among these words for magical skills is the intriguing 'burgrune' – derived from 'rune', meaning 'one skilled in mysteries', and 'burg' – any 'high place'. Practitioners who fulfilled these two qualities were diviners and seeresses: women who could see into the future. We know that such seeresses were highly valued all through the thousand years of Middle-earth. In the early centuries AD, when the Romans were seeking to extend military control into the tribes who lived north of the Rhine, they met their match. In the dense forests, the tribal peoples knew how to hide and use guerrilla tactics. Ambushes destroyed many a Roman incursion. And when the Roman generals sought to negotiate peace terms with the Germanic tribespeople, they were stunned to discover that they had to negotiate not with the chieftains – but with the seeresses!

The Roman historian Tacitus, writing in the first century AD, said of the Germans, 'They believe that there resides in women an element of holiness and a gift of prophecy.' Certain women were believed to be anointed, or born with the gift of being able to receive inspiration and information from the spirit world. Tacitus named some seeresses: 'In the reign of the Emperor Vespasian we saw Veleda long honoured by many Germans as a divinity; and even earlier they showed a similar reverence for Aurinaia and a number of others.' Roman chroniclers made references to other practitioners, including Ganna, a priestess of the Semnones, and another 'wise woman' of the Chatti tribe.

Veleda was a famed seeress of the tribe of the Bructeri in the Rhineland. She 'enjoyed extensive authority,' Tacitus writes, 'according to the ancient German custom which regards many women as endowed with prophetic powers, and as the superstition grows, attributes divinity to them'.

Veleda prophecied the outcome of battles. Her enormous popularity among the Germanic tribes rested especially on her foretelling of the unexpected destruction of the Roman legions in the German revolt of AD 69. And when the Romans wanted to agree peace terms with the Bructeri, it had to be done through Veleda. The representatives they sent were not allowed direct access to her. She remained isolated, sitting in a high tower constructed for the purpose of her prophecies:

> . . . any personal approach to Veleda or speech with her was for-
> bidden. This refusal to permit the envoys to see her was
> intended to enhance the aura of veneration that surrounded
> the prophetess. She remained immured in a high tower, one
> of her relatives being deputed for the purpose carried to her
> the questions and brought back the answers, as if he were the
> messenger of a god.

We are not told how Veleda arrived at her visions of foretelling – dreams, visions, casting runes, or by directly achieving a connection with spirit forces which knew more than she did, and imparted to her their information.

Celtic Seeresses

It seems likely that the name Veleda was more a title designating a seer, rather than a personal name. It is derived from *veles*, 'seer'. And in Ireland, the term for 'seer' was 'filidh', a word closely related linguistically to 'veleda'. This also suggests that these magical capa-bilities transcended tribal boundaries and applied also to the Celts. Among the Celts of Ireland, Wales and Brittany, at the beginning of the first millennium, the druids were elite mystics and learned men. Among them also, filidh was the term applied to those druids who specialized in divination.

The divination technique used by the filidh was referred to in manuscripts as 'imbas forosnai', which appears to have involved the sacrifice of an animal and the chewing of its flesh, with incantations. In the ancient Irish story the Tain bo Cuailnge, (Cattle-raid of Cooley), written down in the twelfth century but reckoned by some experts to be based on events in Ireland as far back as 500 BC, and preserved in oral form since then, we hear of a seeress called Fedelm. She claims to have the imbas forosnai. She appears in the story suddenly, standing on a moving chariot drawn by two black horses. She was a young woman, and she was armed. The text says that she was weaving lace, holding in her right hand a light weaving-rod of silvered bronze with seven strips of gold inlay. It then describes her fully:

> She had fair-golden hair, worn long in three braids, two wound around her head, the other hanging down almost to her calves. A many-spotted green cloak fastened around her and clasped at her bosom with a bulging, strong-headed pin of gold; she had a a red-embroidered hooded tunic and open-toed sandals with gold buckles. Her brow was broad, tapering to a narrow jaw, her eyes were blue-grey with a laughing aspect, and had triple irises. Dark and black were her eyebrows; her lashes cast shadows halfway down her snow-white cheeks. You would think her lips were inset with Parthian scarlet. Shiny and pearly were her teeth.

After this very full description, the story says that Medb spoke to her and asked her name.

'I am the prophetess Fedelm, from the Sid [the Fairy Mound] of Cruachan, a poetess of Connacht.' She had a melodious voice and attractive way of speaking.

'Where have you come from?' Medb asked.

'From Alba, after learning prophetic skill,' the girl answered.

'Have you the imbas forosnai, the Light of Foresight?' asked Medb.

'Yes I have,' the girl said, explaining that she was here to impart fortune-telling.

'Look, then, for me, how will my undertaking be?' asked Mebd, who had plans to gather an army to go into battle. The maiden looked. Then Medb said, 'Good. Now tell, O Fedelm, prophet-maid, how do you see our army?'

'Crimson-red from blood they are; I behold them bathed in red!'

'That is no true augury,' said Medb, unable to believe it. The prophetess confirmed three times what she had seen. But then she began to foretell the coming of the hero Cuchulain to the men of Erin, and, says the story, she 'chanted a lay', or spell.

While the story is reckoned to be very ancient, the version we have is presumably expressed in the more elaborated style that a thousand years of story-telling has engendered. The original version may have been simpler. Nevertheless, it is reasonable to suppose that the elements of the story are constant. Legendary tales retain their power to enchant because their themes transmit a perennial truth. And what this one tells us is that the woman may have been born with special qualities (triple irises), been trained (melodious voice, chanting a spell), had a way of 'looking' to see into the future, had received instruction in prophecy in Alba, and had status as a magician (she offers her professional services to Medb). She does not tailor her vision to suit Medb for she is confident of her powers.

Perhaps surprisingly, the story does not describe any preparation for the seeress to achieve her visions – she merely 'looks'. This may be because the people originally hearing the story would know what the ritual involved, or it may be that Fedelm was able to prophesy without elaborate activity.

Some cultures, especially in Siberia and South America, have survived into the twenty-first century with their magical traditions intact. The practitioners of these arts are usually called, by anthropologists, 'shamans'. They often prepare for their magical activities – such as healing and divination – by working themselves into a state of frenzy or ecstasy. These states of mind take them out of the limitations of their bodily identity and enable them, they believe, to journey to the spirit world in search of information, inspiration, and the lost souls of the sick. This approach was used originally by Celtic seers in the real Middle-earth. An author known now as Gerald of Wales, writing in the late twelfth century, describes a style of seership known as 'awenyddion'. Practitioners of this magic gave their visionary advice in a state of ecstatic trance:

> . . . they immediately go into a trance and lose control of their senses, as if they are possessed. They do not answer the question put to them in any logical way. Words stream from their mouths, incoherently and apparently meaningless and without any sense at all, but all the same well expressed: and if you listen carefully to what they say you will receive the solution to your problem. When it is all over, they will recover from their trance, as if they were ordinary people waking from a heavy sleep . . .

The magicians reported experiencing in their trance something being pressed against their lips. Sometimes it felt like something sweet. At other times it was more like a sheet of paper with writing on it –

presumably with the inspirational message coded there. The most common experience the magicians described was as if they were seeing visions in their dreams.

The listeners had to read into the messages for themselves, it seems. The words must have sounded, at worst, like gibberish, and at best a poetically-inspired stream of magical advice – presumably more often the latter, or the practice would have died out pretty quickly.

Fedelm, however, resembles another kind of seer, described in the Norse tradition. They were called 'thulr', which is often translated into modern English as 'sage'. In the *Havamal*, an ancient Icelandic poem, Odin is referred to as using this sort of magic. He is called 'fimbulthulr', meaning 'mighty sage'. This suggests that males could use it too, although Odin was famously reputed for being a male figure who unusually, and even notoriously, used techniques of magic more often reserved for females.

A term for this style of seer existed also in Old English as 'thyle', usually glossed in manuscripts as an 'orator'. This suggests that this type of seership is marked more by the style of delivery of the vision, rather than any complicated means to achieve it. The word is derived from the verb 'thyla', which means 'to chant', or 'to murmur'. Perhaps this is how Fedelm delivered her advice to Medb . . . in a kind of murmuring chant, in her melodious voice.

Norse Seeresses

Women seers thrived throughout the thousand years of Middle-earth culture, from the early Germanic peoples documented by Tacitus, to Celtic seeresses like Fedelm, right on to the end of that millennium. At this later date, we have an account of such a woman, one among many, we are told, in Norway. She is a character in a story, but one with such documentary detail that historians reckon that we can gain from it a reasonably accurate sense of how this magic was practised. The Icelandic *Eirik's Saga*, written in the late thirteenth or early fourteenth century, contains this vivid description. The saga depicts the lives of people in Greenland during the period of approximately 930–1030, but historians think it likely that the spellcraft documented in the tale was carried out in Norway in the tenth century and earlier. The protagonist is a seeress named Thorbiorg. She may have been a historical person on whom the story was based. In the account it is clear that she was widely renowned; we are told that she was nicknamed 'Little Sibyl'. She was known to be the last of a group of nine 'sisters', seeresses all, who journeyed around the country offering advice from the spirit world.

The saga describes a time of famine, and a land covered in snow. Winters were hard, and the preceding year had been one of critical food shortages. Men who had braved the icy waters to hunt seals and catch fish had often come back with very little. Some of them had not returned at all. So, late that winter, the leading farmer of the area, Thorkel, was given the responsibility of inviting a seeress to prophesy when the terrible famine would end. When she was due to arrive, most of the local community struggled through the snow to gather in his farmhouse to greet Thorbiorg and, 'A good reception was prepared for her, as was the custom when a woman of this kind should be received.'

Her appearance was dramatic. She wore a black lambskin hood lined with white cat-skin, a long cloak, and cat-skin gloves which were furry and white on the inside. On her feet she had shaggy calf-skin shoes, laced with long leather straps ending in big brass balls. She carried a tall staff adorned along its full length with brass, and topped with a brass knob surrounded by 'magical' stones.

Thorbiorg removed her cloak to reveal a blue tunic, fastened at the front by leather straps, and sparkling with precious stones all the way down to the hem. A necklace of glass pearls glowed at her neck. She had strapped a tinderbelt around her waist, and from it hung a large animal-skin pouch in which 'she kept the magical stones, feathers, implements and objects of her craft'.

She was greeted with great ceremony, and was served a specially prepared, ritual meal created from 'the hearts of all living creatures obtainable', along with a porridge of goats' milk. She ate the food with her own implements; a brass spoon and copper knife with a hilt of walrus teeth, clamped together by two rings around the handle. Afterwards, she explained that she needed to sleep in the house overnight before embarking on the seance. Preparations for the spirit seance were completed the following day, and by evening everything was ready, including a ritual 'high seat' topped by a cushion which had to be stuffed with hen feathers. At the appointed time, Thorkel took her by the hand and led her to her special seat.

Thorbiorg asked if there was anyone in the hall who could sing the necessary charm to summon the spirits. At first it appeared as if no one would know the necessary spells, because most of the people in the community had by this date been converted to Christianity, and spirit spells replaced by hymns. But a young woman called Gudrid knew. 'I am unversed in magic, nor am I a prophetess,' said Gudrid, 'but Halldis my foster-mother taught me in Iceland the chant which she called Varthlokur.'

'Then you are wise in good time,' said Thorbiorg.

Gudrid was reluctant to sing the charms: 'But this is a kind of proceeding I feel I can play no part in,' she protested, 'for I am a Christian woman.'

'Yet it might happen,' encouraged Thorbiorg, 'that you could prove helpful to folk in this affair, and still be no worse a woman than before. But it is Thorkel I must look to, to procure me the things I need.'

Thorkel, the host of the seance, persuaded Gudrid to help Thorbiorg. The women formed a circle around the platform on which Thorbiorg was seated, the men around the edge of the room. Gudrid sung the chant so beautifully and so well that 'no one who was present could say he had heard a chant recited by a lovelier voice'. The seeress thanked Gudrid for the song, said that it was sung well, and that now there are many matters open to my sight which before were hidden both from me and from others'.

When she was ready, Thorbiorg said that she was prepared to answer questions, for the answers had been given to her by the spirits. According to the saga, the farmer asked her about the outcome of the famine and accompanying plague. 'I can easily see many things that were previously hidden both from me and others. I may say that this year of dearth will not last longer than this winter; in the spring everything will be better. The plague, which has been raging for a long time, will cease sooner than you think.'

Then others asked about personal fortunes and misfortunes, possibilities, troubles, anything they wanted, and Thorbiorg answered all the questions. For example, in reply to one young woman who had enquired about her fate, Thorbiorg replied, 'I now see thy fate clearly. Here in Greenland thou shalt get that marriage which is the most honourable, although it will not be lengthy, for thy ways go to Iceland. And from thee will come a kindred which will be both great and good, and over thy descendants there will shine a bright light. But now, farewell, and good luck, my daughter.'

The saga manuscript says that she was most willing to impart information, and concludes with, '. . . and it was only a little that did not happen of what she said'.

The Women Diviners

The term used for Norse seeresses like Thorbiorg was 'spakona', meaning a woman with prophetic gifts. A more precise term for a woman practising divination was 'volva', usually translated 'seeress', and for this there is no masculine form. The divination rite in which the volva took part was known as 'seidr'. The etymology of the word seidr connects it with the large group of terms based on the Indo-European root *sed*: a seidr, then, was literally a seance; a 'sitting' to commune with the spirits.

Another of the ancient Norse stories was called *Norna-Gest*. It is one of a collection preserved in the fourteenth century *Flateyjarbook* (yearbook of Flatey Island, off the coast of Iceland) for which scribes spent two years copying and illuminating now lost editions of ancient sagas. The tale tells us that 'At that time wise women used to go about the land. They were called 'spae-wives' and they foretold people's futures. For this reason folk used to invite them to their houses and give them hospitality, and bestow gifts on them at parting.'

In Eirik's saga, Thorbiorg was said to be the last survivor of a company of nine women, and the sagas elsewhere present the seeresses going about in groups. Perhaps at an earlier time isolated seeresses were less common.

The practice of seidr magic was reserved for women only, and presided over by the goddesses Frigg and, especially, Freya. These closely related goddesses both appear at times as the beneficent goddess helping women and girls at the times of marriage and childbirth, as well as shaping the destiny of children. Freya's name is specifically linked by Snorri Sturluson to seidr, for he states that she was a priestess of the Vanir who first taught this knowledge to Odin.

The document called *Landnamabok* (Book of Settlements), was originally compiled by Ari the Learned in the first half of the twelfth century, and is the major historical source about the original settlement of Iceland. It tells of one volva who is said to have worked sorcery over a coastal inlet of water, causing it to fill with fish. The seeresses thus sometimes went beyond divination, in which they offered wise counsel concerning personal and worldly events. In addition, they mediated the power that created new life and brought increase into the fields, among the animals, and in the home – the kind of role usually ascribed to goddesses like Frigg.

Magical Implements and Rituals

Thorbiorg's seance used special objects of magical power, and ritual procedures to connect her with the spirit world.

The Pouch – The saga reports Thorbiorg as having a large animal-skin pouch, suspended from a tinderbelt around her waist. In the pouch 'she kept the magical stones, feathers, implements and objects of her craft'. Historians reckon that some of the ancient bodies recovered well-preserved from bogs were wizards who had sacrificed themselves to journey to the Otherworld on behalf of their community. Or perhaps they had been ritually executed when their magic went wrong.

Intriguing objects are sometimes found with the bodies. A bog burial over two thousand years old preserved a prehistoric medicine pouch, one of thirty such bags that have been found in Bronze Age Danish graves. These bags are therefore a thousand years earlier than that of Thorbiorg – contemporary with Veleda and other early seeresses – but the bag may have been similar in function to the pouch strapped to Thorbiorg's belt. The contents of one bag gives us an impression of the sorts of items wizards and seeresses, including Thorbiorg, might have been carrying. Inside the bag were extraordinary objects: a piece of amber bead, a small conch shell, a small cube of wood, a flint flake, a number of different dried roots, a piece of bark, the tail of a grass-snake, a falcon's claw, a small, slender pair of tweezers, a bronze knife in a leather case, a razor with a horse's-head handle, a small flint knife stitched into an intestine or bladder, a small, inch-and-a-half long leather case containing the lower jaw of a young squirrel, and a small bladder or intestine containing several small articles. The archaeologists recovering these materials concluded that the contents of the bag had been used for 'sorcery or witchcraft'. They were the tools of the trade of a magician, and had belonged to a medicine man.

Some of the tools were probably of immediate practical benefit; the 'slender pair of tweezers', for example, could be for making ritual objects, or for extracting injurious materials from the skin of a patient. The 'small flint knife' stitched, presumably for safety, into a bladder bag, could have many pragmatic purposes.

But the other objects are resonant of magical action. The piece of amber bead, for example, does not have an obvious practical use, but may have been part of the paraphernalia of a spell, and amber could have had properties important to a healer. The amber had been converted into a bead, with a hole drilled through it, so already prepared for some purpose or other; alternatively it may have been from the personal decoration of someone significant in the healer's life.

The small conch shell may have been used for listening to voices and advice from the spirits. The small cube of wood could have been from a tree of particular significance such as one tree struck by lightning, or with which the healer felt an affinity, and gained power from. Such a tree may have represented the World Tree, joining together the spiritual worlds of the Upperworld and the Lowerworld with the realm of everyday reality – Middle-earth. The piece of bark may have had a similar connection, and may indeed have been from the same tree as the cube of wood.

The various dried roots were presumably either for the power of their connection with the plants from which they were extracted, or may have had a direct benefit in being used to make drinks or potions, perhaps from scrapings of the root mixed with water or other substances.

The tail of the grass-snake, the falcon's claw, the horse's head handle on the razor, the lower jaw of the young squirrel; all of these could have symbolic referents. The World Tree, for example, was described in Norse literature as having a squirrel scurrying up and down its length, crossing between the worlds of Lowerworld, Middle-earth and Upperworld, exchanging insults between the bird of prey which stands on it highest branches, and the serpent which devours its root. These three objects could have been talismans of the World Tree, claws of the bird, tail of the squirrel, bark of the tree, all adding up to the calling card of a Middle-earth magician.

This is speculation, of course. But there are plenty of parallels when we remember Thorbiorg's bag is reported to have 'magical stones' (the amber bead), 'feathers' (relating to the falcon's claw), 'implements' (like the tweezers, flint flake and small flint knife) and 'objects of her craft' (perhaps corresponding with the World Tree objects outlined above).

The bronze knife in a leather case could have had simple practical usage, although it is intriguing to remember that Thorbiorg had a special copper knife with a hilt of walrus teeth. The saga account says that the point of the blade had been broken off, possibly in a different sort of ritual. In the *Lacnunga* medical manuscript, a short charm to protect against being 'shot' by invisible arrows from elves also requires the use of a knife with a yellow horn handle, and mounted with three brass nails. This implement, too, might be similar to the special knife with which Thorbiorg eats her ceremonial meal, with the walrus teeth representing the same defensive, weaponry function as the brass nails.

It could also be used for cutting runes. The making of runes seems to have been a magical process for healing, or for bringing benefits to people, animals, farmland and so on. But of course, the same power could also be used against people. In the *Grettis Saga*, an old woman called Thurid makes a cursing rune against Grettir in this way:

When they reached the shore she hobbled on by the sea as if directed to a spot where lay a great stump of a tree as large as a man could bear on his shoulder. She looked at it and bade them turn it over before her; the other side looked as if had been burned and smoothed. She had a small flat surface cut on its smooth side; then she took a knife, cut runes upon it, reddened them with her blood and muttered some spells over it. After that, she walked backwards against the sun round it, and spoke many potent words.

This paraphernalia, easily carried in a leather pouch attached to a belt, sums up the essential implements of the seeress. Working practically with deep intuition, making the realm of the inner imagination manifest for the purposes of healing or otherwise, was aided by manipulations with these special objects.

The pouch of magical implements seems to have been present in, presumably, a more amateur fashion among women in general – or at least, among those women in a community who were responsible for various healing and divination practices, even if they were less than fully fledged seeresses. Excavations at such places as West Stow, in Suffolk, England, have uncovered in women's graves small personal collections contained in pyxides, 'little cylindrical bronze boxes,' worn suspended from a woman's waist, containing items such as scraps of thread, cloth, herbs, and so on. These seem less likely to have practical applications than magical ones.

The Ritual Meal – When she arrived, Thorbiorg was served a special meal. Some translaters of the saga suggest that the meal included not goat's *milk*, but rather *colostrum*, a sustenance more concentrated than ordinary milk, full of antibodies as well as nutrients, secreted for a few days after birthing to fortify newborn mammals in the weakest phase of their lives. The colostrum of goats is yellow-orange, thick, and very strong-flavoured – nowadays people tend to recoil from it. Along with this drink, Thorbiorg takes as her meat the hearts of all animals in the vicinity. Her eating of the hearts of a variety of wild animals, using her own special implements, suggests that she needed to integrate their essence into herself in order to gain their strength and help in contacting the spirits. Tribal people often consider the heart a source of spirit strength, and it is sometimes eaten by hunters. By imparting animal power, the meal strengthens her for her ecstatic journey.

The Seeress's Staff – The ceremonial pole carried by Thorbiorg is similar to those common in surviving cultures in which the shaman carries a staff which is placed on the ground foot down, knob up, and represents the World Tree. These shamans were regarded as having the ability to traverse the various spiritual realms, and carrying a ceremonial pole was symbolic of these journeys. The fact that Thorbiorg's staff was decorated with brass all down the side, and ending with a brass knob adorned all round with magical stones, suggests that the brass decoration may depict the journey she makes to the spirit world. The 'magical stones' which decorate the top of the staff perhaps represent the worlds of knowledge of the Middle-earth cosmology.

As the symbol of journeying, or 'flying' to the spirit world, the staff also represents a means of flight, a symbol of spiritual transportation. Centuries later in the European female shamanic traditions, when the surviving practises were labelled as 'witchcraft', the witches were depicted as flying on staffs in the form of broomsticks, which for them represented spirit travel.

The High Seat – For her divinatory ceremony Thorbiorg was placed on a high seat or stool, and in the story of *Norna-Gest*, we hear how three women – 'described as spakonur, seeresses and as nornir – go from house to house and predict the future. When the women visit his house, Gest is a baby; two of the women predict that he will have fame and luck, but the third, after being pushed from her seat, becomes angry and declares that the boy will die when the candle beside him burns down.

Seidr divination rituals seem often to raise the seeress on to a high seat, probably representing her flight to the spirit world, or place her in an elevated position from which the spirits could find her, and she could receive visions of worlds beyond. The volva's journey to the spirit world was often depicted as being like flying as a bird, and Thorbiorg's high stool was topped by a pillow filled with hen feathers. Freya, the archetypal shamaness represented in Middle-earth by seeresses such as Thorbiorg, was reported by Snorri Sturluson to have a 'falcon coat' which was borrowed by a god called Loki to fly to Giantland. And Freya was able to adopt a 'feather' or 'falcon' shape – when she flew she shapeshifted into a bird and travelled vast distances.

Sometimes, as the volvas 'flew' to the spirit world by sending their souls out of their bodies, people would claim to have seen them, usually in the form of women with hair streaming out behind them. But it was a dangerous journey, because if the soul was wounded or killed on its travels in the spirit world, the body of the seeress showed corresponding wounds or even died.

Singing the Spirit Trance – In other, more fragmentary accounts of seidr rituals it is implied that the seeress obtained her knowledge while in a state of trance. She was said to 'gape', to fall down as though dead, to be roused with difficulty, to be utterly exhausted when the ceremony was over, and so on. And in some old Norse accounts of similar divinatory rituals, seeresses travelled with a number of singers trained in the incantations necessary for the spirit work. One lone seeress travelled to divinatory ceremonies with thirty trained singers, half men and half women, taking this trance-inducing and spirit-catching function to a sophisticated level. The effect of these chanters, performing in a farmhouse – trained singers able to exploit the potential of the human voice, in range and volume – would be overwhelming.

It seems that these singers may have had several functions. They could have created a sound meditation to help the seeress go into a trance. The songs themselves may have called the spirits, or even exerted some measure of control over them. And surely they would have made an impressive impact on the states of mind of the participants in the ceremony from the local community.

The singers accompanying shamanesses sang songs in a magical way. As with the shamans of more recently surviving cultures, the skill of drawing in the spirits depended upon pitching and rhythmically pulsating the air in a manner which enabled, catalysed the trance-entering of the seeress, and opened the doors of heaven for the entry of other forces.

While the shaman journeyed to the spirit world, the song also induced a receptive and appropriately creative state of consciousness in the audience, who after all were participants rather than mere observers. It was important that they were 'taken out of themselves' and that the audience became as one, literally and metaphorically 'in the spirit' of the occasion, in the beginnings of sacred intoxication, and therefore ready to receive the messages to be transmitted by the shaman.

While the rhythm of drumming or chanting might induce altered states of consciousness relevant to the rituals being carried out, the words of the chants also carried significance. The title of the spell-song required by Thorbiorg for her ceremony was Varthlokur, related to the Scottish dialect word 'warlock' (meaning wizard), and the meaning is thought to relate to the power to shut in or enclose. This might be interpreted in two ways: first, the song could attract and hold the helping spirits who enabled the volva to obtain the knowledge. Alternatively it could mean that the song had the power to arouse the volva from her state of trance and summon back her wandering soul from the spirit world, and return it to the enclosure of her body.

In Thorbiorg's ceremony, the song used was obviously generally known to elicit the spirits. But in all shamanic traditions, reference is made to songs which are unique to particular practitioners, and which sometimes play a part in their initiation. Certainly they have a quality different from melodic entertainment. A shaman from a Lapp culture in the Arctic, interviewed early in the twentieth century, described the way songs took him over, and how the words were induced by other forces: 'Songs are thoughts, sung out with the breath when people are moved by great forces and ordinary speech no longer suffices.'

In many cases, these songs are connected with the initial experience of spirits which occurs before initiation begins, and it is possible that Thorbiorg had at one time such a primary encounter. A Norse shamaness from the early twentieth century had such an experience. She was called Uvavnuk. Knud Rasmusson, an Arctic explorer of those years, heard the story of Uvavnuk's initiation. He reports that one evening she had gone out to pass water. It was a dark winter's evening, and suddenly a shining ball of fire showed in the sky. It came down to earth, directly toward the place where Uvavnuk sat. She wanted to run away, but before she could do so she was struck by the ball of fire. 'She became aware all at once that everything in her began to glow. She lost consciousness and from that moment on was a great summoner of the spirits. The spirit of the fire ball had taken up residence within her . . .'

Apparently, Uvavnuk went running into the house, half unconscious, and sang a song which since that time became her magic
formula whenever she was to help others. As soon as she began to
sing, she became delirious with joy, because the people she was
seeking to help became cleansed of all that burdened them. 'They
lifted up their arms and cast away everything connected with suspicion and malice. All these things one could blow away like a speck
of dust from the palm of the hand with this song.'

Perhaps the songs sung by Thorbiorg and her trained singers
were similar – songs that transcended the entrapment of everyday
'suspicion and malice', and instead induce a sense of love 'delirious
with joy'. This is indeed a healing state.

Divination

The gift of divination brought by the volva was a mysterious and
magical one, essential for an understanding of the forces at work in
the real Middle-earth. When Tolkien wrote about Gandalf and
Galadriel in *The Lord of the Rings*, he incorporated many of the
magical techniques which were used in the historical cultures of
early Celts, Anglo-Saxons and Norse. Tolkien describes Gandalf as
carrying a staff which was a potent magical implement, like that
of Thorbiorg. Also like the real Middle-earth seeress, he used song
with it. When he is accused by Wormtongue of being in league with
Galadriel, the 'sorceress of the Golden Wood', Gandalf sang a song
in homage to the wisdom of Galadriel. It is said that he sang softly,
and then suddenly changed and cast a spell with his staff which
caused a roll of thunder and put out the fires in the hall. Wormtongue
was angry, for he had counselled the Lord to forbid Gandalf's staff
from being brought into the hall.

And like Thorbiorg and Fedelm, Galadriel is described as seeming
young, and yet ageless. Her braided hair was still golden with no
streaks of grey, and she had a clear, smooth face and skin and shining,
grey eyes. But he is especially struck by how knowing was her glance,
as if she was deep in knowledge. Her appearance was magical too.
Like Thorbiorg and Fedelm, Tolkien describes Galadriel as wearing
a silver lace cap, threaded with white gemstones. She says of her

prophecies that they are things that may be – if not deflected from their path. She articulates a theory of compromise between fate and free will once more at least a millennium old. This is how seeresses like Thorbiorg practised their magic in the historical Middle-earth.

These seeresses and sorcerers span the thousand years of the Middle-earth culture, from the prophetess Veleda and other tribal seers in their high towers described by Tacitus, all the way to Thorbiorg on her platform in *Eirik's Saga*. Furthermore, the continuing presence of magical practitioners is confirmed through the testimony of Christian objectors. They specified punishment for people using diviners: 'Whoever employs diviners or predicters, and devilish talismans, and dreams, or herbs . . . if a cleric, let him do penance five years, if a layman, three years.' Clearly some people ostensibly baptized as Christian were still following the traditional ways of spirit of Middle-earth – but if they were caught, the process of 'doing penance' often included being allowed only bread and water to eat.

Theodore's Penitential, ch. 27, lays out even more serious punishment for 'Christians' who sought the advice of wizards: 'Those that consult divinations and use them in the pagan manner, or that permit people of that kind into their houses to seek some knowledge by the evil art, or for the sake of averting some omen, they, if clergy, shall be expelled [from the Church] . . .'

Sometimes the punishments were directed at the magicians: 'If anyone is a wizard, that is seeks to control someone's mind through the invoking of demons, let him do penance for five years, one on bread and water.'

These Church penitentials often bemoaned the widespread magical practices, because they seemed to gain their power of action from forces outside of the Christian concept of God. The wizards of Middle-earth and the priests of the new Christian religion both accepted that magic existed, but disputed the source of power behind that magic.

DWARVES, GIANTS
AND MONSTERS

17. Ents

The medieval streets of Cerne, a village about seven miles north of Dorchester, meander around the ruins of an abbey and an ancient church, fine old inns, and thatched yellowstone houses. It is a tranquil setting. But on the high hill just half a mile to the north of the village it is a different story. For seeming to stride straight out of the hill, brandishing a gnarled club gripped aggressively in his right hand, is the huge image of a naked, male giant. And aggression is not the only action he suggests: his enormous presence includes not only his height – 200 feet from the top of his club down to his feet – but also his erect phallus, which measures 30 feet! In ancient times people here had climbed the hill, and carved the giant's outline by cutting ditches into the grassy hillside, exposing the white chalk beneath. He has glowered over the village beneath for centuries since.

Actually, no one knows for sure the Cerne giant's origins. Some believe he may be only a few hundred years old – a sixteenth-century caricature of Oliver Cromwell, cut into the hillside by his critics. But many believe he may have been originally cut into the hillside at the start of the age of the real Middle-earth – in Celtic times, before the Romans came. They think he was a Celtic god who once clutched a severed head – a Celtic religious symbol which, they argue, is represented by a mound below the giant's left hand. Some writers speculate that he was created a little later, during the Roman occupation of Britain. In this case, he could be the god Helith or Hercules, ordered to be cut by the Emperor Commodus (who believed he was a reincarnation of Hercules) during his reign from AD 180 to 193. The figure does bear a resemblance to representations of Hercules – naked and wielding a club – discovered on Romano-British archaeological finds from Norfolk.

But the idea of the Cerne Abbas giant as the revered figure of a god, lovingly carved into the turf as an act of worship, strays far from the deep, abiding terror associated with the giants in Middle-earth. After all, they were beings who had the ability to crush a person easily in their grip, and tear humans limb from limb as the monster Grendel did in *Beowulf*. In his classic study of ancient Germanic mythology, Grimm derives 'eotan' from Gothic 'itan', to eat, and 'thyrs' from Gothic 'dry': these two words would thus signify creatures with an inordinate desire for eating and drinking. Their superhuman appetites could be satisfied, if Grendel is a model, by gorging on human flesh and blood.

More likely is that the giant was carved into the hillside to keep him under control. Perhaps it was to fix his 'real', mobile presence by a spell, paralysing his limbs from action by their bound image in the ground. This idea fits better with the legend that the giant had been terrorizing the local people. When he lay down on the hill to sleep, a posse of locals crept slowly up the hill, their footsteps drowned out by his thunderous snores. They gathered around him, and with a hundred spear strokes slew him where he lay. They then carved his outline into the turf – thus rendering the Cerne giant the oldest forensic chalk outline in history!

Giants were a species of being that cast huge shadows over the imagination of the people of Middle-earth. They were believed to be the first forms of life at the creation of the cosmos. They had seen how Middle-earth was constructed. They were possessed of elemental powers – and so were both terrifying and wise.

Ymir, the Melting Giant

According to the later Norse literature, people of Middle-earth believed that a cosmological cataclysm created the original spark of life. At the beginning of time 'there was nothing but the Yawning Gap', says Snorri Sturluson. He describes a state of suspended power in which, before the cosmos was formed, there were two immense polarities of fire and frost. *Muspellheim* was a region of pure heat and flame, raging, burning. *Niflheim*, freezing fog, was deep chill, locked, bound, creaking cold. These two mighty forces held each other in balance. The space between them was *Ginnungagap*, highly charged, explosive energy. The vision was like an ancient Norse version of the 'steady-state universe' theory of modern astrophysics, explaining the formation of our galaxy.

And then came the Big Bang. In one fateful instant, the two mighty polarities intersected. Fire and Frost exploded into each other's domain. In the Yawning Gap between the formerly separate realms, in Sturluson's words, '. . . where the freezing met the livid heat it melted and dripped away. From the fermenting drops fusing to life by virtue of the power which threw up the heat, there was shaped the likeness of a man. He is called Ymir.'

Ymir had emerged from the primeval hoar frost in human form. But although he took the form of a man, he was not human. He was huge, for the ice had melted into giants as big as mountains. Possibly they are ancestral memories of Ice Age glaciers – ice giants moving only a few feet each year, their immense footprints leaving tracks the size of valleys and gorges shaping the contours of the earth's skin.

But the concept was even bigger than this. For out of the material being of this first giant was formed the entire world as we know it. Sturluson quotes from *Grimnismal*: 'Out of Ymir's flesh was the earth fashioned and from his gushing gore the seas; mountain tops from his bones, trees from his hair, heavenly sky from his skull. Then out of his brows the joyous gods built Middle-earth for the sons of men; and from his brains there burgeoned all the clouds.'

Today cosmologists say we are all composed of stardust which came from a big bang – or the detritus of space for the less romantically inclined! The elements which comprise our bodies – like iron or oxygen – were all forged in the burning cores of distant suns, before being catapulted across space by the tremendous impact of stellar explosions. The ancient figure of Ymir was the image which connects these celestial realms with our earthly bodies.

As the earth was created other human forms appeared, some as people, others giant-sized. One of the humans was Buri, who had a son called Bor. A giant called Bolthor had a daughter named Bestla. Bor and Bestla had a child. This child was Odin. So the giants came before the gods.

The giants were slow-witted, but had knowledge. Cleverer beings, like dwarves and humans, have come along since and *elaborated* the world, but the basic structure and dynamics of life were in the hands of the giants. They retained a kind of brute wisdom; knowledge from the beginning. It is intriguing to imagine this wisdom residing within the primeval forces of the cosmos – not in our minds, not in our libraries, our scientific laboratories, or our computer banks. Truth not in *our* hands, but in the earth's forces. *Out* there, in the dynamic waters of creation, condensed in deep pools of wisdom.

Ents, Orcs and Thyrs

In Anglo-Saxon, there are many different words depicting various sorts of giant. Some of them have terrifying aspects. 'Fifel' is a term applied to Grendel in *Beowulf*, and so must have indicated a large monster. Other terms represent giants occurring in watery places, such as Thyrs, a 'spectre' 'that shall dwell in the fen'. Thyrs giants occured in place names elsewere too, as in Thursford in Norfolk, and Thyrspittes in Lincolnshire.

The form orc-thyrs is also found, the prefix showing the connection with the Lowerworld, for orcs were demons emanating from the realm of the dead. An Anglo-Saxon note written on a manuscript in Latin glosses 'orcus' as meaning 'orc, giant or demon of hell'. It is from this name that Tolkien conjured his 'orcs', which he treated in his tales as the perpetual enemy, to be slain in great numbers.

In Anglo-Saxon, many giants were referred to as 'ents'. In size they ranged from the immense ice-giants, the first beings after the formation of the cosmos, down to smaller ents which stood like mighty oaks, rooted to the ground but with their heads in the clouds, like Tolkien's ent, Treebeard. Even these were of impressive presence. Treebeard is described in *The Lord of the Rings* as having eyes which seemed to have behind them aeons of memory.

Such giants were tall as huge oaks, feet splaying yards across the ground, heads sometimes ethereal-looking as they stuck up into the clouds. One story concerned a giant who had something in his eye that pricked him. It was making his eye water. He tried to get it out with his finger, but that was too bulky. So he took a sheaf of corn and with that he managed to remove the speck in his eye. Then he picked it up and examined it on the end of his finger. 'Why, it's a fir-cone!' he said. 'Who would have thought that a little thing like that could have hurt me so?'

The Old English word 'ent' carries the connotation of a fallen race of wise and faithful giants, whose passing was spoken of regretfully in the later Norse *Prose Edda* at the end of the age of Middle-earth.

An Anglo-Saxon text tells the story of a child giant. As she was walking in enormous bounds across the hills, she looked down and saw something moving. Bending to her knees, she picked up a ploughman with his ox and plough. Putting them in her lap, she watched with curiosity as they crawled and slipped about in panic. Finally she carried them to her mother, and asked, 'What kind of beetle can this be, mother, that I have found rooting up the ground in tiny furrows?'

The mother looked at the ploughman crawling in her daughter's palm. 'Put it away, child,' she said. 'We will have to leave this land one day, and they will live here instead.'

A sad story for the giants. A hopeful one for the people of Middle-earth.

According to the German folklorists the Grimm brothers, giants could be as good-natured as lambs. But when angered, they raged, thundered, uprooted trees, hurled rocks and squeezed water out of stones. In temper they stamped their huge feet on the ground with such force that their legs were buried up to the knees. Their very size, allied with their temper, made them volatile neighbours in Middle-earth. If provoked, the giants of legend could be very dangerous. Especially when they argued.

Elemental Rages

A giant like this appears at Wilmington in Sussex. He is another ancient giant cut into the turf to reveal his outline in the chalk below. To see his feet from heel to toe requires a person to swivel their head to take them in. His body stretches away up the hill, this time in simple outline – no facial features, nipples, ribs, or exciting features like club and penis, as in the Cerne figure – his head near the top, facing out over an impressive landscape into the distance.

He is even bigger than the Cerne giant – 226 feet from head to toe – and holds a staff in each hand. His feet are positioned as if walking towards the viewer – perhaps he is facing out from the doorway entrance to his home inside the hill.

In local legend the Wilmington giant had a counterpart at Firle Beacon, a hill about three miles away across the Cuckmere Valley. When the two giants quarrelled, they tore enormous boulders from the ground and began to hurl them at each other. Where the stones had been ripped away the holes caused the flint mines and quarries on Windover Hill to be formed. The Firle Giant eventually killed the Wilmington one by hurling his hammer at him, crushing his skull. Perhaps, like the Cerne giant, the outline of The Long Man of Wilmington, as he is called, marks his burial mound under the hill. It is a place where legend is manifested in the physical landscape.

In ancient Teutonic myth, giants and trolls were often personifications of natural elements in their most terrifying forms – in the later Norse literature, the giants and trolls were often responsible for the crashing rockfalls and cascading waterfalls, growls and roars in river chasms, for landslips, flashing lightning and rumbling thunderstorms. The awe-inspiring colours in the sky near the North Pole, called the Northern Lights, were reckoned to be caused by fire giants; and avalanches, glaciers, ice-caps, freezing seas and rivers by ice or frost giants. The elemental forces embodied by these ents constituted the very fabric of the world we inhabit.

Sometimes giants turned nasty and could be vicious towards people. Aegir and his wife Ran were violent Norse giants who lived in the sea. Their underground great hall glowed with gold objects plundered from wrecked trading boats. Ran stirred up the waves and lashed them against boats, and cast her vast net over the ocean, trying to ensnare every fisherman who dared venture out onto the grey swells of the sea.

Thor Challenges the Giants

The legends of the people of the historical Middle-earth captured the nature of this elemental wisdom of the giants. When the cosmos was formed, say the Norse tales, the giants were eventually pinned back in a huge, mountainous kingdom over the sea, and on the very edge of Middle-earth. From time to time they threatened to return and battle the gods, and overturn the forces of balance in the cosmos. The ancient Norse god Thor, who was called Thunor in Anglo-Saxon England, was as a huge, bushy-eyebrowed, red-bearded god of thunder. He wielded a mighty, magic-forged hammer as his weapon. It was called 'Moljnir', which meant 'The Destroyer'. When he threw it at his enemies, it never missed its mark. Afterwards it would return of its own accord to his hand. Many of the legends from the historical culture of Middle-earth feature Thor doing battle with the giants. His role was to keep the giants in their lands beyond the sea, and dissuade them from invading the realm of the gods.

At the very edge of the realm of Middle-earth, across the ocean, loomed Jotunheim, the land of the giants. It was one of the nine worlds of knowledge on the World Tree, constructed on an enormous scale, as befitted its residents. The landscape was dominated by towering forests, plunging rivers, vast caverns, soaring mountains and mind-boggling distances. The ancient Norse book of legends, the *Prose Edda*, recounts that one time when Thor went to Jotunheim, he and his companions saw soaring high above them a castle set in the middle of an open plain. Even though they pressed back the crowns of their heads onto the napes of their necks they still couldn't see its battlements.

Thor banged on the doors. 'I admit to my hall only those who are masters of some trial' boomed an immense giant from inside. He peered through a crack in the door, saw Thor, and his lips curled into a sneer. 'What can a puny individual like you hope to achieve against my giant warriors?' Thor was big, but seemed a dwarf next to the giants.

Thor could not resist such a challenge, though he knew he would be up against it. His brow furrowed in thought for a moment, trying to find a challenge he dared issue against these enormous beings. 'There is no one in your Hall can eat faster than I!' he retorted, pulling himself up to his full height. At full stretch, he almost reached the kneecap of the giant.

Chuckling, the giant admitted Thor to his hall. The giants gathered round to watch the sport. They called for an immense trencher of meat to be brought in. Thor sat down at one end, a giant

warrior at the other, and they both ate as fast as they could. Thor
crammed the meat into his mouth and swallowed without chewing.
The two met face-to-face in the middle of the trencher and Thor
thought he had at least matched the giant in the contest. But then
he saw that while he had left only the bones of his meat, the giant
had eaten all his meat, bones and his side of the trencher as well.
Thor had lost the contest.

Thor was fighting mad. Heroically, though some would say
foolhardily, he challenged any giant in the hall to a drinking contest.
This he was really good at and fancied his chances. The giants
stopped laughing long enough to drag out an enormous ale-horn,
filled it, and challenged Thor to empty it. He put it to his lips and
took three immense draughts, until his eyes popped and he thought
he would explode. But the horn was not emptied. The giants were
helpless with mirth at Thor's efforts.

Thor stood up to them, his eyes blazing, feet astride: 'Now I am
really angry!' he shouted above the uproar. 'I will show you how
strong I am. I challenge any of you to a wrestling match.' When
he heard himself say this, Thor felt a slight twinge of doubt. But he
quickly conquered it. He had a mighty heart, full of optimism and
self-belief. He would try his utmost. As he pumped himself up as big
as possible, the giants seemed to be dithering over who should wrestle
with him. But then an old crone shuffled into the arena, and the
giants roared their approval; Thor would wrestle with her. He tried
to object, furious that the ents would impugn his dignity so. But as
he was remonstrating with them, the crone suddenly started grappling
with him. She was surprisingly strong, and although Thor tried with
all his strength, he could struggle only evenly with the old woman
and eventually she threw him to the ground.

Thor felt humiliated. Slowly he climbed to his feet, and crept
toward the door, his head hung in shame. But as he reached for the
latch, the Mighty Giant called him back.

'Wait! Noble One, had I known you were so powerful I would
have never admitted you to my hall, for I would have been afraid of
you.'

Thor thought the giant was mocking him, but when he turned
he saw that all the giants were regarding him with a new respect.
'How can that be?' he asked. 'I lost all three contests.'

'Yes,' said the giant, 'but you did not realize who it was you were contesting. You first competed for eating speed with Wildfire itself, which can consume entire forests at one sitting.' Thor took a step back into the hall. 'And the enormous drinking horn had been connected to the oceans, and in each of your three draughts, you managed to lower the level of the sea by one inch.' The giants were nodding their huge heads and smiling in approval.

'But the old crone?' said Thor. 'She threw me to the ground.' The mighty Giant laughed. 'She was your most formidable opponent. She who threw you to the ground was Old Age herself. She defeats us all eventually!'

To the people of Middle-earth, the giants were beings who understood elemental truths. They saw the unfolding of events against a timeless backdrop. Their questions were always big ones. For the people of Middle-earth, the giants reminded them that human life existed within a universe of immense forces.

18. The Dwarves' Forge

A great gold buckle, weighing nearly half a kilogram, was pulled from the burial mound during the excavations at Sutton Hoo. It had lain in the ground for over 1,300 years as part of the treasure hoard belonging to King Redwald. He died in AD 625, and historians reckon him to be the most likely chieftain to have been buried in that barrow. In life, the buckle, hollow with two sliding clasps at the back, may have been attached to a sword-belt strapped around his waist to hold the magnificent weapon also found in that hoard. Of course, a beautifully-crafted gold buckle would have been of enormous value, and undoubtedly worn for show. Along with Redwald's other riches, it was meant to impress the powerful warlords in his court. It reminded them of his pre-eminence and of the gifts he could bestow on his most loyal retainers. Also, princes visiting from other kingdoms would have been left in no doubt that Redwald was a mighty and wealthy chieftain. His gold radiated his presence and power, his luck and his charisma as a leader born to rule.

But the gold buckle transcended the psychology of boasting and status. In the Middle-earth of a thousand years ago, many of these pieces of artwork were much more than aesthetically pleasing artefacts – they carried subtle depths of meaning. Master gold and silversmiths locked into the design of much of the finest jewellery the secrets of the cosmos. And when King Redwald slid shut the catches on the great gold buckle, he fastened upon himself a defining image of Wyrd, the arbiter of his destiny, and that of his kingdom.

Jewellery

Of course, at all levels of society, people's hair, arms, fingers and clothes were often decorated with necklaces, brooches, pins, arm and finger rings made with a variety of metals and stones. Circular clasps to fasten cloaks at the neck or on the shoulder were crafted from gold, silver, with cheaper versions from bronze. Women wore ornate pins in their hair.

By the middle of the Middle-earth period, smiths making this jewellery used well-established methods. A Saxon craftsman, for his best work in gold and garnets, first hammered a baseplate of solid gold. He then lit his fire, and brazed or soldered gold wires to the baseplate to make a pattern of shallow holes. Into each hole he carefully fitted a piece of gold foil, and then a small piece of garnet. The roughened surface of the gold foil reflected light, making each tiny stone sparkle brilliantly in finger rings, necklaces, brooches and ornate hairpins.

For everyday jewellery, many pieces were made to the same pattern, but jewellery for the king and other nobles was usually custom-made to unique designs. And the smiths also worked on a larger scale, weaving metal fibres into pattern-welded swords, decorated shields and helmets with symbols which imbued the warrior with magical protection and powers. The work of these craftsmen was valuable, because it represented many hours of toil in the forge. A fine pattern-welded sword could have taken a team of smiths weeks or months to produce.

Most of the extensive collection of gold jewellery recovered from Redwald's burial mound is reckoned by experts to have been made in one workshop – perhaps even by one goldsmith. This master jeweller, presumably Redwald's chosen craftsman and renowned for his special skills, had laid strands of gold across the gold baseplate, and interwoven them. The interlaced design of strands covered the front of the buckle. The strands twined among each other, eventually terminating in the stylized curved beaks, claws and staring eyes of birds, snakes and dragons. The interlace is intricate, on a fine scale, and the surface of each thread is detailed with two parallel lines running along its length. The space between them is punctuated by dots. It looks uncannily like strands of DNA, the fundamental structure of life in modern molecular science.

All over ancient England, Scandinavia and western Europe, hundreds of such skilled smiths created these fantastic and intricate swirling thread designs. While fashions in jewellery evolved over the thousand years, these interlace features shared similar aspects to Anglo-Saxon, Scandinavian and Celtic jewellery.

Historians often talk about these designs, and the ways they changed over the centuries, as if they were simply evolving fashions. Today, essentially religious icons, like the Christian cross, are often reproduced as a conventional design for jewellery, as in gold necklaces. They are worn for personal ornament, and not necessarily for profound expression of sacred values. And at some level, the interlace designs of Middle-earth jewellery may also have been recognized as the conventional, and accepted, image of wyrd.

Except that, in times past, the very process of gold- and silversmithing was considered a magical process. Even iron had an almost supernatural status itself. It was harder than copper, tin or bronze, and had a lustre. Iron-forged objects were considered to be effective in counteracting malevolent spirits – the use of horseshoes over doors as a magnet for good luck, and iron nails as weapons against witchcraft continued in popular usage right into recent times. A charm for healing a horse of elfshot begins: 'If a horse be shot, then take that knife of which the haft shall be yellow ox's horn, and let three brazen nails be on it . . . If it be elves which are on him, may this be a cure for it.'

A figure called Weland featured in legends as a spirit who inspired the work of smiths – his smithcraft was considered the most advanced possible, and imbued with magic. When Beowulf boasts of the fine mail coat he is wearing, the lines of the poem have him say 'best of battle-shirts, it protects my breast – foremost of garments – it is Hrethel's legacy, Weland's work'. There is a prehistoric long barrow in Berkshire, situated on the Ridgeway not far from the White Horse of Uffington, which was named after this smith-spirit. It is called Wayland's Smithy. King Alfred refers to it, so we know that it extends back at least as far as Anglo-Saxon times.

The Dwarf-Smiths

The people of Middle-earth thought of the dwarves as living in the Lowerworld as magical smiths. In everyday life, it was the smith's 'power over fire', and especially the magic of metals, which gave them the reputation of a kind of sorcerer. It rendered them a special kind of power. They used heat to transmute elements of the earth into knives, swords, and beautiful jewellery. They created, and wove, fibres of beauty and strength in pattern-welded swords, and the fantastic and intricate swirling thread designs of Anglo-Saxon, Scandinavian and Celtic jewellery. Theirs was thread magic of a material kind.

The dwarves in the ancient stories of Snorri Sturluson's *Prose Edda*, were responsible for making magical objects for the gods and goddesses. The animal most sacred to Freya was the sow, and for Frey it was the boar. The dwarves made golden images of these animals on which the goddess and god rode. Freya's sow was called Hildisvin (Battle Pig) and Frey's boar was called Gullinbursti (Gold Bristled). These magical, golden animals could outrun any horse.

The dwarves also made Freya's famous necklace. There is no doubting the fame and fortune of the necklace itself. One of the various references to it is in the Anglo-Saxon poem *Beowulf*: 'Never under heaven have I heard of a finer prize among heroes since Hama carried off the Brising necklace to his bright city, that gold-cased jewel . . .' It was called the Necklace of the Brisings. Scholars debate the identity of 'the Brisings', but most reckon them to be four dwarfs of the Lowerworld. Dwarves were known for driving hard bargains for their magical smithwork, and to obtain the necklace, Freya slept with all four dwarves. As a result, most of the myths, stories and ceremonies which concerned Freya were either not written down at all, or were written but later destroyed because of the often erotic nature of her mysteries and myths, and were especially singled out for eradication by the monkish missionaries to the north. Even in normally tolerant Iceland, her poetry – the 'mansongr' (love song) – was prohibited.

The Old Norse 'brisingr', means fire, so the Brisings means fire-dwarves – referring either to their goldsmithing or to the fire they use in their work.

The necklace of the Brisings is much more than a pretty trinket. It gave Freya great powers. The object was said to be worn either as a belt or as a necklace, depending on how the goddess wished to use its power.

In their alchemical abilities as magical smiths, the dwarves focused on magical manipulations. For example, the myths tell a story about Alvis, a dwarf living in the World of Dark Elves. In a twelfth-century Norse poem he reveals some of his wisdom about the various realms of the universe. The name for night varies, he says, from one realm to another. The war gods, fertility gods and giants refer to it by its quality of a dark blanket (Darkness, Hood and Lightless respectively), and the elves call it Sleep's Soothing. The Dwarves, however, refer directly to the Magical Quality of Night, its use as a special, ritual time, its relation to their function as spinners of spells. They call it 'The Weaver of Dreams'.

Reflecting the deep level of their work, smiths were often regarded with awe, and treated as a version of wizards. Their power over fire was a kind of sorcery, because they were able to transmute elements of the earth into shapes of their own desire. The smith had a magic power peculiarly his own – a trait common in tribal societies where forging iron retains the mystery of a miraculous skill governed by taboo and mastered by an elite group of craftsmen. So crafting symbols of the underlying structure of life from gold – at the behest of the greatest kings and chieftains – was to make magic.

Interlace Design

So, common to Saxon, Celtic and Viking artwork throughout the thousand years of Middle-earth culture, were ornate and detailed designs like Redwald's gold buckle, in which lines of decoration twist and enmesh within each other to form an unbroken web of gold strings. The interwoven strands created a seemingly never-ending pattern. The interlaced patterns seem sinuous and organic. They embody the soft contours of nature, rather than the sharper angles of human engineering. But it is when the designs are studied closely, that we can see how the jewellery reflects the deeper dimensions of Middle-earth magic. The gossamer-threads of the silver and gold-formed knots appear impossible to unpick. A pull on any thread would surely produce an inevitable and complementary pull on another. The jewellery designs convey an impression of constant but controlled motion. The overriding impact is of tremendous vitality and energy contained within a finite universe. And this is where the jewellery design concurs with the earlier examples of the Middle-earth vision of life in weaving. The sensuous curves and interlaced folds of the jewellery designs parallel, like a microcosm, the every-day life of the people of Middle-earth. The designs seem to form an almighty web of veins and threads, so sensitive that in life, any movement, any thought, any happening no matter how small, would reverberate throughout the web. Their mutual interdependence ech-oes a vision of life in which all things are interconnected. And this is the fundamental meaning of the Anglo-Saxon concept of Wyrd, in which that which unfolds in life is the natural outcome of all that went before. As we have seen elsewhere in this book, the magic of the Middle-earth mind is in knowing that everything involves and implies everything else.

This view of life is deeper and more complex than our everyday experience of it. Our minds work much more like individual strands of these interwoven designs. We have an independent identity. In making our way through life, we are aware of many influences, barriers, forces, obstacles, but we cannot see it in all its complexity. And in Middle-earth, in daily life people must have done as we do – look for elements that are predictable and apparently logical. But even so, as the flow of events unfolded for each person with the minutiae of daily life, individual happenings must also have seemed capricious – even chaotic. Some things happen with no pattern, no theme, no rhyme or reason. But while this is perhaps how life could seem subjectively in the daily round, the concept of Wyrd underlay the belief that there was a logic to complex events, but it was beyond our capacity to perceive it. There were so many causes that no one but the spirits, and perhaps the Wyrd Sisters, could ever see them all at once. Individuals could follow individual threads, and observe where they crossed others. But there were too many to see the pattern formed by the web of threads. The wizard Gandalf says that even the wise could not see all ends. And in the real Middle-earth, this was exactly true of interlace jewellery. Redwald, when he wore his interlace gold buckle, showed that his presence as king was part of the natural flow of events in the cosmos.

19. Spellbinding

In AD 679 the young warrior Imma – a bodyguard for the Northumbrian King Egfrid – was badly wounded in the great battle of the River Trent. He was left on the battlefield as dead. He lay all that day and the next night among the bloody corpses. As dawn broke over the devastation, he roused himself back to wakefulness. Sitting up, and in pain, he bound his wounds as best he could. He rested from these exertions until he felt strong enough, then struggled to his feet, and staggered off to find any remnants of his army that might take care of him.

But soon he was discovered and captured by some of the enemy's army – those fighting for King Ethelred of Mercia. They took him before their leader, who was an earl in King Ethelred's court. The earl ordered his wounds to be dressed; and when he began to recover, to prevent his escaping, he ordered him to be bound. But as soon as the guards who bound him were gone, his bonds became loosened and fell off.

Imma's captors tried to bind him in chains, but they continually burst open. Alarmed, the Mercians dragged Imma before the earl, who immediately suspected sorcery. He demanded '...whether through witchcraft or through runes he brake his bonds?' Imma retorted that it was neither. He explained that his brother, who was an abbot, and believing Imma dead from his wounds sustained in the battle, was having masses said for his soul, '...the celebration whereof occasioned that none could bind him without his being immediately loosed again'.

It turned out that his brother was a monk called Tunna. Hearing that his brother had been killed in the fight, he had gone to the battlefield to find his body. He found another very like him in all respects and, concluding it to be his, he carried the same to his monastery, and buried it honourably, and had been taking care often to say masses for the absolution of his soul. These had resulted in the chains breaking.

The earl let him live, and sold him as a servant in London. All the way to London to deliver him to his new master, his guards tried to bind him with several sorts of bonds, but they repeatedly fell off. When they reached London, the buyer, perceiving that he could in no way be bound, gave him leave to ransom himself if he could. Imma took an oath that he would either return, or send him the money for his ransom. He raised the money through well-placed friends, bought his freedom, and eventually returned home to Northumbria. And thanked his brother!

Bede reported this story in his *Ecclesiastical History of England* in order to present the power of prayer as a rival to the indigenous magic of Middle-earth. Here it shows just how accepted these remarkable sorts of events were.

This sort of magic was reflected in *The Lord of the Rings*, when the elf Legolas exclaimed his amazement when a tightly-bound prisoner was able to escape from the orcs and horsemen. Even stranger was the fact that the prisoner, having escaped, then stopped to cut his bonds from his legs. Yet if his legs had been tied up, puzzled Legolas, how could he have used the knife to cut his bonds at all? His companion Gimli concludes that the prisoner's escape from being bound was sorcery.

Such spellbinding in the historical Middle-earth was a practical matter. Wizards cast spells on people by placing or releasing magical bonds which held them fast – literally spellbound. And like the wizards for whom he was the deity, Odin had spells which spun people's threads into knots, so that the interwoven forces of life became stuck. The knots shackled the mind, and paralysed movement, thought and will. These spells rendered his enemies helpless in battle.

Ancient stone carvings surviving in Sweden today show Odin beside his spell-bond – three interlinked triangles, forming a kind of knot. Symbols representing Odin's knots are also found on cremation urns from early cemeteries in East Anglia, along with figures of the horse and the wolf.

Wargs – Wolves of the Otherworld

A story of a wolf from the Norse myths, at the end of the Middle-earth period, tells us a lot about the magic of spellbinding, and the nature of the interlace threads which represent the complexity of Wyrd. Where did the story come from? The answer is the Otherworld journeys of wizards.

In magical ceremonies and sacred trances, they went to the realm of spirits, and returned with secrets, mysteries and healing remedies. The stories depict happenings in the realms of the Upperworld and Lowerworld, and in those regions at the edge of Middle-earth, like the lands of the giants. These are the worlds which were discovered by Odin, when he journeyed in the World Tree on his magic horse Sleipnir. These are deep stories. Like myths, their meaning reaches into the archetypal regions of people's psyches. They represent wisdom from the spirits, and from the ancestors.

Binding the Wolf

In Middle-earth, one such story that was told about binding spells and the threads of wyrd was recorded by Snorri Sturluson. He was writing 200 years or more after the end of Middle-earth, and historians reckon he had access to written documents that are long since lost. Also he knew a raft of folk tales and oral lore which had been passed down the ten generations or so since Christianity finally reached Iceland in the year AD 1000. His stories are possibly therefore more literary than the originals – although we should also remember the tremendous elaboration of the Anglo-Saxon poem, *Beowulf*, which may have been composed as early as the eighth century. This story reveals a lot about the magic of being spellbound.

In the legends of historical Middle-earth, a story was told about a great wolf called Fenrir, who represented all the forces of chaos. Not at first, though. He began life as a beautiful and cuddly cub, and three of the gods adopted him. Their identities alter between versions of the story, but usually they were Thor, god of thunder and battler with the giants; Odin, god of magic and wisdom, as well as war; and Tyr, a very ancient sky-god.

They named the wolf Fenrir. Silver and sleek, he was an impressive pet, and the gods were proud of him. For a while, that is, while he was small. But then he began to grow – rapidly. The gods began to feel nervous around him. Then one day, the gods heard a fateful prophecy. It said that Fenrir's chaos would overwhelm all of civilization. In fact, his wildness would destroy the cosmos.

In a panic, the gods formed a plan to control the wolf. They commissioned a huge chain to be built, a very strong chain which they could wrap around the wolf, and fetter him to the rocks so that he would not be able to break free. They named the mighty chain Loeding. They played to the wolf's vanity by challenging him to be strong enough to try his strength against the chain. He agreed. Eagerly they wrapped the chain tightly around the wolf, banged the end spikes deeply into the rocks and secured it. But as soon as they stood back smugly, Fenrir strained against the fetter. It snapped. He had escaped from Loeding.

When the gods saw this, the blood drained from their faces. They knew they had to do something drastic. Immediately they commissioned a fetter twice as long, twice as thick, and twice as strong as the first one. They called it Dromi. The gods played on Fenrir's vanity again: 'Fenrir, if you could break this really big chain, you would be ever so famous. Your name would go down in history.' The wolf considered it. He reasoned to himself that although the fetter was very strong, he had grown in might since he had broken Loeding. And, he thought, one has to take risks in order to achieve real fame. He allowed the gods to place the enormous fetter around him.

When the chain was on, Fenrir snarled, shook himself, and banged the chain against the ground. Then, digging his feet hard into the ground to get a grip, he arched his back and strained against the mighty links. With an almighty explosion, the fetter burst. The pieces of metal shot far and wide into the sky, where they formed the stars. They twinkled prettily, but unfortunately for the gods, Fenrir had now escaped also from Dromi.

The gods were terrified. The still-growing wolf looked uncontrollable. Reluctantly, Odin decided they must journey to the Lowerworld to seek the help of the dwarves, magical smiths and weapon-makers who could, surely, forge an unbreakable chain. It was a humiliation for the mighty gods to so beg for dwarfish help, but there was no other course of action open to them. The gods explained to the dwarves what had happened, and begged them to make a fetter strong enough to hold the giant wolf. The dwarves drove a hard bargain. Eventually a deal was struck. They agreed to make a fetter that would stop Fenrir from rampaging through the heavens.

On the appointed day, the gods went back to collect their massive chain, the one that would really tie down the rapacious wolf once and for all. They were horrified by what they saw. The dwarves had made a chain that looked so flimsy it couldn't fetter a fly.

'Just a minute,' cautioned the dwarves. 'You don't yet know what this fetter is made of. It is a very special one. It is called Gleipnir.' Proudly they started to list the materials of their work: 'It's made up of six ingredients. One is the noise that a cat makes when it moves. The second is the bushy beard of a woman. The third is the growing roots of a mountain. The fourth is the breath of a fish. And the fifth is the spittle of a bird . . .' The gods were beside themselves with anger; so far the fetter contained nothing of any substance at all. None of these things existed. 'And the final thing is the sinews of a bear.' Which was actually the only material part of the whole chain. 'But what is the value of these ingredients?' bellowed the gods. 'Apart from the sinews of the bear, the ingredients are nothing at all!'

'Precisely!' retorted the dwarves. 'And that is what gives it its power. Plus our magic of course.' And then the truth dawned on the gods. The dwarves, renowned for their magic, had made a bond of spells. It was a magic fetter. 'Well,' said the gods reluctantly, 'we've paid for it, we'd better go back and try it on Fenrir.'

The gods took the fetter, which was as smooth and soft as a ribbon of silk, back to Fenrir. The enormous wolf was not impressed. 'It's so slight a cord that I would gain no fame by breaking it.' The gods' hearts sank. 'And anyway,' concluded Fenrir, who was quite an intelligent wolf, 'if it has been made by magic, guile and cunning, it's getting nowhere near my legs.' They tried all means of persuasion, to no avail. Finally, they said, 'Look, Fenrir, if we put this fetter on you and you cannot break out of it, we promise that we shall unwrap the chain and let you free immediately. Only a coward would refuse such a challenge.'

Fenrir's hackles rose, and his eyes glowered coldly. It was his weak point – a provocation he could not resist. 'Rather than be accused of cowardice by you three,' he snapped, 'I'll do it. But only on one condition: that one of you place his hand in my mouth as a pledge that your promise is made in good faith.' This cunning device put the gods in a bit of a bother. They knew that, if the fetter did bind Fenrir, they had no intention of keeping their promise to free him. But finally, one of them agreed to place his hand in the wolf's mouth.

Fenrir was surprised, but now felt obliged to go through with the bargain. Eyeing his teeth nervously, the gods settled the magic fetter around the enormous wolf, and scuttled back to a safe distance – the two who hadn't got their hands in his mouth, that is. Fenrir started pulling, tugging, digging his paws in, as he had done before with Loeding and Dromi, trying to tear the cord free of the ground or burst it asunder. It did not budge. He thrashed around, growling and howling, but the more fiercely he struggled, the more tightly bound he became. Soon he was completely fettered. The gods danced and laughed in relief. All except Tyr, who lost his hand!

Chaos and Spontaneity

In the historical Middle-earth there was a strong sense of the proper order of things, the balance of forces in life. The wolf was the creature which represented the threat to this natural order. He represented the forces of chaos, always shadowing the structured world of the gods like a hidden predator, looking for any chance to strike.

In the ancient stories of north-west Europe, another legendary character called Loki played the part of the trickster. He brought mischief and confusion into the Upperworld of the gods, and the Lowerworld of the dwarves. His exploits challenged, and threatened to turn upside down, the 'natural order' of things. There was nothing charming or amusing about Loki, as there sometimes is in trickster figures in other cultural traditions. Loki 're-ordered the cosmos' from time to time, and his actions often threatened to cause disharmony and destruction. He represented the forces of chaos, always shadowing the structured, interconnected world of the gods like a hidden threat, and looking for any chance to strike.

Now, Loki had three children, with a giantess called Angrboda. One child became the World Serpent; a second became the Queen of Lowerearth, a terrifying spirit-woman who presided over the darkest recesses of the realm of the dead. The third child was the wolf Fenrir. As an offspring of Loki, the wolf represented the always threatening forces of chaos, the potential destruction of order. Loki did go too far in his tricks when he contrived the death of Balder, one of the most loved Norse gods. On a surviving ancient cross at Kirkby Stephen in Cumbria, is carved the image of what happened to him when the other gods captured and fettered him in a cavern, while serpents fastened to the roof dripped venom onto his face.

But then, in the Norse myths, the day came when Fenrir *did* escape from the dwarves' fetters that bound him. At Andreas, on the Isle of Man, there survives a carved panel depicting Odin on this fateful day, his leg disappearing into the maw of a rampant Fenrir while he tries to defend himself with his spear. Fenrir's escape to freedom marked the end of the world. Absolute chaos ensued. The entire world fell to uproar and burned to the ground. And yet, says the myth, out of this devastated landcape, a new dawn arose. Life began anew. So perhaps pure chaos gave the power, the spark of life to a magic universe. It needed to be fettered to keep it from exploding out of control and becoming destructive. When the force of Fenrir did escape, there were devastating results for a time, but then life was reborn.

So in Middle-earth, as long as Fenrir was fettered, his potentially chaotic energy had within it dynamic elements of freedom, spontaneity and vitality. The very limitations made the escape from them more intense and potent. The people of Middle-earth felt themselves to be part of an interleaved set of forces, as represented symbolically on their jewellery. And like Fenrir, they found themselves at every moment in their lives to be constrained and limited by these many subtle, unseen bonds. Some of these restrictions on spontaneity and freedom were part and parcel of the nature of life – everyone was subject to these same forces which governed the turning of the stars, the journey through the sky of the sun and the moon. Other binding threads were personal to an individual's life, reflected the ways they had been spun at birth by the Wyrd Sisters. And yet others were part of people's own volition, restrictions not inevitable but placed on themselves. Everyone's lives were necessarily involved with fetters, like the dwarves magic fetters which bound Fenrir.

The fetters were all-encompassing. They restricted the ways in which people in Middle-earth were able to deal with issues. But as we have seen, Wyrd was not the same thing as unalterable fate. To shift the pattern, to change the world, made possible by the unbinding spells of wizards, sometimes required just the lightest and most subtle alteration, adjustment, or refinement to the way a person thought or acted.

Using Dwarfish Magic

The gods in this story enacted a scenario with which we are all familiar from time to time. They faced a problem which was potentially dangerous, and threatened to bring chaos to their lives. They attempted to shackle it by fighting strength with strength, fire with fire. They tried to 'nail down' the problem, the world.

But sometimes problems are more intractible than that. They do not go away, but like Fenrir they resist, and grow bigger. Panicked, the gods tried again with more of the same – same materials, the same approach. But the problem rose up and broke free with devastating effect.

The gods were using a non-magical path to problem-solving. To meet force with force, is sometimes like trying to bite our own teeth. In Middle-earth magic, to solve a problem required finding a way of revisioning the fibres, replacing threads around problems, using subtlety and insight.

The dwarves, magicians who could make wondrous jewellery and magical weapons, used intuitive and subtle approaches of great power. Rather than identifying the obvious obstacle and the ready-made remedy, they looked for underlying forces; the language of the threads. As with the powerful, magical fetter, the ingredients of such an approach are subtle, even inconsequential in themselves, but are very potent in combination. By engendering an awareness of all the subtle forces impinging on an issue, a fetter could be constructed which was more powerful and longer lasting than a more dramatic and obvious 'fix'.

Tolkien used a similar idea in *The Lord of the Rings*. In his account, when the elves got ready to cast-off in their small boats, among the goods stowed on board were coils of rope. They looked delicate yet strong, silky-smooth and grey. An elf said they were made of 'hithlain', which means a 'thread of mist'. They were like the mysterious and powerful ropes in the historical Middle-earth story, conjured by the dwarves.

In the Norse legend, because the gossamer, magical fetter which finally chained Fenrir down *looked* insubstantial at first sight, the gods almost rejected it. But the dwarves had created something which, while looking soft and unchallenging, nevertheless became tighter and tighter the more the wolf used his great strength to struggle against it. The dwarves realized that Fenrir could be fettered by wrapping him in something which used his strength against him, which tied him up as a result of, not in opposition to, his struggling. It was the language of fibres and threads, imagination and dwarfish magic.

In historical Middle-earth, wolves were certainly feared by lone travellers. Because they hunted and ate the same food as humans – from rabbits to deer – they seemed to occupy a particularly ominous presence in the minds of humans. Also, humans inhabited settlements carved out of cleared areas of the forest, whereas wolves lived in the thick of the forest itself. Threatening human food sources, they seemed to be the essence of wildness pressing in on the fragile civilization, maintained at considerable cost in such primitive times. Social outcasts – robbers and thieves – were known as 'wolves'. The threat posed by wolves pitched them beyond being simply material animals – they became abstract forces, malevolent, magical beings.

Tolkien reflected this in the *Lord of the Rings*, where Gandalf and his companions were attacked in the forest by a pack of wolves. They heard the wolves encircling them with their night howls, and glimpsed the gleaming eyes of the animals stalking them, getting closer. The enormous shadow shape of a wolf loomed, standing stock still and close by. He howled, calling his pack. Gandalf grew menacingly large. Brandishing a blazing branch from their fire, he marched towards the wolves. They backed off, and he flung the firestick at them.

Eventually the wolves came and attacked again. Gandalf and his company of hobbits fought them off again with swords and axes, killing many of them. But the next morning, no bodies could be found. Gandalf declared that it was as he had feared. These were were no ordinary pack of hunting wolves. They were Wargs, evil wolves, allies of the orcs, the terrible race of Middle-earth.

In the real Middle-earth, people experienced life as finely balanced between chaos and order. Spells which could bind, like the ones which fettered Fenrir were therefore considered to be powerful magic indeed.

20. The Spider Monster

Preserved in the British Library are the thousand-year-old vellum pages of the Anglo-Saxon *Lacnunga* manuscript. In there, carefully transcribed in a round hand, are some remarkable spells. They offer a glimpse into the initiation of wizards in the real Middle-earth, and how they came by their magical powers. They suggest that in the historical Middle-earth, apprentice wizards encountered a spider monster – but a monster with a positive agenda, for she had the function of taking a person to initiatory Otherworlds.

The *Lacnunga* is usually thought of by Anglo-Saxon historians as a tenth-century collection of medical remedies. And much of it is. But there are a number of entries which deal with a different order of material. They are not merely remedies for physically expressed ailments. Rather they are rituals and incantations for traversing the divide between the mundane world of material reality and the deeper realm of the spirits. They step over the boundary into the Other-world. One such spell in the *Lacnunga* describes a journey in which an apprentice wizard is taken from this world and tested in the Otherworld. In the ritual, supervised by a wizard, a spider creature appears, wraps the apprentice in its web, and flies on the apprentice's back to a place of initiation.

As the apprentice is in a fevered state, and therefore more open to the wizard begins to provide some structure for them. The entry is listed in the Spellbook as a 'Night Mare'. We shall see why!

The lines of the spell read, in modern translation:

> Here a spider-creature came stalking in.
> He had his bridle-web in his hand.
> He said that you were his steed,
> he laid his bonds on your neck.

Soon they began to set off from the land.
And as soon as they came off the land,
then their limbs began to cool.

Then the sister of the creature came stalking in
She made an end to it, and oaths she swore
that never this one the sick should harm
Nor him who could understand this charm
Or understand how this charm to sing.

Sickness and the Spirit World

It is not surprising to find such esoteric techniques of magic in a compendium of folk medicine. In all shamanic and magical cultures, through the ages, sickness was a gateway to wisdom. In the fevers of illness, the mind alters and visions of another reality became possible. Today we call these sometimes bizarre images, hallucinations, and tend to assume that the senses are disordered during such trance states, and that we mistakenly see and hear things in delirium that we know are not 'really there'. Magical cultures like Middle-earth take a different view. While they seek to heal the sick person, they believe that the gift of these fevered states is the ability to see things that are in another world, but which are not normally accessible to us. It was during these episodes that, in such cultures, certain people were chosen by the spirits to become shamans, healers, wise women and wizards. In shamanic traditions which have survived into the twentieth century, in Siberia and South America especially, accounts of illness as a prelude to inititation reveal that the illness was sometimes sudden and severe, but it could also be marked by a progressive change in demeanour and well-being, in which the future shaman becomes meditative, seeks solitude, sleeps a great deal, seems absent-minded, has prophetic dreams and even acute symptoms like seizures. Dreams and visions experienced during the throes of sickness were highly valued, especially fevers in which the patient would see 'other worlds'.

Of course, in the process of initiation these visions were not random. They were conditioned, shaped and driven by the structure imagination of the magical tradition. As the apprentice enters heated 'fever' body-mind realms, the images that spontaneously arise are 'interpreted, discussed, and empowered by the shaman'. So the apprentice shaman may be having experiences structured for him by the poetry of the shaman who sings of the visions, and narrates their action. After that, once someone has been allowed to see such things, as a shaman they are taught techniques for generating inner heat, and for entering the Otherworld at will. And it is in these states of consciousness that the *Lacnunga* spell's invisible threads of Wyrd manifest. They are visible in the wizard's vision.

Sometimes it took great courage, for journeying from the physical body into the Otherworld was a transforming experience in itself. Myths all over the world feature apprentice shamans being carried into the Otherworld by an animal spirit on its back, or holding him in its jaws, or 'swallowing' him to 'kill and resuscitate him'. The spirits come from every quarter – and speak through the shaman's voices.

Tolkien expressed the darkness of this sort of encounter in *The Lord of the Rings*. Shelob, a monstrous spider is associated with unpleasant darkness, and it is said that she weaved webs of shadow, and that she vomited darkness. She lived on men, elves and orcs. Her presence in Tolkien's story is quite horrific. Described as an evil thing in spider form, when she captured creatures, she curled her legs and arms around them. Such things happened to people in the real Middle-earth.

The Spider Spell

The spider incantation, even when rendered into modern English, still retains some of the impressive imagery of its native Anglo-Saxon. It is a spell which tells the story, in highly condensed and coded form, of the journey of an apprentice to the Otherworld, the initiatory testing grounds for a man about to become a wizard. The lines are short, the clues small, and so we have to build up a possible context for this ritual from other things we know about Anglo-Saxon England, and from other cultures in which magical practitioners have survived into the more recent past.

As with the rest of the *Lacnunga*, this shamanic ritual was recorded by Christian monks or scribes, who were the only people in western Europe, before the first millennium, to use secular rather than sacred writing. The earlier Anglo-Saxon tribes depended on oral transmission of knowledge, and used the symbolic language of runes for healing and spellcasting, but not usually for the purposes of recording larger tracts of information.

It was a common activity for monastic scribes to copy out medical manuscripts from classical sources in Latin. But the document from which the initiation spell is taken was, unusually, recorded in the vernacular Anglo-Saxon. And since it was a record of pagan practice, the historians reckon that it was written by apprentice scribes rather than monks.

The preface to the lines of the spell is almost certainly Christianized, with the most blatant pre-Christian elements replaced with appropriate Christian terminology and ritual. It prescribes a preliminary ritual, saying, 'You must take seven little wafers, such as are used in worship, and write these names on each wafer . . .' and there then follows a list of Biblical names. This Christian introduction very likely replaces the carving of nine rune-sticks as an accompaniment, for the instruction then goes 'and then let a virgin go to him and hang it on his neck. And do so for three days.' The use of virgins was unlikely in a Christian ritual! And the number nine was the primary sacred number in rituals of the Germanic and some of the Celtic tribes of ancient Europe. Rune-writing was the carving of shapes and designs, according to set patterns, each of which carried a weight of symbolic meaning. And a number of them together formed a spell.

In the original pre-Christian version, then, the virgin brings to the person undergoing the ritual the rune-stave, cut with the appropriate runic message and then strung around the neck perhaps with a leather strap or piece of rope. The involvement of a virgin marks out the power of this ritual as *female* magic. Indeed, it is possible that the woman who performed the presentation of the rune sticks was more than a young female playing a subsidiary role in the ceremony. She may have been a shamaness, with the requirement for a 'virgin' being another Christian compromise interpolation.

In most cultures where this sort of ritual was practised, it would take place with some theatre. The wizard present might be in full regalia, an animal-skin cloak covering a tunic sewn with magical objects. The apprentice would wear around his neck the rune-stave, as he had been doing for three days. If the ritual paralleled at all the shamanic rituals of later cultures, he may have spent the time in a spirit-house, or a house decorated with symbolic objects to set up the ritual.

In order to achieve this journeying ability, shamans in recent tribal societies themselves 'engineered' their states of consciousness in a number of ways. Many of them consciously undermined the 'supports' which help us to maintain the everyday state of consensual reality. Most of us have experienced the disorienting effects of a lack of sleep from time to time. They, however, would systematically deprive themselves of sleep, staying up for extended numbers of hours all through the nights and days. They fasted, thus setting aside the confirming, relaxing, comforting and conventionalizing effect of eating regularly, calming hunger pangs and maintaining a high blood-sugar level. They went without drink, which soon releases the mind from the usual range of psychological states, and enables it to explore regions previously uncharted. These practices are suggested in Middle-earth literature, when the god Odin is described as fasting for nine days and nine nights on the World Tree, without food or drink.

The shamans also danced, marathon dances, so that the rhythmic bodily undulations and beatings of the feet on the floor attuned the mind-body to the rhythm of the spirits. They chanted and sang, shouted and called, intuiting the language of the spirits, and using their voices to take them into other realms. This practice echoes the rituals of the volvas like Thorbiorg described in Chapter 16.

Shamans also imbibed various concoctions prepared from selected plants to help to induce visions, glimpses of the other world, sensations of flying, and a number of supporting experiences which empowered their travel out of this mundane world.

In the spider spell, during the three days, the apprentice may also have been fasting, and drinking from a specially prepared brew which helped him in his visions. Mentioned elsewhere in Old English, the word 'lybcraeft' means 'skill in using healing drugs' with magical overtones, and its practitioners are the 'lyblaeca', or 'wizard', and 'lybbestre', or 'sorceress'. Perhaps the wizard gave the apprentice a plant concoction to drink, to speed the journey to the otherworld.

In many shamanic cultures, including those of the Norse, the shamans used drums to drive their journeying into the spirit world. Odin is accused of 'drumming in the cove' when practising seidr. Recent psychological research shows that listening to rhythmic percussion encourages brainwaves which override the propensity of the mind to wander and lose concentration. The drumming drives along the imagination, increases the flow of images, and perhaps even aids psychic sensitivity to messages from 'another realm'. Shamans can keep up a vivid spirit journey for hours at a time.

The spider creature's incantation was perhaps used in a setting in which a 'patient', or sick apprentice, was visited by a wizard who chanted the lines we have in the document. Throughout the time of Middle-earth, from the Celts to the Norse, the practical application of magic by voice implied a singing or chanting 'delivery'. The word indicating charm, incantation, or spell was 'galdor' meaning to sing or chant. It is based on the verb 'galan', to sing, from which we have the word 'nightingale', or night-singer. The use of the voice in chanting potent words in the right way was considered the heart of much spellcasting. Although 'spell' is a useful term for this and other techniques of summoning magical forces, in Old English it was more often used simply to mean 'speak' – as in our modern usage when we want someone to clarify a communication, we ask them to 'spell it out'. As time went on, the term became more specific to a magical context.

The instructions require the spider spell to be sung over the initiate three times, in either ear and above the head. Three times three is nine, a sacred number in the real Middle-earth. In indigenous cultures whose traditions have survived into the twenty-first century, healing and initiatory rituals are often carried out in public. When the spider spell was chanted, perhaps in a crowded fire-lit and smoky room, the effect would have been spellbinding.

Journey with the Spider Monster

The first lines of the chant are by the shaman to the patient, framing and setting up the apprentice's visions: 'Here a spider-creature came stalking in. He had his bridle – He said that you were his steed, he laid his bonds on your neck.'

Certainly in Tolkien's fictional account, the grip of Shelob is terrifying. He describes it as a soft, clinging grasp, but with a lot of strength. It felt, as the creature squeezed hard, as if it were pulling tight ropes around the victim. Shelob felt for the throat and then bit sharply into the shoulder.

In the Anglo-Saxon spell, harnessed by the bonds of the spider creature, the apprentice is about to be ridden. Now the shaman talks to the audience, describing the flight into the air of the apprentice spider: 'Soon they began to set off from the land. And as soon as they came off the land, then their limbs began to cool.'

And then came the initiation by the Wyrd Sisters: 'Then the sister of the creature came stalking in. She made an end to it, and oaths she swore that never this one the sick should harm, nor him who could obtain this charm or understand how this charm to sing.'

So the lines relate how the apprentice is 'captured' by one of the Three Sisters in spider form, wrapped in her fibres as a bridle, ridden into the sky and taken to a place where one of the other sisters proclaims that he cannot be harmed.

What Happens in the Spirit World?

The image of the spider, wrapping the initiate in a web and riding him into the sky, is awesome. But what is intriguing is what happens to the apprentice after he is delivered, bound by the web, to the place where the sister 'made an end to it', protects him, and shows him the secrets of the charm. The sister is perhaps one of the Wyrd sisters, representing all three of them, and the web is the very web of Wyrd.

Mythologies from all around the world depict the ascent to the sky by the shaman to be, along with other images, in a spider's web. A similar experience, in which the initiate can see the fibres and the other things which come with it, comes from the Australian shaman of the Yaralde tribe, who also have traditions closely paralleling Wyrd. This describes the initiatory terrors that accompany the vision of the spirits:

When you lie down to see the prescribed visions, and you do see them, do not be frightened, because they will be horrible ... If you get up you will not see these scenes, but when you lie down again, you will see them, unless you get too frightened. If you do, you will break the web threads on which these scenes are hung. If you see and hear these things without fear, you will never be frightened of anything.

The web of Wyrd holds visions which are gateways to spiritual insight and transcendence.

Even more revealing, the spider spell has remarkable affinities with a shamanic ritual from the Malekulan culture, a twentieth-century 'Stone-Age' tribal society in the New Hebrides. They are separated by thousands of miles of land and a thousand years of history, but comparative research on shamanism has shown similarities the world over in initiatory techniques and narratives which seem to persist across time as well as distance. This is not surprising, since shamanic rituals tap an archetypal level of human functioning – the fundamental way in which people encounter the world psychologically and psychically.

The narratives of the Malekulans can help us to gain an idea of how the full story of the experience undergone by the Anglo-Saxon shaman may have developed beyond the few lines afforded by the *Lacnunga* manuscript. The Malekulans have, at the centre of their shamanic initiation rituals, a labyrinth dance, in which the initiate must show that he is knowledgeable about the prescribed pattern of approach into a cave, wherein he is taught secrets. The dance is for men, and it is presided over by women, as goddesses of the labyrinth. The labyrinth is dedicated to the spider goddess Le-hev-hev, the spinner of fate who is also a 'Mother of Rebirth'.

For the Malekulans the newly 'dead' (apprentice shamans undergoing illness and ritual death), after being bodily abducted and taken into the sky by spider spirits, will arrive at a cave by the sea. There a labyrinth design is traced by Le-hev-hev on the sand at the entrance to the cave. On seeing the 'dead' person, the spider goddess obliterates half the design.

The apprentice has to show that he knows the pattern well, and dances the maze, completing the pattern in the sand. The guardian ghost of the cave, satisfied that the soul of the apprentice shaman knows its dance, releases the soul to join other ancestors in the depths of the cave, where it is taught great secrets known only to the dead. And then the soul is reborn, as the shaman, with knowledge, wisdom, magical powers and skills.

Dreams and Trances

This is speculative, but we may imagine the vivid visions of the spider spell entailing an apprentice gripped by a spider creature which rode him into the sky, cooling his heated body, landed him on an Otherworld island, where he perhaps performed a ritual akin to the Malekulans' dancing a pattern in the sand, thereby being admitted into the presence of the Spider Goddess, and then being given access to the secret knowledge of the dwarves. This scenario goes well beyond the lines of the spell, but suggests the sort of experience which may have befallen the Anglo-Saxon apprentice.

One name for the spider creature rendered into modern English is the Night Mare. Such images are not outside our own experience, therefore; almost everyone has at some point in their life experienced deep and disturbing dreams. So we all have the psychological capacity and the images to enter the world of the nightmare.

Our ancestors thought that such images, such journeys as were undertaken by the apprentice with the spider creature, were as *experientially* valid as everyday 'material world' activities. They were never regarded as 'just' dreaming. They were as important to the understanding of life and of ourselves as waking activity.

But dreaming is an involuntary entry into an image world akin to that of the spider creature, since most of us do not have direct control over the content and structure of our dreams. In cultures in which shamans functioned as 'dream doctors', which covers almost every traditional society which has ever been, their task was to set up for people, especially those who had been shown to be especially gifted in being able to enter the vivid world of the spirits, psychological settings in which entry to and return from such worlds was created specifically and consciously.

Today we generally regard such powerful experiences as being a by-product of brain 'over-activity' while we are trying to sleep – we have had a 'bad night'. In traditional societies however, including that of our ancestors in ancient Europe, such dreams were regarded as having special significance and value. They were an essential element of the range of human experience, and the images were seen as emanating from the deep, universal pool of the spirit world.

The nearest concept to this in the modern west is the collective unconscious. This idea was developed by the Swiss psychiatrist C. G. Jung during the first half of the twentieth century, in which he characterized some of our deeper dream and art images as being shared among all humans, and expressing certain propensities to see the world in ways which are a consequence of our biological and neurological nature. These deep dreamings are dipping into a shared pool of imagery which also inspired the magical consciousness of the real Middle-earth.

VOYAGE TO THE OTHERWORLD

21. Journey to the Edge of Middle-earth

I am sitting on top of King Redwald's burial mound. It was built by the Anglii people in around AD 650, at Sutton Hoo in Suffolk. This large, oval pile of earth covers one of the most famous graves in the world. The original vista from the top of the mound would have been breathtaking, and can still be glimpsed between the stand of trees planted in the nineteenth century. Beyond them, almost immediately below one end of the mound, the ground drops away steeply to the Deben river below – from where Redwald's ship and others would have sailed the short distance to the North Sea, and directly to what is now Denmark.

All around still, today, are the undulations of other mounds in this graveyard of kings and warriors. In the background are views across distant fields. This would be the last sight of the dead, about to embark on their final journey down the River Deben and out into the ocean, sailing to the edge of Middle-earth.

The Anglii tribe, like many in seventh-century Anglo-Saxon England, celebrated their great chiefs by interring them in coffins and then piling earth over them to make a great mound to identify the place. These burials were once the occasion of great rituals. Most historians reckon that the chieftain honoured in this mound was Redwald, buried with a full-sized, 90-foot long ship, and a great hoard of treasure. The site has been excavated by archaeologists, and the treasure removed to the British Museum. Redwald's body had completely disappeared by the time the mound was excavated. Experts reckon that the acid in the soil might well have disintegrated him within the first seven of the 1,300 years that the mound has existed. It is just possible, although highly unlikely, that the mound was built simply to house his valued belongings. It could also be that something else happened to his body – as would be the case if he had been lost at sea in a storm or a battle.

Archaeologists have estimated that originally the mounds would have been visible from the site of Ramsholt Church, four miles away – perhaps even from as far away as the Roman Saxon Shore fortress at Walton, formerly situated eight miles to the south on a cliff (now lost through coastal erosion).

So the mounds, now smaller as a result of weathering over the last 1,500 years, once stood high and dominant on the East-Anglian skyline. Visitors sailing the short distance upriver from the east coast to reach the king's stronghold would have seen, looming up on the right, these impressive tributes to the former chieftains of these tribes. Their substantial size, and the valuable nature of the buried treasure hoard, would certainly have impressed incomers to the kingdom with the earthly influence, mana and luck of the buried chieftains and, by extension, the whole tribe.

Kings were aware of the eternal glory emanating from having erected to their memory and their honour one of these barrows, as the mounds are called. In the Anglo-Saxon poem *Beowulf*, the hero lies mortally wounded from his battle with the dragon. In his dying speech, he instructs his warriors to have the greatest of them erect him a barrow: 'Bid the famed-in-battle build me a splendid mound on the headland after my pyre; it shall be a reminder to my people, rising high on Hronesnaesse, so that seafarers will call it Beowulf's Barrow.' The barrows seem to have served for generations to come as sites of honour and veneration of dead chiefs.

Burial Mounds in Britain

Burial mounds in Britain stretch back in time as far as Stonehenge. The earliest ones were long mounds, with ditches dug around them. Usually they contained a chamber of wood or stone that enclosed the body. Then around 2300 BC people – perhaps incomers from the Iberian peninsula – started building round barrows. These were constructed of an earth bank and surrounded by a ditch. They eventually replaced the long barrows, although archaeological evidence shows that people re-used the old barrows as well.

In the first millennium, the Celtic people of early Middle-earth used flat burials like in modern cemeteries until around the mid-sixth century, when people started burying their dead in the ancient burial mounds left by earlier civilizations, along with cremation burials. In the seventh century the building of mounds began again, like the ones at Sutton Hoo.

Historians have suggested that the reasons for the return of burial mounds may have been the evolving of more hierarchical kingship societies, rather than the small-scale tribal and extended-family settlements of earlier times. The impressive mounds mark the return of the big chiefs. There were also continuing influences from Scandinavia with later waves of settlers, and the tradition may have been transported from there.

There are many burial mounds still visible in England. In addition, we can identify the sites of former mounds by the evidence of place-names that have survived, or can be read in ancient documents. For example, in Derbyshire, the word 'hlaw', meaning mound, appears in placenames as '-low'. Over thirty of these can be shown to have been burial mounds. At least eleven of them have a personal name as the first element, identifying the person who was buried there – for example, Bassa at Baslow, Eatta at Atlow, Hucca at Hucklow and Tidi at Tidelow.

Some other names include Taplow in Buckinghamshire, which means Tappa's Mound – he was a warrior. There are many in Shropshire also, including Beslow, Longslow, Munslow, Onslow, Peplow, Purslow and Whittingslow and in Herefordshire, Wolferlow. All these appear to be named after individuals, probably chiefs of early Anglo-Saxon settlements in these regions.

The Anglo-Saxons practised two kinds of burial – either interring the body in a grave, or cremation, in which the body was burned, and the ashes buried in a pot. In either tradition, people in pre-Christian burials were often laid to rest with some selected personal effects, usually assumed to be used in the afterlife.

The nature of the objects buried with the individual seems to reflect the status of the person. Male burials sometimes included a spear, or spear with shield, sometimes neither. Such standard practice would reflect the status of warrior class and serf. The placing of swords with burials are rare. Perhaps these expensive weapons served as symbols of a more potent power and rank.

Between the sixth and seventh century, some Anglo-Saxons were cremated, while others were buried. The reason is still a mystery. Perhaps the differences in practice were to do with tribal customs stretching way back in history and reflecting differences in the gods being honoured. It may have been a choice of the person in their lifetime. Or it may reflect on the character or status of the person concerned in some way that we do not yet understand.

On the continent, the Romans tell us that the early Saxons cremated their tribal chieftains with specially designated kinds of wood – oak, beech, pine or juniper. So it was obviously a finely-tuned ritual. Cremation seems to presume that the afterlife could be reached without the physical body, although since the soul was believed to journey beyond the body in life, this is hardly surprising.

Redwald's Burial Mound

As the afternoon light begins to fade, the power of the Sutton Hoo looms larger. I feel some unease, sitting on King Redwald's mound. Some years ago it was opened for archaeological excavation, and then covered again. Today visitors to the site are ushered onto its surface for historical talks. But beneath me, the burial took place of a great king, amid much pomp and ceremony. And presuming that Redwald's body was inhumed in the part of the boat where the treasure hoard was located, he would have been directly beneath where I am sitting.

A light mist begins to creep up from the river. Energy forces all around. If the Anglii were here today, they would probably feel that Redwald's spirit could still be contacted on this mound. We know that these people assumed a continuing spirit, for we have accounts of their going to burial mounds and leaving offerings, in order to converse with the spirits of the dead. And as so often before, we know what rituals were being practised from the complaints and laws of the Christian authorities. Aelfric for example, railed that 'Still witches resort to heathen burial-sites with their evil rites, and call upon the devil, and he arrives in the form of the person who lies buried there as if he had arisen from death.' So Aelfric imagined a kind of ghost form for the person who has died, which came in response to the ceremonies, the evil rites – except that Aelfric believed it was not the person himself who had arisen from the dead, but only the devil impersonating him. Aelfric went on to explain that a witch could not bring about this appearance of a person from the dead, when he said, '... but she can not achieve that, that a dead person arise by her witchcraft'. When Aelfric says that the witch can manifest a figure from the burial mound, but not the real person, he is reserving for the Church the exclusive right to resurrection.

Seeking to speak with the dead at burial mounds was not only the preserve of witches. Ordinary people tried it too, at least towards the end of the Middle-earth period. One of the Icelandic sagas tells the story of a shepherd named Hallbjorn. He sought inspiration for his poetry by sitting, and then even sleeping on the mound where the poet Thorleif was buried. To make initial contact with his spirit, he started to compose a poem in Thorlief's honour. But Hallbjorn was overwhelmed by the emotion of what he was trying to achieve, and found it impossible to complete.

One night as Hallbjorn slept on the mound, he dreamed that the figure of a person came out of the mound, and showed him how to compose such a poem properly. As he came to wakefulness, he thought he glimpsed the figure re-entering the mound. The story reassures us that the poem he wrote as a result of 'the dream' was a successful one – as indeed was all the poetry he wrote after that.

Even the gods talked to the dead. In the *Ynglinga Saga*, Odin would '... wake up dead men from the earth, or sit down under men hanged' as ways of seeking knowledge. The sitting under hanged men perhaps refers not to burial mounds, but the practice of executing criminals at crossroads.

We also know that in Norse legend, Odin journeyed like a shaman to the Lowerworld to gain knowledge from seeresses who had died. A disturbing dream suggested bad omens regarding the fate of the god Balder. Odin rode to the Lowerworld to raise a seeress from the dead, in order to consult her about the meaning of the dreams: 'On Odin rode ... till he came to the lofty hall of Hel. Then Odin rode to its eastern gate, where he knew the Sibyl's barrow stood. He chanted the mighty spells that move the dead, till she rose all unwilling, and her corpse spake ...' This story also seems to indicate that the seeking of knowledge from dead people was not a mere mental process like meditation. It involved some sort of manifestation of a person, as if in ghost form.

Sometimes the corpse could not speak of its own accord. We have a report of a ritual for requiring a corpse to speak prior to burial. In another saga, the character Hading and his female companion Harthgrepa sought shelter for the night at a house, 'where they were celebrating in melancholy manner the funeral of the master, who had just died. Desiring to probe the will of the gods by magic, she inscribed most gruesome spells on wood and made Hading insert them under the corpse's tongue, which then, in a voice terrible to the ear, uttered these lines . . .' We do not know whether rune staves could be similarly inserted under the tongue of a ghost raised from the dead.

The relationship between the people and the dead spirits was not all one-way. The corpses still retained some sense of character. Sometimes they simply did not feel inclined or obligated to answer the call from the living. In 'The Waking of Angantyr', in the ancient collection of Norse poems called the *Elder Edda*, a character called Hervor summons her father Angantyr from his grave with this invocation: 'Angantyr, wake! Hervor calls you,/ Your only daughter whom you had by Tofa . . . / Hervard, Hjorward, hrani, awake!/ Hear me, all of you, under the tree-roots . . .'

This spell does not result in any response, and Hervor has a tantrum. She curses all of the spirits who are ignoring her: 'May ants shred you all to pieces,/ Dogs rend you; may you rot away.' She seems to damn their physical corpses to destruction as a way of insulting their spiritual beings. At this, Angantyr manifests before her, and tells her she is crazy: 'Your words are mad, without meaning to them.' Perhaps he is saying here that her damnation of the physical corpses is nonsense, and that she misunderstands the nature of their relationship.

Ship Funerals

When the people of the Anglii tribe constructed the large mound as a monument to King Redwald, they buried not only his body and a treasure hoard. Remarkably, they also interred with him in his honour an entire ship, complete with its 38 oars. Archaeological exploration revealed the impression the ship left in the soil of the mound. It was slender and elegant and nearly 90 feet in length. Historians presume that it must have been dragged up from the river below the hill, and moved on log rollers to its position in the mound.

This procedure seems to have a long history. From very early times in the north, ships have been associated with fertility and the cycle of birth, life and death. Bronze Age carvings have been found in Scandinavia depicting ship and horse in conjunction with the sun wheel, the prime source of life.

And in the Celtic tradition, the beautiful maids from the Land of Youth in the Irish legends often arrive in boats – the voyage over the water is remembered in Celtic tradition as an entry into the Other-world. So ship burials seem to symbolize the journey beyond death in this world, and entry into life in another.

Certainly they could be magical. In one of the stories, Skidbladnir was a marvellous ship made by the dwarves for the god Frey. It was golden, and large enough to hold all of the gods, fully armed. As soon as its sail was hoisted, a breeze sprang up and filled it, projecting the boat forward. But then, when no longer needed, Frey could dismantle the ship, fold it up and put it into a pocket.

Ship burial was widespread in the Nordic countries during the Viking Age and among the Anglo-Saxons in Britain. In Bronze and Iron Age peat-bog sites in Scandinavia, small model ships have been found. By about AD 600, the dead were buried in real boats that were lowered into the ground and, if the deceased was a king, accompanied by weapons, jewellery and various treasures.

Tolkien used this powerful image in *The Lord of the Rings*. Boromir was a powerful and dedicated warrior. He died in battle fighting Orcs, and in defending Merry and Pippin. He was given a full funeral, and his body was set afloat down Anduin, the greatest river of Tolkien's fictional Middle-earth. The characters Aragorn, Legolas and Gimil placed Boromir in the middle of the boat, his head resting on his folded cloak. Around him they laid his weapons, and beneath his feet the swords of his enemies. The funeral boat was towed out into the river behind another, and when they were in the swift running river they cast loose the funeral boat. It rode the whole river, over fall and rapids, and eventually took Boromir out into the Great Sea, at night and under a starry sky.

In the real Middle-earth, the dead may have been cremated on their ships. This happened in Snorri Sturluson's account in the *Prose Edda* story of Balder's funeral. He was burned on his ship, in the presence of all the gods. In fact, the burning of a ship may have been necessary to ensure a satisfactory outcome, for it could have been a macabre and somewhat anti-climactic ending to find the ship ground onto the beach at the next tide, or stuck in the reeds at the edge of a river.

Over the Edge of Middle-Earth

Why a ship? There are prosaic possibilities. Perhaps Redwald sailed often himself to the Danish shore, trading or fighting. Possibly ships were, along with treasure, the ultimate sign of wealth, and burying a whole ship was a symbol of Redwald's power. But the evidence below, following on from what we have just considered, suggests that the burying of a ship enabled the honoured deceased to undertake a journey after death.

The *Beowulf* poem relates such a ship burial. After loading the body of the 'beloved folk-king, lord of rings, the mighty one by the mast. There was much treasure, a fortune fetched from afar . . .' – just like Redwald. Then something different happened. 'There now they set up for him a golden sign, high over head, and let the waters bear him, gave all to garsecg . . . No man, whether the wise under the hall's roof, or heroes under the heavens', can know and truly say who received that lading.'

Garsecg is the ocean. But it is more than the sea as we know it. Anglo-Saxon cosmology featured a vision of Middle-earth ringed with garsecg. It was a waterway that marked the boundary between this world and the next. So this ocean went to infinity. The ship, whether that described in Beowulf, or belonging to Redwald at Sutton Hoo, was a means of voyaging out of this Middle-earth, and across the encircling waters of garsecg, the boundary between worlds.

The weapon of the Norse giants, Aegir and Ran, seems to have been a net, with which Ran would entrap seafarers. All waters had a presence, and a spirit, but the ocean in particular was powered by a personality which moved the people. We can see this in one of the many Anglo-Saxon riddles, in which the task of the listener was to guess what, or whom, is speaking. The lines of this riddle, originally written over a thousand years ago, translate into modern English as follows:

> Sometimes I plunge through the press of waves, surprising men, delving to the earth, the ocean bed. The waters ferment, seahorses foaming . . . The whale-mere roars, fiercely rages, waves beat upon the shore; stones and sand, seaweed and saltspray, are flung against the dunes when, wrestling far beneath the waves, I disturb the earth, the vast depths of the sea . . . Sometimes I swoop to whip up waves, rouse the water, drive the flint-grey rollers to the shore. Spuming crests crash against the cliff, dark precipice looming over deep water; a second tide, a sombre flood, follows the first; together they fret against the sheer face, the rocky coast. Then the ship is filled with the yells of sailors . . . Tell me my name.

The voice is that of Aegir, god of the sea, who is creating a storm. The lines portray the sea storming, a personality with attributes, actions, powers, and they leave it to us to name it. This act of water is seen as a force with vitality and a sacred name, rather than an abstract meteorological process, mapped and tracked on satellites and computer screens.

A folk-belief referred to in one of the Icelandic sagas suggests that when people were drowned, they were thought to have gone to Ran, and if they appeared at their own funeral feasts, it was a sign that she had given them a good welcome. In a late saga, *Fridhjof's Saga*, it is said to have been a lucky thing to have gold on one's person if lost at sea. The hero went so far as to distribute small pieces of gold among his men when they were caught in a storm, so they should not go empty-handed into Ran's hall if they were drowned. It may be that the gold in Redwald's tomb was not for use in the afterlife, but rather to ensure that he did indeed reach that next world.

The Return of Middle-Earth

As the sun sinks towards the west over the River Deben, shadows gradually creep from the woods and up onto the ancient funeral grounds of the East Angles. All around me, the grassy landscape swells with the large, ancient barrows entombing the bodies and prized belongings of historic kings and battle heroes from the real Middle-earth. It is like a symbol of the end of this remarkable era. A thousand years where, above the usual turmoil of tribal warfare and difficult times, the lives of people were enchanted by an advanced imagination. And there lay the deeper dimension to the ancient history of these times. The realms of the imagination made possible the insights of Middle-earth.

As a psychologist, I do of course value the welcome advantages of twenty-first-century science, engineering and medicine – and some would say that such a fantastical culture as that of ancient England is irrelevant to the imperatives of contemporary life. But sophistication comes in many forms. What I find so important, and such a revelation, is that Middle-earth, both Tolkien's epic fantasy and the real historical culture I am writing about here, sweep us away on seemingly essential journeys into our own imaginations. We are familiar with all of the ingredients of these people's imagined world – concepts like 'life-force' feature hugely in fantasy books and film entertainment like *Star Wars*. Our hunger for it is so all-embracing that we hardly note its strangeness. But we should be aware of the implications of the fact that, in the western world, we spend literally billions of dollars each year on 'leisure time' stories which reconnect us with the sense that there is a dimension beyond the pragmatic parameters of the material world. It is there that, while being absorbed by the vivid stories and visions, we encounter deep, timeless elements of our psyche.

And now, a thousand years after that era closed, Middle-earth is returning. The huge interest in fantasy literature and films inspired by those times shows that it never really left our minds. It just lay fallow, until it was needed again. And now is perhaps when we most need to once again recognize that beyond the bounty of our rational, scientific, engineered society, the forces of fantasy, intuition, and imagination may yield some deeper perspectives which could help us better understand our place in the world.

For thousands of years, people have been enthralled by essentially the same adventures, whether told by Stone-Age storytellers or cyber-age producers of feature films. The stories are so compelling because they emanate from dreams that animate the most ancient depths of our consciousness. Like all mythology, they are stories which capture the essential spirit of our lives, from all cultures. Often they came from the visions and dreams of people identified as wizards, sorcerers, shamans and seers – those in the community whose imaginations were believed to receive material from the spirit world. We are most disconnected, fragmented, exposed, frail when we are separated from the deep dream – the story of the earth's mind, the rhythm of its beating heart. It is the landscape of our deep imagination. And when we read about the real Middle-earth, we feel reconnected with ourselves.

Notes

1. The Real Middle-earth

There are now many editions of Tolkien's books. Most recent is J. R. R. Tolkien, *The Lord of the Rings* (London: Collins 2002; first published 1956). Tolkien maintained a full correspondence with readers who wrote asking him detailed questions about his work, and was invariably open and informative about the sources for his fiction. Many of the letters are collected in H. Carpenter (ed.), *The Letters of J. R. R. Tolkien* (London: Allen & Unwin 1981).

Introductions to what we know of the peoples of early north-west Europe include R. Collins, *Early Medieval Europe 300–1000* (Basingstoke: Palgrave, 2nd edn, 1999), J. M. Wallace-Hadrill, *The Barbarian West 400–1000* (Oxford: Blackwell, 1996) and H. Wolfram, *The Roman Empire and its Germanic Peoples*, T. Dunlop (trs.) (Berkeley: University of California Press, 1997) and with good illustrations is R. Rudgley, *Barbarians: Secrets of the Dark Ages* (London: Macmillan 2002). A readable and informative overview of the archaeology of the period is in M. Welch, *Anglo-Saxon England* (London: Batsford and English Heritage 1995). On the strong parallels between e.g. Celts and Anglo-Saxons, see the informed discusson of this point in R. Hutton, *The Pagan Religions of the Ancient British Isles* (Oxford: Blackwell 1990, especially chapter 7), and H. R. Ellis Davidson, *Myths and Symbols in Pagan Europe: Early Scandinavian and Celtic Religions* (Manchester University Press 1988). P. B. Ellis, *Celt and Saxon: The Struggle for Britain AD 410–937* (London: Constable 1993) provides a counterbalance to this new togetherness and a full account of the warfare between Saxons and Celts over the centuries.

Practical details of life in England at the close of the first millennium are engagingly detailed by R. Lacey and D. Danziger in *The Year 1000* (London: Little, Brown 1999) and reviewed in R. I. Page, *Life in Anglo-Saxon England* (London: B. T. Batsford 1970).

S. O. Glosecki, considers how early Anglo-Saxon societies fulfil the main characteristics of oral, tribal cultures in *Shamanism and Old English*

Poetry (New York: Garland 1989). The Worldwide Indigenous Science Network, funded by the Ford Foundation, researches the wisdom of surviving indigenous tribal cultures today. They have recently added a project to recover the ancient Anglo-Saxon tribal tradition. Their work is summarized at www.wisn.org.

There are now many renditions of Beowulf from the Anglo-Saxon into modern English, each offering a slightly different atmosphere and interpretation of the lines. The classical editions are by E. Dobbie, *Beowulf and Judith* (The Anglo-Saxon Poetic Records, 4: A Collective Edition, 6 vols, New York: Columbia University Press 1953) and R. K. Gordon (1926) republished as *Beowulf* (New York: Dover 1992), both of which read well. I like M. Alexander, *Beowulf* (Harmondsworth: Penguin, 1973). A recent translation by S. Heaney, *Beowulf* (London: Faber and Faber 1999) won the Whitbread Book of the Year Award.

The original 1000-year-old Anglo-Saxon medical manuscript is now in the British Library, where its reference is Harley 585. It is one of the central sources for this book. Provided below is a sample of references for those wishing to explore further. Discussions of the background to this document and translations of some of the materials came first in the classic work by T. O. Cockayne, *Leechdoms, Wortcunning and Starcraft of Early England* (Bristol: Thoemmes 2001, 3 vols; first published by Longman 1864–6). Cockayne gave the document the name 'Lacnunga', which is still used today. In the twentieth century came G. Storm's very good early treatment, *Anglo-Saxon Magic* (The Hague: Martinus Nijhoff 1948), analysis of the remedies by J. H. G. Grattan and C. Singer, *Anglo-Saxon Magic and Medicine* (Oxford University Press 1952); and W. Bonser's comprehensive volume *The Medical Background of Anglo-Saxon England* (London: Wellcome Historical Medical Library 1963). Anthropological perspective is in N. F. Barley, 'Anglo-Saxon Magico-Medicine', *Journal of the Anthropological Society of Oxford*, 3, 1972, pp.167–77, and a generally wider ancient medical context is by M. L. Cameron, 'Anglo-Saxon Medicine and Magic' in *Anglo-Saxon England* (17, Cambridge University Press 1990) and *Anglo-Saxon Medicine* (Cambridge University Press, 1993). The Lacnunga manuscript, encapsulating some of the most central 'magical' beliefs of the real Middle-earth has, in the last few years attracted renewed scholarly attention. Most recent editions are E. Pettit (ed.), *Anglo-Saxon Remedies, Charms and Prayers from British Library MS Harley 585* (Lewiston, NY: Edwin Mellen Press 2001); most accessible of all is S. Pollington's excellently informed and comprehensive volume *Leechcraft: Early English Charms, Plantlore and Healing* (Hockwold-cum-Wilton: Anglo-Saxon Books 2000).

For a scholarly introduction to runes, R. W. V. Elliott, *Runes* (Manchester University Press, 2nd edn, 1989). A. Bammesberger (ed.), *Old English Runes and Their Continental Background* (Heidelberg: Carl Winter University, 1991) provides a Europe-wide context for the development of runes. Modern esoteric interpretations of runes are in, e.g., E. Thorsson, *Runelore* (New York: Samuel Weiser, 1987).

M. Swanton, *Anglo-Saxon Prose* (London: Dent 1975) includes translations of Anglo-Saxon land charters.

Tacitus' account of the early Germanic peoples was written in about AD 98. It is available in modern translation in H. Mattingly (ed.) and S. A. Handford (trs.), *The Agricola and the Germania* (Harmondsworth: Penguin, revised edn, 1970). Cassius Dio's description of Boudicca is in vol. 8 (of 9) of *Dio's Roman History*, E. Carey (trs. 1925) and Strabo's description of the Celts is included in vol. 2 (of 8) *The Geography of Strabo*, H. L. Jones (trs.1923). Both sources are cited in A. Fraser, *Boadicea's Chariot, The Warrior Queens* (London: George Weidenfeld and Nicolson 1988).

Wulfstan is quoted in M. Swanton, *Anglo-Saxon Prose* (London: Dent, 1975) and a whole sermon is reported on pp. 116–25. More of Wulfstan's perspective is provided by D. Bethurum (ed.), *The Homilies of Wulfstan* (Oxford: Clarendon Press, 1957).

The central work of Snorri Sturluson is *The Prose Edda: Tales from the Norse Mythology*, there are various translations and I have used the one by J. I.Young (Berkeley: University of California Press, 1954). Some scholars used to suggest that this poetic vision of the Norse spiritual cosmos – written a little later in the thirteenth century than most of the material in this book – is too sophisticated to be used in conjunction with the less complete but cognate sources for ancient England and Germanic Europe. But, in cautioning against a literal interpolation of the later literature, these scholars have gone too far and, as is shown by Brian Branston and others, there are so many strong parallels between the Anglo-Saxon and the later Scandinavian material that over-caution takes us further from, rather than closer to, the truth. See B. Branston, *The Lost Gods of England* (London: Thames and Hudson 1984, especially pp. 45–55) and K. Crossley-Holland, *The Norse Myths* (London: Deutsch 1980 p. 133). A lively review of the saga literature is in M. Magnusson, *Iceland Saga* (London: The Bodley Head 1987).

The eventual full dialogue between the secular and rational age is explored comprehensively by Keith Thomas in *Religion and the Decline of Magic* (London: Blackwell, 1971).

2. The People of Middle-earth

Reviews of the tribal communities of early Europe are provided in R. Collins, *Early Medieval Europe 300–1000* (Basingstoke: Palgrave, 2nd edn, 1999), their military practices are in J. Laing, *Warriors of the Dark Ages* (Sutton 2000), and details of specific tribes are covered in some of the following books: on the Celts, see J. L. Bruneaux's analysis in *The Celtic Gauls: Gods, Rites and Sanctuaries* (Seaby 1988); archaeological background in B. Cunliffe, *The Ancient Celts* (Oxford University Press 1997); for an overview, M. Greene (ed.), *The Celtic World* (London: Routledge, 1991). Of the very many books which have considered aspects of the Celtic sacred tradition in detail, the most interesting include N. Tolstoy, *The Quest for Merlin* (London: Hamish Hamilton 1985), exploring the historical and legendary material on Merlin; J. Markale, *Women of the Celts* (Rochester, Vermont: Inner Traditions 1986), on the role of women as evidenced in lore and legend; J. Matthews, *Taliesin* (London: Aquarian 1991); on the Celtic poet Taliesin; A. and B. Rees, *Celtic Heritage: Ancient Tradition in Ireland and Wales* (London: Thames and Hudson 1961, reprinted 1994) is a masterly interpretation of the spiritual themes of mythology.

Introductions to the influences on early Britain is in A. Ross, *Pagan Celtic Britain* (London: Constable, revised edn, 1992) and R. Hutton, *Pagan Religions of the Ancient British Isles* (Oxford: Blackwell 1991), especially chapter 6 'The Imperial Synthesis AD 43–410'.

On the west Germanic peoples and Anglo-Saxons, the period from the departure of the Roman overlords up to the end of the first millennium is reviewed in J. Campbell (ed.), *The Anglo-Saxons* (Harmondsworth: Penguin, 1991). The background to the arrival and settlement of the tribal groups from mainland Europe is described in varying detail in almost all general introductions to Anglo-Saxon England. For readers interested in the transposition of tribal groups from the Continent into early England, and the nature of the early settlements, useful books for overall reviews include: N. Higham, *Rome, Britain and the Anglo-Saxons* (London: Seaby 1992); M. Todd, *The Early Germans* (Oxford, 1992); and M. Welch, *Anglo-Saxon England* (London: Batsford 1992). D. Hooke (ed.), *Anglo-Saxon Settlements* (Oxford: Basil Blackwell 1988) and J. N. L. Myres, *The English Settlements* (Oxford: The Clarendon Press 1985) consider the way communities developed. J. Hines (ed.), *The Anglo-Saxons from the Migration Period to the Eighth Century: An Ethnographic Perspective* (Woodbridge, 1997) provides for a range of essays on early culture. For the formation of kingdoms see T. Dickinson and D. Griffiths, *The Making of Kingdoms: Anglo-Saxon Studies in Archaeology and History* (Oxford, 1999, vol. 10). A classic source which is still fascinating reading, even though some of the material has been supplanted by more recent research, is H. M. Chadwick, *The Origin of the English Nation* (Cambridge University Press 1907). Introductions to the tribal cultures of the Huns and Goths are in P. Howarth, *Attila, King of the Huns* (London: Constable 1994), E. A. Thompson, *The Huns* (Oxford: Blackwell, revised edn, 1996) and P. Heather *The Goths* (Oxford: Blackwell 1996).

The Vikings are well covered in P. Cavill, *Vikings: Fear and Faith in Anglo-Saxon England* (London: HarperCollins, 2001) who considers their impact on Christian developments. E. Roesdahl, *The Vikings* (Harmondsworth: Penguin, revised edn, 1988) is useful for a general overview and H. R. Ellis Davidson, *Gods and Myths of Northern Europe* (Harmondsworth: Penguin, 1964) on the spiritual perspectives of the Norse. J. Graham-Campbell, *The Viking World* (London: Weidenfeld and Nicolson, revised edn, 1989) includes excellent illustrations of archaeological artefacts.

The nature of Anglo-Saxon kings, queens, and chieftans, is analysed in W. A. Chaney, *The Cult of Kingship in Anglo-Saxon England* (Manchester University Press, 1970).

On Bede, an introduction to his life and works is in P. Ward, *The Venerable Bede* (London: Geoffrey Chapman 1990). P. Hunter Blair, *The World of Bede* (Cambridge University Press, revised edn, 1990) considers the historical and cultural context in which Bede lived. An accessible edition of Bede's writing is *Bede, A History of the English Church and People*, L. Sherley-Price (trs.) (Harmondsworth: Penguin, 1968).

3. How They Lived?

Details of the replica Anglo-Saxon village at West Stow can be found in S. West's very readable and informative publication, *West Stow Revisited*, (St Edmondsbury Borough Council, 2001). The village, in West Stow Country Park, about 6 miles north-west of Bury St Edmunds, is open to the general public. A colourful account of the activities of an Anglo-Saxon village, in addition to the West Stow publications, is in R. Lacey and D. Danziger *The Year 1000* (London: Little Brown 1999).

King Ine's laws gave specificity to customs which had been in existence in Germanic tribal societies for a long time. See F. Stenton, *The Anglo-Saxon England* (Oxford University Press, 3rd edn, 1971), and chapter IX 'The Structure of Early English Society' for a clear and authoritative summary of the early law-givers, including Ine.

Tacitus' accounts of the society of the early Germans is in H. Mattingly (ed.), S. A. Handford (trs.), *Agricola and the Germania* (Harmondsworth: Penguin, revised edn, 1970). S. Schama gives an interesting consideration of Tacitus and other writers on the early Germans in *Landscape and Memory* (London: HarperCollins 1995, pp. 75–100).

Technical aspects of sword making and fighting are reviewed in S. Pollington, *The English Warrior from Earliest Times till 1066* (Hockwold-cum-Wilton: Anglo-Saxon Books 2001).

The ways in which the early Anglo-Saxon evolved into modern English is described in R. McCrum, R. MacNeil and W. Cran, *The Story of English* (London: Faber and Faber, 1992).

Techniques of food growth, preparation and cooking are detailed in A. Hagen, *A Handbook of Anglo-Saxon Food: Processing and Consumption* (Pinner: Anglo-Saxon Books, 1992) and in A. Hagen, *A Second Handbook of Anglo-Saxon Food and Drink: Production and Distribution* (Hockwold-cum-Wilton: Anglo-Saxon Books 1995). For gender roles see also C. E. Fell, *Women in Anglo-Saxon England*, (London 1984).

4. The Magic of the Forest

The age and significance of yew trees, including the tree called Ankerwyke, the burial at Taplow Court under a yew, and a gazeteer of ancient yews across Britain are in A. Chetan and D. Brueton, *The Sacred Yew* (Harmondsworth: Penguin 1994). Ancient oaks in Windsor Park are photographed beautifully in T. Pakenham *Meetings with Remarkable Trees* (London: Weidenfeld and Nicolson 1996).

The debate about the actual extent of forest cover is still going on. Earlier estimates of forest cover based on geological research were later reassessed more modestly, and now the pendulum is swinging back again as place-name research is identifying new areas of woodland. Forest cover had been cleared considerably by human use even early in the Middle-earth period, cf. O. Rackham, *Trees and Woodlands in the British Landscape* (London: 1990) and P. Marren, *Britain's Ancient Woodland* (London: 1990). But certainly, trees were still far more of a feature of the landscape – and of the human worldview – than in more recent centuries. D. Hill, *An Atlas of Anglo-Saxon England* (Oxford: Blackwell 1984) concludes, on p. 17, from the available evidence that 'there were then important forests in England, and that the country was more heavily wooded than in later periods'. For a more general survey of the natural landscape then, see also P. Dark, *The Environment of Britain in the First Millennium AD* (London: Bristol Classical

Press 2000). Details of the forest of Andresweald are in P. Brandon (ed.), *The South Saxons* (London: Phillimore 1978, pp. 138–59). The atmosphere and high aesthetics of forests and their significance for the early Germans is in S. Schama, *Landscape and Memory* (London: HarperCollins 1995). A fine analysis and review of forest management practice, the concept of barnstokkr, the relation between the words for 'tree' and 'trust', the magical powers of maiden ash trees and ash wands, the drawing of circles of protection, and the hag-riding of horses, are all in S. Pollington, *Leechcraft: Early English Charms, Plantlore and Healing* (Hockwold-cum-Wilton: Anglo-Saxon Books 2000), especially the section called 'Tree Lore', pp. 493–506.

Tolkien explains the source of Mirkwood and his strong feelings about the beauty of trees in his letters, in H. Carpenter, *The Letters of J. R. R. Tolkien* (London: Allen & Unwin 1981).

Banishments of indigenous Anglo-Saxon practice by the Christian authorities are reviewed in G. R. Owen, *Rites and Religions of the Anglo-Saxons* (Newton Abbot: 1981) and detailed in W. Bonser, *The Medical Background of Anglo-Saxon England* (London: Wellcome Historical Medical Library 1963, pp. 129–36), including the laws of King Cnut and the proclamations of St Eligius. Further details of the indigenous magical practices are in W. Bonser, 'The Significance of Colour in Ancient and Medieval Magic, with some Modern Comparisons' *Man*, XXV, 1925, pp. 194–8. For the objects used see A. L. Meaney, 'Anglo-Saxon Amulets and Curing Stones', *British Archaeological Reports*, British Series no. 96, 1981, and for the nature of the practitioners, see A. L. Meaney, 'Women, Witchcraft and Magic in Anglo-Saxon England' in S. G. Scragg (ed.), *Superstition and Popular Medicine in Anglo-Saxon England* (Manchester University Press, 1989). On the nature of magical ritual in general see S. J. Tambiah 'Form and Meaning of Magical Acts: A Point of View' in R. Horton (ed.), *Modes of Thought* (London: Faber 1973). S. O. Glosecki's analysis of the imaginal in Anglo-Saxon England shows how features of nature had many layers of significance in *Shamanism and Old English Poetry* (New York: Garland 1989). For the close relationship between the literal world and the imaginal 'Otherworld' see N. Tolstoy, *The Quest for Merlin* (London: Hamish Hamilton 1985, p. 162) and J. Markale, *Women of the Celts* (Rochester, Vermont: Inner Traditions 1986, pp. 194–5). On Pope Gregory and the general co-option of pagan rites by the Christian missionaries, see V. Flint, *The Rise of Magic in Medieval Europe* (Princeton University Press, 1991) and for Gregory's letter to Augustine see B. Colgrave and R. A. B. Mynors (ed. and trs.), *Bede's Ecclesiastical History of the English People* (Oxford: Clarendon Press 1969).

English place names are in K. Cameron, *English Place Names* (London:

Batsford, 1961) and in G. J. Copley, *English Place-Names and Their Origins*, (London: David & Charles 1971).

Descriptions of the Norse cosmos and creation are reviewed in H. R. Ellis Davidson *Myths and Symbols in Pagan Europe: Early Scandinavian and Celtic Religions* (Manchester University Press 1988). A Germanic culture analysis is provided in R. Metzner, *The Well of Remembrance* (Boston: Shambhala 1994, esp. pp. 192–211), and perspectives from the Norse tradition is in E. O. G. Turville-Petrie, *Myth and Religion of the North* (London: Weidenfeld and Nicolson, 1964). Vivid accounts are in B. Branston, *Gods of the North* (London: Thames and Hudson 1980) and M. Magnusson, *Hammer of the North* (London: Orbis 1976). Odin's vision of the structure of the cosmos in realms and worlds is described engagingly in K. Crossley-Holland, *The Norse Myths* (Harmondsworth: Penguin 1980, pp. 15–17). The Germanic world tree, called Irminsul, is discussed in P. G. Bauschatz, *The Well and the Tree: World and Time in Early Germanic Culture* (Amherst: University of Massachusetts Press 1982).

The shamanic perspective in Anglo-Saxon culture is reviewed by S. O. Glosecki *Shamanism and Old English Poetry* (New York: Garland 1989). The primary source for the Havamal is Snorri Sturluson, J. I. Young (trs.), *The Prose Edda: Tales from the Norse Mythology* (Berkeley: University of California Press, 1954, p. 40–6). N. Tolstoy, *The Quest for Merlin* (London: Hamish Hamilton 1985, p. 177); and B. Branston, *Gods of the North* (London: Thames and Hudson 1980, pp. 114–15) discuss the shamanic significance of Odin's by-name Ygg. The initiation experiences of shamans worldwide are described in M. Eliade, *Shamanism: Archaic Techniques of Ecstasy* (London: Routledge, 1964) – the Siberian example of scaling a birch tree as world tree is on p. 469. For the various kinds of landscape used for initiation around the world see J. Swan 'Sacred Places in Nature: One Tool in the Shaman's Medicine Bag', in G. Doore (ed.), *Shaman's Path* (Boston: Shambhala 1988, pp. 151–60). The importance of an extended imagination for the shamanic vision is considered in S. Greenwood, *Magic, Witchcraft and the Otherworld: An Anthropology* (Oxford: Berg 2000) and the role of imagery in M. Tucker, *Dreaming with Open Eyes: The Shamanic Spirit in Contemporary Art and Culture* (London: HarperCollins 1993). A review of the psychological states of mind typical of shamanic activity is in R. Walsh, *The Spirit of Shamanism* (Los Angeles: Tarcher 1990) and a range of essays introducing the shamanic perspective provided in S. Nicolson (ed.), *Shamanism: An Expanded View of Reality* (Wheaton, Illinois: The Theosophical Publishing House, 1987). For an attempt to illustrate the various visions of shamanic states of consciousness through artwork, costume, mask and ritual see J. Halifax, *Shaman: The Wounded Healer* (London: Thames and Hudson, 1982).

Odin's initiation journey took 'nine nights', but in mythological time it can seem much longer or shorter. A. and B. Rees, *Celtic Heritage: Ancient Tradition in Ireland and Wales* (London: Thames and Hudson 1961, reprinted 1994) has excellent discussions of mythological time. See M. Eliade, *Shamanism* (pp. 274–9) for a consideration of the shamanic significance of the number nine.

For early magical practice see R. Kieckheffer, *Magic in the Middle-Ages* (Cambridge University Press 1989), and for its embodiment in names of gods and other evidence see F. P. Magoun, 'On Some Survivals of Pagan Belief in Anglo-Saxon England' in *Harvard Theological Review* 1947. See also T. J. Csordas, 'Imaginal Performance and Memory in Ritual Healing', in C. Laderman and M. Roseman (eds), *The Performance of Healing* (London: Routledge 1996, pp. 91–114).

5. Towers of Doom

The desertion of Roman buildings in the south-east of Anglo-Saxon England are mentioned by J. Blair, 'Roman Remains' in M. Lapidge (ed.), *The Blackwell Encyclopaedia of Anglo-Saxon England* (Oxford: Blackwell 1999, pp. 396–8), in C. J. Arnold, *Roman Britain to Saxon England* (London: Croom Helm 1984) and in B. Branston, *The Lost Gods of England* (London: Thames and Hudson 1984, pp. 22). Recent archaeological analyses are reviewed by N. Faulkner in 'Decline and Fall', *British Archaeology*, 55, October 2000. For the high quality of Roman roads see C. Taylor, *Roads and Tracks of Britain* (London: 1979) and also D. Hooke, *The Anglo-Saxon Landscape: the Kingdom of the Hwicce* (Manchester University Press 1985). The abandoned Roman villa at Fawler is discussed by T. Shippey, *The Road to Middle-earth* (London: Harper Collins 1982). The historian's opinion that urban life is more sophisticated than rural is mentioned in H. Finberg, *The Formation of England 550–1042*, p. 75.

The significance of crossroads and 'spirit' in the landscape is considered by P. Devereux, *Haunted Land* (London: Piatkus 2001), and by N. Pennick and P. Devereux, *Lines on the Landscape* (London: Robert Hale 1989).

A discussion and diagram of the settlement and buildings of Yeavering is in H. R. Ellis Davidson, *The Lost Beliefs of Northern Europe* (London: Routledge 1993, pp. 22–4).

Early Germanic cultures on the Rhine are discussed in S. Schama,

Landscape and Memory (London: HarperCollins 1995). Our primary source for Nerthus and her procession is in Tacitus, H. Mattingly (ed.), S. A. Handford (trs.), *The Agricola and the Germania* (Harmondsworth: Penguin 1970). Other interesting accounts of the wagons and Nerthus' travels are included in P. Berger, *The Goddess Obscured* (London: Robert Hale 1988). A good introduction to the peat-bog finds is in H. R. Ellis Davidson, *Gods and Myths of Northern Europe* (Harmondsworth: Penguin 1964, pp. 95–6).

The nature of the Roman statues of gods and goddesses is discussed in A. Fraser, *Boadicea's Chariot: The Warrior Queens* (London: Weidenfeld and Nicolson 1988). The notion that 'gods and goddesses' in early Anglo-Saxon culture were more like nature spirits is in B. Griffiths, *Aspects of Anglo-Saxon Magic* (Hockwold-cum-Wilton: Anglo-Saxon Books 1996).

The poem 'The Ruin', probably about Bath, is included in many collections of Anglo-Saxon verse, including R. K. Gordon, *Anglo-Saxon Poetry* (London: Dent, revised edn, 1954, p. 84) and M. Alexander, *The Earlist English Poems* (Harmondsworth: Penguin 1966). The classic source for this and other Anglo-Saxon poems is still G. P. Krapp and E. Dobbie (eds), *The Anglo-Saxon Poetic Records*, 6 vols, which includes 'The Ruin' in vol. 3 *The Exeter Book*. (New York and London: Routledge 1931–53).

The concept of wyrd features in B. Bates, *The Way of Wyrd* (London: Century 1983), and is also considered in A. Stone, *Wyrd: Fate and Destiny in North European Paganism* (self-published, printed by Newark Chamber of Commerce, 1989).

6. The Dragon's Lair

The role of dragons as icons for kings is introduced in W. A. Chaney, *The Cult of Kingship in Anglo-Saxon England* (Manchester University Press 1970, pp. 127–30), and their nature as guardians of treasure hoards is reviewed in H. R. Ellis Davidson, 'The Hill of the Dragon: Anglo-Saxon Burial Mounds in Literature and Archaeology', *Folk-lore*, LXI, 1950, pp. 169–84. Other dragon references are reviewed by G. Speake, *Anglo-Saxon Animal Art and its Germanic Background* (Oxford: Clarendon Press 1980) and earlier by C. H. Whitman, 'The Old English Animal Names', *Anglia I*, XXX, 1907, pp. 389–90. Dragon place names are documented in D. Wilson, *Anglo-Saxon Paganism* (London: British Museum Publications 1992), in P. Drayton, 'Danelaw Gods – The Place-name Evidence: Exploring New Interpretations', *Mercian Mysteries*, August 1993, pp. 7–12, available online 2001 from the archive of B. Trubshaw (ed.) *At the Edge*, www.indigogroup.co.uk/edge, and in M. Gelling, 'Place-names and Anglo-Saxon Paganism', *University of*

Birmingham Historical Journal, 8, 1961–2, pp. 7–24. Dragon names in a more general context are in K. Cameron, *English Place Names* (London: Batsford 1961), C. M. Mathews, *Place Names of the English-Speaking World* (London: Weidenfeld and Nicolson 1972) and P. H. Reaney, *The Origin of English Place-Names* (London: Routledge 1960). For dragon legends, the Celtic dragon legend of Llud and Lefelys is in J. Gantz (trs.), *The Mabinogion* (Harmondsworth: Penguin 1976). The legendary background to dragons is covered in J. Hoult, *Dragons: Their History and Symbolism* (Glastonbury: Gothic Image 1987), B. Griffiths, *Meet the Dragon: An Introduction to Beowulf's Adversary* (Wymeswold: Heart of Albion Press 1996) and F. Huxley, *The Dragon* (London: Thames and Hudson 1979). The primary source for the world serpent is S. Sturluson, J. I. Young (trs.), *The Prose Edda: Tales from the Norse Mythology* (Berkeley: University of California Press, 1954, pp. 56 and 89). Chinese dragons and feng shui are discussed in P. Rawson and L. Legeza, *Tao: The Chinese Philosophy of Time and Change* (London: Thames and Hudson 1973) and N. Pennick *The Ancient Science of Geomancy* (London: Thames and Hudson 1979). By the end of the eighth century most villages had been formed. See H. Finberg, *The Formation of England: 550–1042* (1974). The land charter mentioning Grendel is translated by M. Swanton, *Anglo-Saxon Prose* (London: Dent 1975, p. 12). The nature of Grendel is considered in S. Newton, *The Origins of Beowulf and the Pre-Viking Kingdom of East Anglia* (Cambridge: D. S. Brewer 1993).

The significance of crossroads is considered in N. Pennick, *Earth Harmony* (London: Century 1987) and P. Devereux, *Earth Memory* (Slough: Quantum 1991).

Pennick, *Earth Harmony* (pp. 22–3) elucidates the importance of artistic language for describing the nuances of the 'physical' landscape. For how the spiritual landscape is embedded in our experience of the physical see B. Lopez, *Crossing Open Ground* (London: Macmillan 1988). The parallels between advanced scientific theory and mystical concepts and languages was introduced by F. Capra, *The Tao of Physics* (Berkeley: Shambhala 1975) and is the first book in what is now practically a genre. B. Lancaster, *Mind, Brain and Human Potential* (Shaftesbury: Element 1991) describes how the mind constructs what we presume to be an 'objective' external reality. Psychological geographers recognize that our view of landscape evokes a deep response, see Y. F. Tuan *Topophilia* (Berkeley: University of California Press 1968), and the interaction between human activity and experiences of the landscape are seen more recently in, for example, both Arctic and Australian indigenous culture, described in B. Lopez, *Arctic Dreams: Imagination and Desire in a Northern Landscape* (London: Macmillan 1986, p. 296).

7. A Hoard of Treasure

The White Horse of Uffington is claimed as Celtic workmanship by A. Ross, *Pagan Celtic Britain* (London: Constable, revised edn, 1992), but is considered perhaps more likely to be Saxon by R. Hutton, *The Pagan Religions of the Ancient British Isles* (Oxford: Blackwell 1991), and H. R. Ellis Davidson, *Myths and Symbols in Pagan Europe: Early Scandinavian and Celtic Religions* (Manchester University Press 1988). An example of a Christian image of the dragon as the power of evil and darkness is Carpaccio's *St George Killing the Dragon*, illustrated in F. Huxley *The Dragon* (London: Thames and Hudson 1979, p. 79).

Terms like 'wyrmbed' show how dragons became parts of kennings or 'clue words', the understanding of which depended usually on a knowledge of mythology. In the myths, serpent-dragons were said to lie on golden treaure in burial mounds, which were therefore 'wyrmbeds'. H. R. Ellis Davidson *The Lost Beliefs of Northern Europe* (London: Routledge, 1993).

The Sutton Hoo archeological finds, displayed in the British Museum, are reproduced in many books, including M. O. H. Carver (ed.), *The Age of Sutton Hoo* (Woodbridge: The Boydell Press, 1992) and *Sutton Hoo: Burial Ground of Kings?* (London: British Museum Publications, 1998). The classic British Museum publication is R. L. S. Bruce-Mitford, *The Sutton-Hoo Ship Burial* (3 vols) (London: British Museum Publications, 1975–83). Discussions of the Sutton Hoo treasure and its significance may be found in R. Hutton *The Pagan Religions of The Ancient British Isles* (Oxford: Blackwell 1991, pp. 275–9), C. Hills 'The Archaeology of Anglo-Saxon England in the Pagan Period: A Review', *Anglo-Saxon England 8*, (Cambridge University Press 1979, pp. 318–26) and G. Owen, *Rites and Religions of the Anglo-Saxons* (Newton Abbot: David & Charles 1981, pp. 67–79). A summary of the findings and their significance is in H. R. Ellis Davidson *The Lost Beliefs of Northern Europe*, pp. 17–24. Of particular relevance to Anglo-Saxon magic is S. O. Glosecki 'Wolf Dancers and Whispering Beasts: Shamanic Motifs from Sutton Hoo?', *Mankind Quarterly*, 26, 1986, pp. 305–19.

For a consideration of the concept of 'luck' see A. R. Smith, 'The Luck in the Head: Some Further Observations', *Folklore*, LXXIX, 1963, pp. 396–8, W. Chaney, *The Cult of Kingship in Anglo-Saxon England* (Manchester University Press, 1970) and S. Pollington, *Leechcraft: Early English Charms, Plantlore and Healing* (Hockwold-cum-Wilton: Anglo-Saxon Books 2001), which considers also the debts, obligations and spiritual level of gift-exchange.

There are various renditions of *Beowulf* from the Anglo-Saxon into modern English, referenced earlier. Analyses and commentaries on Beowulf run into the hundreds. For readers wishing to explore further, some sources of relevance to this book include J. R. R. Tolkien, 'Beowulf: The Monsters and the Critics', *Proceedings of the British Academy*, 22, 1936, pp. 245–95, C. Watkins, *How to Kill a Dragon: Aspects of Indo-European Poetics* (Oxford University Press 1995), A. Bonjour, 'Beowulf and the Beasts of Battle', *Proceedings of the Modern Language Association*, 72, 1957, pp. 563–73, N. K. Chadwick, 'The Monsters and Beowulf', in P. Clemoes (ed.), *The Anglo-Saxons* (London: Bower and Bower 1959), G. N. Garmonsway, *Beowulf and its Analogues* (London: Dent 1968), G. Hubener, 'Beowulf and Germanic Exorcism', *Review of English Studies*, 11, 1935, pp. 163–81, M. Osborn, *Beowulf: A Verse Translation with Treasures of the North* (Berkeley: University of California Press 1983) and D. Whitelock, *The Audience of Beowulf* (Oxford: Clarendon Press 1951). For the oral performance of Beowulf as a magical charm, or galdor, see S. Pollington, *Leechcraft: Early English Charms, Plantlore and Healing* (Hockwold-cum-Wilton: Anglo-Saxon Books 2000).

L. Dossey, *Space, Time and Medicine* (Boulder: Shambhala 1982) provides a clear exposition of the principles of cyclic time.

A primary source for Norse legends is S. Sturluson, J. I. Young (trs.), *The Prose Edda: Tales from the Norse Mythology* (Berkeley: University of California Press, 1954). On the death and rebirth of the snake/dragon, A. Mindell, *Dreambody* (London: Routledge 1984, p. 129).

8. Elves' Arrows

Elfshot appears in the Lacnunga in a magical charm to protect people from their arrows, as in S. Pollington's *Leechcraft: Early English Charms, Plantlore and Healing* (Hockwold-cum-Wilton: Anglo-Saxon Books 2000, p. 229). The picture of the man shot with elves' arrows in the Utrecht Psalter is in the British Library, MS Harley 603, folio 22r. The Utrecht Psalter, and its illustrations, is discussed in J. Brantley, 'The Iconography of the Utrecht Psalter and the Old English Descent into Hell', *Anglo-Saxon England*, 28, 1999, pp. 43–63. Discussions of the nature of elfshot appear in R. North, 'Heathen Gods in Old English Literature', *Cambridge Studies in Anglo-Saxon England*, 22 (Cambridge University Press 1997), K. L. Jolly, *Popular Religion in Late Saxon England: Elf Charms in Context* (Chapel Hill: 1996), M. L. Cameron, *Anglo-Saxon Medicine* (Cambridge University Press 1993), W. Bonser 'Magical Practices Against Elves', *Folk-Lore*, XXXVII, 1926, pp. 356–63 and N. Thun 'The Malignant Elves: Notes on Anglo-Saxon

Magic and Germanic Myth', *Studia Neophilologica*, 41, 1969, pp. 378–96. For the nature of elves generally in Anglo-Saxon England, and elves being a general word for spirits, see B. Griffiths *Aspects of Anglo-Saxon Magic* (Hockwold-cum-Wilton: Anglo-Saxon Books 1996, p. 50); and G. Storms, *Anglo-Saxon Magic* (The Hague: Martinus Nijhoff 1948). Tolkien explained his perspective on elves in a letter see H. Carpenter, *The Letters of J. R. R. Tolkien* (London: Allen & Unwin 1981, p. 176). T. Shippey, *The Road to Middle-earth* (London: Allen & Unwin 1982) discusses the beauty of elves. For Saxo's description of elves and the practice of going to a gifted person for seeing into the Otherworld see H. R. Ellis Davidson (ed.) *Saxo Grammaticus – The History of the Danes, Books 1–9*, vol I, P. Fisher (trs.) and vol II, commentary H. R. Ellis Davidson (Cambridge University Press 1979–80). For cross-cultural material on such 'gifted' people in more recently surviving cultures see M. Eliade, *Shamanism: Archaic Techniques of Ecstasy* (London: Routledge, 1956).

Anglo-Saxon terms for wizards and witches are legion, and are reviewed in Pollington, *Leechcraft: Early English Charms, Plantlore and Healing* (Hockwold-cum-Wilton: Anglo-Saxon Books 2000), W. Bonser *The Medical Background of Anglo-Saxon England* (London: Wellcome Historical Medical Library 1963) and B. Griffiths, *Aspects of Anglo-Saxon Magic*, p. 89). This latter book also introduces 'Cormac's Saga' (p. 53), and the practice of alfablot.

The contributions of Aelfric are documented in M. M. Gatch, *Preaching and Theology in Anglo-Saxon England: Aelfric and Wulfstan* (Toronto: University of Toronto Press, 1977).

The belief in landspirits is discussed in H. R. Ellis Davidson, *The Lost Beliefs of Northern Europe* (London: Routledge 1993), and the development of the 'races' of gods, the Aesir and Vanir, in R. North, 'Heathen Gods in Old English Literature', *Cambridge Studies in Anglo-Saxon England*, 22, 1997. Almost all general books on Scandinavian mythology and religions have good sections on Frey, regarded as a fertility god, and in some ways elaborating the early belief in spirits, see E. Turville-Petre *Myth and Religion of the North* (London: Weidenfeld and Nicolson 1964), a review of his saga appearances in M. Magnusson, *Iceland Saga* (London: The Bodley Head 1987), insightful perspectives on his nature and significance are found throughout H. R. Ellis Davidson, *Myths and Symbols in Pagan Europe: Early Scandinavian and Celtic Religions* (Manchester University Press 1988). Snorri Sturluson's 'original' description of Frey is in J. I. Young (trs.), *The Prose Edda: Tales from the Norse Mythology* (Berkeley: University of California Press, 1954). A particularly interesting account and discussion of Frey's wooing of Gerd is in B. Branston, *Gods of the North* (London: Thames and Hudson 1980).

9. Plant Magic

The Old English Herbarium and the Lacnunga, the enchantment of plants, Hildegard's attitude to mandrake, and Pliny's comments on early Celtic plant magic, are discussed in W. Bonser, *The Medical Background of Anglo-Saxon England* (London: Wellcome Historical Medical Library 1963). Mugwort and celandine are considered by G. Storms, *Anglo-Saxon Magic* (The Hague: Martinus Nijhoff 1948). These magical/medical manuscripts are newly translated and analysed in S. Pollington, *Leechcraft: Early English Charms, Plantlore and Healing* (Hockwold-cum-Wilton: Anglo-Saxon Books 2000), including mention of the magical healing reputation of vervain (p. 163), a consideration of the concepts of 'haelu' and health (pp. 453 and 488), and the spirit force suffusing the cosmos in Anglo-Saxon England. For the concepts of vital power, and the intimate interrelation of people with the landscape and the gods, see R. H. Wax, *Magic, Fate and History: Early Scandinavian and Celtic Religions* (Manchester University Press 1988), especially chapter IV 'The Ideal Typical Enchanted Point of View'.

For examples of ancient European notions of life force in people see R. B. Onions *The Origins of European Thought* (Cambridge University Press 1954, pp. 129 and 474).

Dolores Krieger developed the approach to healing now known as Therapeutic Touch.

10. Spirit Nights

The source for the Norse myth about Night is S. Sturluson, J. I.Young (trs.), *The Prose Edda: Tales from the Norse Mythology* (Berkeley: University of California Press, 1954, p. 37–8), and comments about ironwood are on p. 39.

Tacitus' comments are in H. Mattingly (ed.), S. A. Handford (trs.), *The Agricola and the Germania* (Harmondsworth: Penguin, revised edn, 1970).

The picking of periwinkle by the seasons of the moon is discussed in S. Pollington *Leechcraft: Early English Charms, Plantlore and Healing* (Hockwold-cum-Wilton: Anglo-Saxon Books 2000) and in G. Storms *Anglo-Saxon Magic* The Hague: Martinus Nijhoff, (1948), who also considers the nature of fertility festivals.

Concepts of liminal moments, spirit nights and the Otherworld are in A. and B. Rees, *Celtic Heritage: Ancient Tradition in Ireland and Wales* (London: Thames and Hudson 1961, reprinted 1994).

Wulfstan is quoted in M. Swanton, *Anglo-Saxon Prose* (London: Dent 1975) and the whole sermon is reported in pp. 116–25.

11. Wells of Wisdom

Well dressing and other well traditions are discussed by J. and C. Bord, *Earth Rites* (London: Granada 1982), by J. A. MacCulloch, *Religion of the Ancient Celts* (London: Constable 1991, first published 1911, pp. 181–97), including the association of the River Seine with the goddess Sequana; by N. Pennick *Celtic Sacred Landscapes* (London: Thames and Hudson 2000, pp. 63–77) and by J. Michell, *The Earth Spirit* (London: Thames and Hudson 1975, pp. 76–7).

Wells in Wales are documented in F. Jones, *The Holy Wells of Wales* (Cardiff: University of Wales Press 1954). Fritwell as site of divination is in C. Hough, 'The Place-Name Fritwell', *Journal of the English Place-Name Society*, 29, 1997, and is discussed in Pollington, *Leechcraft: Early English Charms, Plantlore and Healing* (Hockwold-cum-Wilton: Anglo-Saxon Books 2000). The honouring of Coventina is considered in A. Ross, *Pagan Celtic Britain* (London: Constable, revised edn, 1992, p. 56), who also mentions the River Glen in her discussion of sanctuaries associated with springs, wells and rivers (pp. 46–59). For a collection of river names, see E. Ekwell, *English River-Names* (Oxford: Oxford University Press 1928); for precious Celtic art objects found and probably dedicated to the Thames in London see C. Fox, *Pattern and Purpose: A Survey of Celtic Art in Britain* (Cardiff: 1958). Women going to wells for fertility rituals is in J. M. McPherson, *Primitive Beliefs in the North-East of Scotland* (London: Longmans and Green 1929 pp. 50–1).

S. Sturluson, J. I. Young (trs.), *The Prose Edda: Tales from the Norse Mythology* (Berkeley: University of California Press, 1954) is the source for the Norse vision of twenty-seven great rivers of the Upperworld, the description of Yggdrasil (pp. 42–6) and the vision of the water in the sacred wells (pp. 45–6).

Joseph Campbell discusses water and women in *Primitive Mythology: The Masks of God* (New York: Viking, revised edn, 1969). Related discussions are in G. Owen, *Rites and Religions of the Anglo-Saxons* (Newton Abbot: 1981) and M. Sjoo and B. Mor, *The Great Cosmic Mother: Rediscovering the Religion of the Earth* (New York: Harper and Row 1987).

Research into the sensitivity of water is reported in T. Shwenk, *Sensitive Chaos* (New York: Schocken Books 1976); this work is also discussed in L. Watson, *Earthworks* (pp. 120–1).

Pilgrims' badges in the River Thames are reported in R. Merrifield, *The Archaeology of Religion and Magic* (London: 1987) and discussed in R. Hutton, *The Pagan Religions of the Ancient British Isles* (Oxford: Blackwell 1990).

12. The Raven's Omen

The poems 'Elene' and 'Judith' are included in R. K. Gordon (ed. and trs.) *Anglo-Saxon Poetry* (New York: Dutton 1926, revised 1977). An analysis is in P. J. Lucas, 'Judith and the Woman Hero', *Yearbook of English Studies*, 22, 1992, pp. 17–27.

Brunanburgh is mentioned in W. A. Chaney, *The Cult of Kingship in Anglo-Saxon England* (Manchester University Press, 1970), which also introduces the story of Ravenlandeye. The warmer weather of part of the first millennium is in J. Rackham 'Environment and Economy in Anglo-Saxon England', *CBA Research Report*, 8, 9, York, 1994.

Mabd, Morrigu and the crows, and the story of Alasdair and bird language, are all in C. and J. Matthews, *The Encyclopaedia of Celtic Wisdom* (Shaftesbury: Element 1994). Babd is summarized in M. Dixon-Kennedy, *Celtic Myth and Legend* (London: Blandford 1996) and discussed in A. and B. Rees, *Celtic Heritage: Ancient Tradition in Ireland and Wales* (London: Thames and Hudson 1961, reprinted 1994). A. Ross, *Pagan Celtic Britain* (London: Constable, revised edn, 1992) considers Owein's board game of wooden wisdom, and the story of Da Choca's Hostel.

Gregory of Tours account of the 'bird prophecies' of the Franks is considered in H. R. Ellis Davidson, 'The Germanic World' in M. Loewe and C. Blacker (eds), *Divination and Oracles* (London: Allen and Unwin 1981), as is the wizard's view of the future.

Amulets are reviewed in A. L. Meaney, *Anglo-Saxon Amulets and Curing Stones* (*British Archaeological Reports*, British Series no. 96 Oxford 1981).

The source for Odin's two ravens is S. Sturluson, J. I. Young (trs.), *The Prose Edda: Tales from the Norse Mythology* (Berkeley: University of California Press, 1954).

A discussion and diagram of the settlement and buildings of Yeavering is in H. R. Ellis Davidson *The Lost Beliefs of Northern Europe* (London: Routledge 1993 pp. 22–4). Yeavering was probably abandoned after Edwin's death see B. Hope-Taylor, *Yeavering: An Anglo-British Centre of Early Northumbria* (London: 1977).

The original account of King Edwin and the crow is the early *Life of St Gregory*, written between AD 680 and 714 by an anonymous monk of

Whitby, and is one of the earliest pieces of literature in England. It is translated and included in D. Whitelock (ed.), *English Historical Documents* (London: Eyre and Spottiswood 1955, p. 688).

13. Shapeshifters

The ancient European belief that people could alter shape from human to animal is introduced in T. O. Rahilly, *Early Irish History and Mythology* (Dublin: 1957, pp. 323–5) and discussed in N. Tolstoy, *The Quest for Merlin* (London: Hamish Hamilton 1985) and S. O. Glosecki *Shamanism and Old English Poetry* (1989), which also has excellent discussions of the concepts of dreams from outside the body, soul, hamr, spirit skin and fetch – especially 'Images of the Animal Guardians', chapter 6, pp. 181–210, including the sensing of the presence of fetches. See also consideration of these concepts in H. P. Duerr and F. Goodman (trs.), *Dreamtime: Concerning the Boundary Between Wilderness and Civilization* (Oxford: Blackwell 1985), B. Collinder, *The Lapps* (Princeton University Press 1949, pp. 148–9) and E. O. G. Turville-Petre, *Myth and Religion of the North* (London: Weidenfeld and Nicolson 1964, pp. 221–30). For shamans in a state of trance and shamans journeying out of their bodies, see J. Halifax, *Shamanic Voices: the Shaman as Seer, Poet and Healer* (Harmondsworth: Penguin 1979) for first-hand narration of experiences of 'animal presence'.

    'Shaman' is today the widely used and accepted umbrella term for practitioners of healing and the sacred in tribal societies. They are believed to be especially gifted in mediating between the spirit world and the everyday world, and to be able to perceive through a kind of dream consciousness during waking life; literally 'dreaming with open eyes' see M. Tucker, *Dreaming with Open Eyes: The Shamanic Spirit in Modern Art and Culture* (London: Harper Collins 1993). H. R. Ellis Davidson in her *Pagan Scandinavia* (New York: Praeger 1967) writing about shamans in the context of ancient Scandinavia, says on p. 23, that 'The shaman . . . could send out his spirit in a trance to discover what was hidden, to heal the sick, to enter the land of the Dead and return to men, to combat evil powers and to assuage the wrath of the spirits. One of the outstanding characteristics of the shaman everywhere is his close relationship with the animal world, emphasized in costume and ritual, and by the belief in animal spirits helping and hindering him in his endeavours.' General source material on the role and activities of shamans in ancient Europe and Scandinavia can be found, for example, in Glosecki *Shamanism and Old English Poetry*, P. Buchholz, 'Shamanism: the Testimony of Old Icelandic Literary Tradition', *Medieval*

Scandinavia, 4, 1971, pp. 7–20, M. A. Arent, 'The Heroic Pattern: Old Germanic Helmets, *Beowulf*, and *Grettis saga*', in E. C. Polome (ed.), *Old Norse Literature and Mythology* (Austin: University of Texas Press 1969, pp. 130–99), C. Edsman, *Studies in Shamanism: A Symposium* (Stockholm: Almqvist and Wiksell 1967, pp. 120–65), H. R. Ellis Davidson, *Gods and Myths of Northern Europe* (Harmondsworth: Penguin 1964 pp. 141–9), M. Eliade, *Shamanism: Archaic Techniques of Ecstasy* (1964 pp. 379–87), V. Salmon, 'The *Wanderer* and the *Seafarer* and the Old English Conception of the Soul', *Modern Language Review*, 55, 1960, pp. 1–10) and N. K. Chadwick, *Poetry and Prophecy* (Cambridge University Press 1952). Shamanic rituals to acquire guardian spirits are described in M. D. Jakobsen, *Shamanism: Traditional and Contemporary Approaches to the Mastery of Spirits and Healing* (New York and Oxford: Berghahn Books 1999), Eliade, *Shamanism*, pp. 110–44, H. Kalweit, *Dreamtime and Inner Space* (Boston: Shambhala 1988, pp. 209–12) and P. Vitebsky, *The Shaman* (London: Macmillan, 1995 pp. 59–63).

The Manannan and Mongan story is included in C. and J. Matthews, *The Encyclopaedia of Celtic Wisdom* (Shaftesbury: Element 1994).

W. A. Chaney. *The Cult of Kingship in Anglo-Saxon England* (Manchester University Press, 1970, pp. 121–35) has a discussion of animals sacred to the Anglo-Saxons. A. Ross, *Pagan Celtic Britain* (London: Constable, revised edn, 1992, pp. 302–446) comprehensively reviews animals sacred to the Celts. In more recently surviving tribal cultures, animals also have significance see Eliade *Shamanism* (especially pp. 88–99), and also J. E. Brown, *Animals of the Soul* (Shaftesbury: Element 1992). On how these attitudes of closeness with animals has now been lost see B. Lopez, *Crossing Open Ground* (London: Macmillan 1988).

For the magical role of the bear, see the excellent analysis of Beowulf references in Glosecki, *Shamanism* p. 198, in K. La Budde, 'Cultural Primitivism in William Faulkner's *The Bear*', in F. Utley (ed.), *Bear, Man, and God* (New York: Random House 1964, pp. 226–33) and in R. Carpenter, *Folk Tale, Fiction, and Saga in the Homeric Epics* (Berkeley: University of California Press 1946).

The concept of berserker is discussed by Ellis Davidson in *Gods and Myths* (p. 66–70), which includes the story of Bothvar Bjarki as a bear, M. Eliade, W. Trask (trs.), *Rites and Symbols of Initiation* (New York: Harper and Row 1975 p. 72) and Duerr and Goodman, *Dreamtime* (p. 62). For the psychology of the warrior, including the berserkers, see S. Pollington *The English Warrior from Earliest Times till 1066* (Hockwold-cum-Wilton: Anglo-Saxon Books, 2001).

The boar-helmets in Beowulf are considered in Glosecki, *Shamanism*

(p. 54) and the military practice of destroying captured, spiritually enhanced weapons is in Ellis Davidson, *Pagan Scandinavia* (p. 70–1).

Tacitus reported that early Germanic peoples wore animal skins in H. Mattingly (ed.), S. A. Handford (trs.), *The Agricola and the Germania*, chapter 17. See also W. Bonser, 'Animal Skins in Magic and Medicine' *Folklore*, 73, 1962, 128–9.

Hrolf's saga and Athils are mentioned in H. R. Ellis Davidson, *Myths and Symbols in Pagan Europe: Early Scandinavian and Celtic Religions* (Manchester University Press 1988).

On Odin travelling in fetch form see Snorri Sturluson, E. Monsen and A. H. Smith (trs.), *Heimskringla* (Heffer 1931). For the Volsung saga Sigmund and Sinjof, see H. R. Ellis Davidson *Gods and Myths of Northern Europe* (Harmondsworth: Penguin 1964, p. 68).

14. The Wizard's Wild Ride

The wild hunt entry in the Anglo-Saxon Chronicle for AD 1127 is in G. N. Garmonsway (ed.), *The Anglo-Saxon Chronicle* (London: J. M. Dent 1953, new edn 1972). The Celtic figure Gwynn ap Nudd, who rode in wild hunt, listed in M. Dixon-Kennedy, *Celtic Myth and Legend* (London: Blandford 1996). For symbolic horses among the Celts, M. Green, 'British Hill-Figures: A Celtic Interpretation', *Cosmos*, 11, pp. 125–138 and J. A. MacCulloch, *The Religion of the Ancient Celts* (London: Constable 1911, reprinted 1991).

The story of the death of Fergus is told in C. and J. Matthews *The Encyclopaedia of Celtic Wisdom* (Shaftesbury: Element 1994, pp. 358–76).

S. Sturluson, J. I. Young (trs.), *The Prose Edda: Tales from the Norse Mythology* (Berkeley: University of California Press, 1954), relates the story of Hrimfaxi, and the magic horse Sleipnir. Hermothr's ride to the Lowerworld is described in the Norse manuscripts with a seemingly objective geography. For the relationship between sacred landscapes and the material world see H. R. Ellis Davidson, 'Mythical geography in the Edda Poems', in G. D. Flood (ed.), *Mapping Invisible Worlds* (Yearbook 9 of the Traditional Cosmology Society, Edinburgh University Press, 1993, pp. 95–106). Shamanic journeys from more recent cultures into the dangerous but wisdom-bestowing environs of the Lowerworld are recounted in, for example, H. Kalweit, M. Kohn (trs.), *Shamans, Healers and Medicine Men* (Boston: Shambhala, 1992) and J. Halifax, *Shamanic Voices: the Shaman as Seer, Poet and Healer* (Harmondsworth: Penguin 1979).

Tacitus describes how the early Germanic peoples consulted prophetic horses see H. Mattingly (ed.), S. A. Handford (trs.), *The Agricola and the Germania* (Harmondsworth: Penguin, revised edn, 1970). For a perspective on the imaginal world of Anglo-Saxon England, see S. O. Glosecki *Shamanism and Old English Poetry* (New York: Garland 1989).

Interesting analyses of the name Yggdrasil appear in N. Tolstoy *Quest for Merlin* (London: Hamish Hamilton 1985, p. 177) and B. Branston *Gods of the North* (London: Thames and Hudson 1980, pp. 114–15).

The balance of forces in Norse cosmology are explored in R. H. Wax *Magic, Fate and History: The Changing Ethos of the Vikings* (Kansas: Colorado Press 1969).

15. The Web of Destiny

For childbirth practices see M. Deegan, 'Pregnancy and Childbirth in the Anglo-Saxon Medical Texts: A Preliminary Survey', in D. G. Scragg and M. Deegan (eds), *Medicine in Early Mediaeval England* (Manchester University Press, 1989).

K. Morris, *Sorceress or Witch: The Image of Gender in Medieval Iceland and Northern Europe* (London: University Press of America 1991) considers the meaning of the term 'hagtesse'. She also discusses Frigg as a Norse and Anglo-Saxon goddess who expressed fertility themes. On this see also B. Branston, *The Lost Gods of England* (London: Thames and Hudson, 2nd edn, 1974) especially pp. 127–34 and K. Crossley-Holland, *The Norse Myths* (Harmondsworth: Penguin 1980). P. Berger, *The Goddess Obscured* (London: Robert Hale 1988) is especially interesting on the fertility aspects of the corn spirit. Women's childbirth celebrations are indicated in M. Eliade *Myths, Dreams and Mysteries* (London: Collins/Fontana 1968). Symbolic approaches to aspects of childbirth are reviewed in B. C. Bates and A. Newman-Turner, 'Imagery and Symbolism in the Birth Practices of Traditional Cultures', *Birth: Issues in Perinatal Care and Education*, 1985, 12, 1, pp. 29–36. Awareness of the biological and cosmological aspects of the female monthly cycle were much stronger then, and are discussed in T. Buckley and A. Gottlieb (eds), *Blood Magic: The Anthropology of Menstruation* (Berkeley: University of California Press 1988) and M. Sjoo and B. Mor, *The Great Cosmic Mother: Rediscovering the Religion of the Earth* (San Francisco: Harper and Row 1987). The latter also indicates the relevance of the great spider woman of the Navajo.

Ancient figures of 'the mothers' from Roman times are in G. Owen, *Rites and Religions of the Anglo-Saxons* (Newton Abbot: 1981) and for further back in prehistory see M. Gimbutas, *The Civilisation of the Goddess* (San Francisco: HarperCollins 1991) and M. Gimbutas, *The Language of the Goddess* (San Francisco: Harper & Row 1989).

B. Branston, *The Lost Gods of England* (London: Thames and Hudson 1974 and 1984 edition) and H. R. Ellis Davidson, *Myths and Symbols in Pagan Europe: Early Scandinavian and Celtic Religions* (Manchester University Press 1988) both discuss the significance and cross-cultural parallels of the Wyrd Sisters.

The Bishop of Worms and the tradition of the Parcae can be found in H. R. Ellis Davidson *Gods and Myths of Northern Europe* (Harmondsworth: Penguin 1964). The Norns and Bralund appear in the opening stanzas of *The First Lay of Helgi*; my source is P. B. Taylor and W. H. Auden (trs.), *The Elder Edda. A Selection* (London: Faber and Faber, 1969).

On gewif and weaving destiny in Viking cosmology, R. H. Wax, *Magic, Fate and History History: Early Scandinavian and Celtic Religions* (Manchester University Press 1988), 'Another intrinsic aspect of the magical world view is the idea that man, the gods, and all the other phenomena are related or connected to each other by a web of empathy' (p. 50). An interesting discussion along similar lines is in N. Pennick, *Games of the Gods* (London: Rider 1988, pp. 27–31). The processes of spinning and weaving in the first millennium are summarized clearly with illustrations in J. Graham-Campbell, *The Viking World* (London: Frances Lincoln 1989, pp. 121–2). Spinning and weaving implements recovered in excavations at West Stow are described in S. West, *West Stow Revisited* (St Edmundsbury Borough Council, 2001).

Saxo Grammaticus tells the story of Fridlef consulting women about his children in his twelfth-century *Gesta Danorum*. Njals saga M. Magnusson and H. Palsson (trs.), *Njal's Saga* (Harmondsworth: Penguin 1960). Kogi cosmological belief systems are described in A. Ereira, *The Heart of the World* (London: Jonathan Cape 1990).

The Solomon and Saturn prose and poetic manuscripts are covered by K. O'Brien O'Keefe, 'Solomon and Saturn, Poetic and Prose' in M. Lapidge (ed.), *The Blackwell Encyclopaedia of Anglo-Saxon England* (Oxford: Blackwell 2001, pp. 424–5); and T. A. Shippey (trs.), *Poems of Wisdom and Learning in Old English* (Cambridge: 1976).

16. The Seeress

Evidence for wizardry and magic in ancient Europe is considered by S. O. Glosecki, *Shamanism and Old English Poetry* (New York: Garland 1989) and

B. Griffiths, *Aspects of Anglo-Saxon Magic* (Hockwold-cum-Wilton: Anglo-Saxon Books 1996), which references Theodore's penitential against employing diviners, and the laws and punishments against wizards. See also A. Davies, 'Witches in Anglo-Saxon England: Five Case Histories' in D. G. Scragg (ed.), *Superstition and Popular Medicine in Anglo-Saxon England* (Manchester University Press, 1989) and N. Price (ed.) *The Archaeology of Shamanism* (London: Routledge 2002). See R. Kieckhefer, *Magic in the Middle Ages* (Cambridge University Press 1989) for the nature of distinctions between priestesses and witches. Tacitus is a major source for information on how the Romans had to negotiate with Germanic seeresses, the name of Veleda, and references to wise women of the Chatti tribe, in H. Mattingly (ed.), S. A. Handford (trs.), *The Agricola and the Germania* (Harmondsworth: Penguin, revised edn, 1970). On the nature and status of seeresses, see K. Morris, *Sorceress or Witch: The Image of Gender in Medieval Iceland and Northern Europe* (1991) and, more generally, J. Jesch, *Women in the Viking Age* (Woodbridge: Boydell Press 1991).

On the name 'Veleda' as a professional title, H. R. Ellis Davidson (ed.) *The Seer in Celtic and Other Traditions* (Edinburgh: John Donald 1989) and H. R. Ellis Davidson 'The Germanic World', in M. Loewe and C. Blacker (eds) *Divination and Oracles* (London: Allen and Unwin 1981), which also deals with the dangers to travelling shamanic souls, the seidr practitioner's 'gaping and falling down', and the significance of the Scottish dialect word for 'warlock'.

There are a number of translations of the saga appearance of Thorbiorg. My source is G. Jones, *Eirik the Red* (Oxford University Press 1961, pp. 135–6). Discussions of seidr include J. Blain, *Nine Worlds of Seid-Magic: Ecstasy and Neo-Shamanism in North European Paganism* (London: Routledge 2002), T. Dubois, *Nordic Religions in the Viking Age* (Philadelphia: University of Pennsylvania Press 1999), S. O. Glosecki, *Shamanism and Old English Poetry* (New York: Garland 1989, pp. 96–102), including an analysis of the drink given to Thorbiorg, N. K. Chadwick, *Poetry and Prophecy* (Cambridge University Press 1952, pp. 9–10), Edsman, *Studies in Shamanism: A Symposium* (Stockholm: Almqvist and Wiksell 1967, pp. 143–5), M. Eliade, *Shamanism: Archaic Techniques of Ecstasy* (London: Routledge, 1964, pp. 385–7) and P. Foote (ed.), G. Johnson (trs.), *The Saga of Gilsi The Outlaw* (University of Toronto Press 1963, p. 79). On Freya: S. S. Grundy 'Freyja and Frigg', in S. Billington and M. Green (eds), *The Concept of the Goddess* (London: Routledge 1996). For the background to the songs necessary for spirits to come, spakonas travelling with trained singers and breathing technique and phrasing etc., see C. M. Bowra, *Primitive Song* (London: Weidenfeld and Nicolson, 1962).

The story of Norna-Gest is considered in A. Stone, *Wyrd: Fate and Destiny in North European Paganism* (self-published, printed by Newark Chamber of Commerce 1989).

For references to the Celtic practice of 'imbas' divination, the seeress named Fedelm, Gerald of Wales on divination trances, chanting or murmuring in divination technique, see C. Matthews, *The Elements of The Celtic Tradition*. (Shaftesbury: Element 1989), C. and J. Matthews, *The Encyclopaedia of Celtic Wisdom* (Shaftesbury: Element 1994) and A. Stone, *Wyrd: Fate and Destiny* relates these approaches to the Anglo-Saxon concept of wyrd.

On the bodies recovered from bogs, and the nature of 'magic bags', P. V. Glob, R. Bruce-Mitford (trs.), *The Mound People* (London: Faber and Faber 1969). On the symbolism of animals' hearts being eaten by hunters, see B. Lopez, *Arctic Dreams: Imagination and Desire in a Northern Landscape* (London: Macmillan 1986).

Freya's falcon coat borrowed by Loki is considered in H. R. Ellis Davidson *Myths and Symbols in Pagan Europe* (Manchester University Press 1988, pp. 212–13). On the trickster figure a classic text is P. Radin, *The Trickster: A Study in American Indian Mythology* (London: 1956). See also H. R. Ellis Davidson, 'Loki and Saxo's Hamlet', in P. Williams (ed.), *The Fool and the Trickster* (Ipswich: D. S. Brewer 1979).

Lapp shaman on inspirational songs in H. Kalweit, *Dreamtime and Inner Space* (Boston: Shambhala 1988).

17. Ents

Theories of the origins of the Cerne giant are reviewed in M. Green, 'British Hill-Figures: A Celtic Interpretation', *Cosmos*, 11, 1995, pp. 125–38 and in T. Darvill, K. Barker, B. Bender and R. Hutton (eds), *The Cerne Giant: an Antiquity on Trial* (Oxbow 2000). Possible origins of the hillside Wilmington giant are considered in R. Castledon, *The Wilmington Giant: the Quest for a Lost Myth* (Wellingborough, Northampton: Turnstone Press 1983).

Various ancient Germanic terms for giants are recorded in the classic nineteenth-century study of folklore and etymological analyses by J. Grimm, J. S. Stallybrass (trs.), *Teutonic Mythology* (New York: Dover 1966, 4 vols, 4th edn). Anglo-Saxon terms for giants are considered in W. Bonser, *The Medical Background of Anglo-Saxon England* (London: Wellcome Historical Medical Library 1963).

The origins of creation, the giant Ymir, and also the story of Thor competing against the giants, are told by Snorri Sturluson, J. I. Young (trs.), in *The Prose Edda: Tales from the Norse Mythology* (Berkeley: University of California Press, 1954).

Stardust reference from J. and M. Gribbin, *Stardust* (London: Allen Lane 2000).

Trolls and elemental aspects of Scandinavian landscape are covered in M. Magnusson, *Hammer of the North* (London: Orbis 1976). See also M. Tucker, 'Not the Land, but an Idea of a Land', in J. Freeman (ed.), *Landscapes from a High Latitude* (London: Lund Humphries 1989 pp. 106–20).

The primary source for Ran, the goddess of the sea, is C. Larrington (trs.), *The Poetic Edda* (Oxford University Press 1996).

18. The Dwarves' Forge

The treasures found in the Sutton Hoo archeological dig are described and put in context in M. Carver, *Sutton Hoo: Burial Ground of Kings?* (London: British Museum Press, 1998), and A. C. Evans, *The Sutton Hoo Ship Burial* (London: British Museum Press 1996) vividly describes all the artefacts recovered from the grave, most of which are illustrated. There are many publications which feature this artwork in good reproductions, including R. Bruce-Mitford, *The Sutton Hoo Ship-Burial* (London: British Museum Publications 1972) for the impressive range of Anglo-Saxon jewellery recovered from this site, including for example the interwoven design of the 'great gold buckle' (colour plate on p. 65), M. Magnusson, *Hammer of the North* (London: Orbis 1976) for excellent photographs of many pieces and also E. Roesdale et.al. (eds), *The Vikings in England* (London: The Anglo-Danish Viking Project 1981).

J. Graham-Campbell, *The Viking World* (London: Frances Lincoln 1989, pp. 114–21) on clothing, jewellery, cleanliness of Anglo-Saxons and Vikings, and even 'an artificial make-up for the eyes' for both men and women. J. Graham-Campbell and D. Kidd, *The Vikings* (London: British Museum Publications 1980) includes discussion of likely clothing designs. B. Branston, *The Lost Gods of England* (London: Thames and Hudson 1984, p. 33) says, 'The womenfolk frequently adorned themselves with two and sometimes three brooches, often with festoons of glass and amber beads looped from brooch to brooch. Their waists were spanned by a girdle from which might hang characteristic T-shaped iron or bronze trinkets, ivory rings, strike-a-lights and knives.' This book also discusses the legendary Weland and his smithy.

See M. Tucker, *Dreaming With Open Eyes: The Shamanic Spirit in*

Contemporary Art and Culture (London: Harper Collins 1993) for a comprehensive analysis of the presence of the sacred in art.

The supernatural status of iron is discussed in S. Pollington, *Leechcraft: Early English Charms, Plantlore and Healing* (Hockwold-cum-Wilton: Anglo-Saxon Books 2000); the magical power of smiths in M. Eliade, *Shamanism: Archaic Techniques of Ecstasy* (1964). The forge in G. Bachelard, *The Psychoanalysis of Fire* (Boston: Beacon Press 1968).

K. Crossley-Holland, *The Norse Myths* (1980) contains an account of Freya's possible relationships with the dwarfs, as does H. R. Ellis Davidson, *The Lost Beliefs of Northern Europe* (London: Routledge 1993, pp. 108–9). Freya's necklace is considered by R. Metzner, *The Well of Remembrance* (London: Shambhala 1994).

The primary source for the dwarf wisdom of Alvis is C. Larrington (trs.), *The Poetic Edda* (Oxford University Press 1996).

Interlace and the mutual interdependence of everything is discussed in R. H. Wax, *Magic, Fate and History: The Changing Ethos of the Vikings* (Kansas: Colorado Press, 1969).

19. Spellbinding

The story of Imma is in S. Pollington, *The English Warrior from Earliest Times Till 1066* (Hockwold-cum-Wilton: Anglo-Saxon Books 2002).

Bede's history of England is in Bede, L. Sherley-Price (trs.), *A History of the English Church and People* (Harmondsworth: Penguin, 1968).

Odin's spellbinding knots are discussed in H. R. Ellis Davidson, *Gods and Myths of Northern Europe* (Harmondsworth: Penguin 1964, pp. 63–4). The 'binding power' of Odin has been compared with the lines and knots of the Indian Varuna, cf. G. Dumezil, *Gods of the Ancient Northmen* (E. Haugen ed. Berkeley: University of California 1973).

The primary source for the stories of Fenrir, Loki and Ragnarok and the ending of the world, is S. Sturluson, J. I. Young (trs.), *The Prose Edda: Tales from the Norse Mythology* (Berkeley: University of California Press, 1954).

On the balance of cosmological forces, R. H. Wax, *Magic, Fate and History: the Changing Ethos of the Vikings* (Kansas: Colorado Press 1969).

For an excellent evocation of the spirit of the wolf see B. Lopez, *Of Wolves and Men* (New York: Dent 1978).

20. The Spider Monster

G. Storms, *Anglo-Saxon Magic* (The Hague: Martinus Nijhoff 1948) and S. Pollington, *Leechcraft: Early English Charms, Plantlore and Healing* (Hockwold-cum-Wilton: Anglo-Saxon Books 2000) for translations of the spider creature spell. S. O. Glosecki *Shamanism and Old English Poetry* (New York: Garland 1989) for a comprehensive consideration of the shamanic bases of these texts. Sickness as a gateway to initiation in shamanic societies is explored in J. Halifax, *Shaman: The Wounded Healer* (London: Thames and Hudson 1982). The use of sleep deprivation, fasting, etc., for the induction of trance states is in P. Vitebsky, *The Shaman* (London: Macmillan 1998). The primary source for Odin 'drumming in the cove' is P. B. Taylor and W. H. Auden (trs.), *The Elder Edda: A Selection* (London: Faber and Faber 1969). Research on drumming and altered states is in M. Harner *The Way of the Shaman* (San Francisco: Harper and Row 1980). Galdor, chanting and spells in Pollington, *Leechcraft*.

Wyrd sisters references in B. Branston, *Gods of the North* (London: Thames and Hudson 1980).

For the use of divinatory dreams in ancient northern Europe see H. R. Ellis Davidson, 'The Germanic World', in M. Loewe and C. Blacker (eds), *Divination and Oracles* (London: Allen and Unwin 1981). Dreaming and imaginal states of consciousness where experiential journeys are 'real' are considered in J. Achterberg, *Imagery in Healing: Shamanism and Modern Medicine* (Boston: Shambhala 1985) and A. Bleakley, *The Fruits of the Moon Tree* (London: Gateway 1984). See also the accounts by shamans of their initiatory experiences in J. Halifax, *Shamanic Voices: the Shaman as Seer, Poet and Healer* (Harmondsworth: Penguin 1979) and the analysis in S. Larsen, *The Shaman's Doorway: Opening the Mythic Imagination to Contemporary Consciousness* (New York, Harper Colophon 1977).

Yaralde tribe images of the web are in M. Eliade, *Shamanism: Archaic Techniques of Ecstasy* (London: Routledge 1964). The Malekulans are discussed in J. Campbell, *Primitive Mythology: The Masks of God* (New York: Viking 1969 revised edn, pp. 444–51). The Collective Unconscious is related to imagery in C. G. Jung (ed.), *Man and His Symbols* (Garden City, N.J: Doubleday, 1964).

21. Journey to the Edge of Middle-earth

For Sutton Hoo, a main source is M. Carver, *Sutton Hoo: Burial Ground of Kings?* (London: British Museum Press, 1998), see also M. S. Midgley, 'Earthen Long Barrows of Northern Europe: A Vision of the Neolithic World', *Cosmos*, 11, pp. 117–23.

My main Beowulf sources here are M. Alexander, *Beowulf* (Harmondsworth: Penguin, 1973) and S. Newton, *The Origins of Beowulf and the Pre-Viking Kingdom of East Anglia* (Cambridge: D. S. Brewer 1993).

The source for Aelfric on witches, burial mounds, ghosts, etc., is P. Clemoes (ed.), *Aelfric's Catholic Homilies: The First Series Text* (Oxford University Press 1997).

Fridjof's saga is mentioned in H. R. Ellis Davidson, *Gods and Myths of Northern Europe* (Harmondsworth: Penguin 1964), the Hallbjorn and Thor-lief story is in H. R. Ellis Davidson *Myths and Symbols in Pagan Europe* (Manchester University Press 1988), which also notes the long history of Scandinavian ship burials.

Odin standing under hanged men to hear their words is mentioned in R. Metzner, *The Well of Remembrance* (Boston: Shambhala 1994).

The primary source for Skidbladnir, for Balder's ship funeral and for Odin riding to the Lowerworld is S. Sturluson, J. I. Young (trs.), *The Prose Edda: Tales from the Norse Mythology* (Berkeley: University of California Press, 1954).

That beautiful maids from the land of youth go to the Otherworld in ships is indicated in C. and J. Matthews, *The Encyclopaedia of Celtic Wisdom* (Shaftesbury: Element 1994).

The concept of garsecg is discussed in Newton, *The Origins of Beowulf* and in B. Griffiths, *Aspects of Anglo-Saxon Magic* (Hockwold-cum-Wilton: Anglo-Saxon Books 1996), which also considers the stories of Hading and Harthgreper, and Angantyr talking to the dead.

The riddle about Aegir, god of the sea, is in K. Crossley-Holland (trs), *The Exeter Book Riddles* (Harmondsworth: Penguin, revised edn, 1993).

Index